Mary Albright • Clay Carr

101 Biggest Mistakes Managers Make

and How to Avoid Them

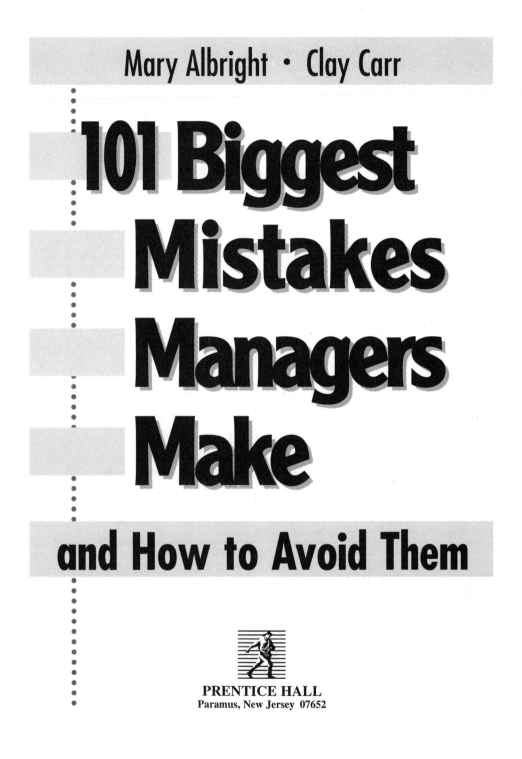

PRENTICE HALL
Paramus, New Jersey 07652

Printed in the United States of America

10 9 8 7 6 5 4 3 2 (C)   10 9 8 7 6 5 4 (P)

ISBN 0-13-234188-3 (C)   ISBN 0-13-234170-0 (P)

PRENTICE HALL
Paramus, NJ 07652

A Simon & Schuster Company

On the World Wide Web at http://www.phdirect.com

Prentice Hall International (UK) Limited, *London*
Prentice Hall of Australia Pty. Limited, *Sydney*
Prentice Hall Canada Inc., *Toronto*
Prentice Hall Hispanoamericana, S.A., *Mexico*
Prentice Hall of India Private Limited, *New Delhi*
Prentice Hall of Japan, Inc., *Tokyo*
Simon & Schuster Asia Pte. Ltd., *Singapore*
Editora Prentice Hall do Brasil, Ltda., *Rio de Janeiro*

We affectionately dedicate this book to

Bernie Lukco
and
Gayle Carr

who brought peace and joy to our lives

INTRODUCTION

"Oops. Nobody ever told me that!"

"Wait a minute. I never knew that before!"

"You mean this was my fault?"

What did you learn in your basic supervisory training? Maybe how to develop a work plan, conduct a meeting, make a presentation, manage your time? Maybe a little bit about how to divide up work, prepare a performance appraisal, handle a leave counseling?

Supervisory training teaches you about a lot of things you *should* do. What it usually leaves out are all the things you *shouldn't*.

That's what this book is about—many of the worst mistakes that can get you into trouble, but that no one ever told you about. Some of these mistakes are readily apparent, like being too strict or too lax with your workgroup, being defensive to criticism, or ignoring customers. But many are less obviously "mistakes." These are errors like using "only one can win" awards, trying to solve performance problems with technology, or giving poorly done work to someone else to complete. They're the actions you take that you learn were mistakes only after you've had to suffer the consequences.

What if you've been a supervisor for three or four or five years? Won't you already know by now what to do and what not to do?

Not necessarily. The effects of many mistakes aren't obvious immediately—and may never become clear. You might complete an entire managerial career oblivious to office politics, ignoring opportunities for networking, rewarding mediocrity over innovation, and saving your workers from their own mistakes–all without ever understanding how much better and more effective you *could* have been.

We all make mistakes, and we all try to learn from our errors. But mistakes continue to haunt us. The job of being a manager is increasingly difficult and prone to errors in both judgment and execution. *101 Mistakes* can help you deal with errors in two different, important ways:

1. It provides you a guide to the most common mistakes made by managers in almost any situation or environment. Although the book is written primarily for managers in traditional organizations, it also addresses problems that arise when you implement teams and give those teams decision-making responsibilities. If you know where the pitfalls lie, you can avoid them more easily.

2. When you do make a mistake, you can get specific guidance on how to recover from it quickly and how to prevent it in the future. (In these days of rapid

change and experimentation, no manager can avoid mistakes entirely. Instead, the critical skill is learning from them.)

How this book is organized

It's easy to find out whether something you plan to do (or have already done) is a mistake. This book arranges 101 of the most common management mistakes into 11 different chapters. Each chapter deals with a specific category of mistakes (such as "Mistakes in Dealing with Performance" or "Mistakes in Your Relationship with Your Boss"). The table of contents lists all 101 mistakes under their chapter headings, so you can quickly home in on the one you're looking for.

Each case in the chapter focuses on a single mistake. It depicts a typical scenario in which a manager makes the mistake, and then describes why it was a mistake and the immediate action you need to take to recover from it quickly. The case also tells you how to avoid making the mistake in the future and how to consistently handle the same kind of situation correctly. Of course, sometimes an action is a mistake in one context but perfectly appropriate in another. The case also tells you whether this action is *ever* right. Finally, each case offers a tip to help you build on the information you've learned. Often the tip extends the principles discussed to other situations; other times it explains the basic idea underlying the case in more depth.

Once you've read the case that deals with the problem closest to yours, you might also want to glance through some of the other cases in the chapter. Sometimes two cases are described in contrast to one another (like "rejecting new technology" versus "getting technology for technology's sake"). Other times a case is a follow-up to a mistake described earlier (such as "not having clear objectives" and "not having clear standards"). And in all the chapters, ideas introduced as marginally related to one case will be explained more fully in another.

Mistake-free management

Is it possible to become a mistake-free manager? Probably not. Even as you conquer one problem, some new situation will present itself which has the potential for a whole new set of mistakes. But what can you do to lessen the risk that you'll fall prone to them?

You can take the information in this book and generalize it to other situations and other cases. You can do that by "learning how to learn" about management issues. Here are some techniques:

• *Whenever you have to take an action you're not sure about, evaluate its consequences afterward yourself.* Was the result of your action what you intended it to be? Did it have unexpected effects? Would it have worked as well if some aspects of the situation were different?

• *Ask for feedback, especially from your own workgroup.* They can tell you better than anyone else how your words and actions are perceived. Make sure your staff know that you're not only asking them to give you input, you expect it. Then use what you've learned to improve your approach next time.

• *Finally, share your experiences with other managers, and ask them to help you work through problem situations.* Use your peers as a sounding board to try out new ideas. Find out what's worked for them in similar cases. As you try new approaches, let your peers know what's worked and what hasn't. That way the whole management group can learn from one anothers' experiences.

These three sources of information about your performance as a manager (your workgroup, your peers, and you) are an unbeatable combination. Armed with these allies, you can figure out how to identify and avoid your own mistakes in the future.

CONTENTS

Introduction   v

CHAPTER 1

MISTAKES IN DEALING WITH WORKERS

1-1 The Mistake: Setting one worker against another

The situation: "You know, Cindy, I thought I had this account all sewn up. We had agreed on an approach, a product, and a price, and I thought my customer was all ready to sign a contract. Next thing I know, I get a call from the guy and he says he's thought it over and decided maybe we should do something else instead. He still wants to work with us, but now he wants to start all over with a whole new analysis. I just don't understand what went wrong."

"Well, I know exactly what went wrong, Felicia. Paul Portris, who's going to do the work on the project, got to him. Paul's one of our best workers—and our worst enemies. You've got to figure a way to outsmart him or all your projects are going to stagnate forever."

Why was it a mistake?

Even workers who don't do exactly what you (or the rest of the staff) would like are part of the team. As soon as you set workers up against one another you undermine the teamwork that needs to occur among everyone in the workgroup. When kids act out, their parents don't tell the other kids, "Go get 'em." And when the right fielder throws the ball away, the rest of the team doesn't go out to beat him up. You can't build a team if the team members are pitted against one another—at home, on the field, or on the job.

How can you recover from it quickly?

You can get together with Felicia and Paul as soon as you possibly can and help the two of them work out their differences—together. Begin the meeting by explaining what you see as their positions: "Paul, it appears that you're not satisfied with the analysis Felicia has done and think it needs to be revised. Felicia, it seems that you think Paul is getting in the way of getting a contract signed and wants to get too much done upfront without a commitment from the customer. Is that a fair characterization? "So how can we change our process to satisfy both your needs?"

Then, when you've resolved the problem between Paul and Felicia, or gotten them to the point where they can resolve it themselves, you need to explain to Felicia that your initial reaction was speaking from frustration—that you don't consider anyone on this team to be an enemy. Whether you agree with them or not, all of your people are working toward the same goals.

How can you consistently do it right from now on?

Follow the pattern outlined above whenever workers have conflicts.

First, get the workers together to discuss their perceptions of what the problem is. Find out what each of them expected and how each was disappointed.

Next, get each of the workers to explain to the other what she would like to see happen in the future. Here, Felicia would like to take her step of the process only to the point that she has enough information to make an agreement with the customer, but Paul wants the process to go further into the details of the proposed project before an agreement is negotiated.

(Note that neither Felicia nor Paul is "right," nor is the other person "wrong." Most conflicts are like that. In most cases, the disagreement isn't so easily solved.)

At this stage, then, you have a choice. Either you can continue your involvement in resolving the conflict, perpetuating your role as the problem solver for the organization, or you can help Felicia and Paul negotiate a solution that's satisfactory to both of them. Smart managers would choose the latter whenever possible and in the process help the workers develop the skills to resolve conflicts themselves in the future without your intervention.

And, from now on, whenever conflicts arise within your workgroup, make sure your first response is always, "Let's hear the other side of the story and try to work this out"—not to make judgments about which side you're on.

Is doing what you did ever right?

There's probably no time when it's ever right to set one worker against another. Some team leaders believe that when you're working to remove a member from the team (for poor performance or behavior problems), you can enlist the help of other workers in the unit to "encourage" the misfit worker to go elsewhere—before you reassign or fire him. But, even then, you have to weigh the strength of the messages you're sending to the rest of the team. Is it more important to get rid of the worker? Or to foster solidarity among your team members? It would seem to be more important to foster solidarity. Dealing with team members who aren't marching to the same drummer is *your* job as team leader, not the job of other workers. Let your workers be the "good guys." When dirty work has to be done, you be the "bad guy."

A tip for mistake-free managing:

Although there will always be workers on your team whom you trust more than others or, in whose judgment you have more faith, it's important not to let those preferences dominate your decisions about how to resolve differences between workgroup members. Every member of the team has something to contribute. And, whether we always want to hear them or not, sometimes those voices in the wilderness are saying things it's important for everyone else to hear. Sometimes the best ideas come from people who have a different perspective from you and from the rest of the group. Listen to them too.

1-2 The Mistake: Showing favoritism not based on performance

The situation: "So, maybe Carl isn't always right, but I feel I have so much in common with him on other things—like golfing together and working with me on charity projects—that I ought to support his position. Of course, I'd never tell the rest of the staff that that's the way I feel. It just seems as if I owe him some loyalty."

Why was it a mistake?

If you want the people who work for you to be loyal to you, you must be loyal to them, too. And that loyalty is demonstrated strikingly by your support (or nonsupport) of them. Most employees enter the job expecting that the single greatest determinant of their success will be how well they perform the work they're assigned. When you allow other factors to sway your judgment, then your employees lose trust and confidence in you, and that lack of confidence is often displayed by higher turnover, lack of loyalty to you or the organization, or mediocre work.

What incentive is there for someone to perform well if rewards and success are based on your personal likes or dislikes?

And the extreme example of favoritism based on other than performance factors is *discrimination*—against workers because of their race or color or age or gender or other job-irrelevant factors.

How can you recover from it quickly?

This is one of those mistakes that you probably can't recover from quickly. By the time you've established a pattern of favoritism that's obvious enough that your workers can perceive it, that pattern is almost certainly so well established (and the damage to your workers' trust in you is so complete) that it will take some time to recover.

Your best bet is to try to watch your own behavior and try to spot your own tendencies toward favoritism before they're noticed by anyone else. By nature, we all are drawn more toward some people than to others—because of similar backgrounds, shared interests, a common approach to work or to life in general. The trick is not to let those natural affinities interfere with your judgment about people at work.

How can you consistently do it right from now on?

The next time you're tempted to favor one worker over another, stop and ask yourself, "Am I on Carl's side because he's right or because I *want* him to be right?" And if it's because you want him to be right, back up, start over, and re-think how you ought to handle the decision. You consistently do it right from now on largely by being aware of when you're tempted otherwise.

If you find yourself drawn to one of the people you manage to such an extent that you're forming a deep friendship or even an intimate relationship, then you need to have a heart-to-heart discussion with that person. It hardly ever works for a friend (or partner) to supervise a friend. Favoritism, or the perception of favoritism, is inevitable. In addition, it's very difficult to separate work and non-work issues and feelings. So, if you are strongly drawn to one of your workers, you need to ask yourself two questions:

First: "Is it more important to me (and the other person) to continue our work relationship or to continue our personal relationship?"

And then, if the answer is that the personal relationship is more important: "Which of us should get a job out of this unit?"

On the other hand, if you find yourself distancing yourself from one or a few people fairly consistently, you should ask yourself whether there is a *legitimate* reason for your feelings. Are you beginning to see a pattern—that you consistently avoid people who are better educated than you, who have certain physical characteristics, who come from certain parts of the country? It's important to build your staff with people you can be comfortable with—people whose working styles are compatible with yours, whose expertise meshes with the demands of the job, who have skills that complement the rest of the staff. But remember that prejudice is not limited to the "official" areas of race, color, creed, national origin, gender, and age. Discrimination based on other non-work-related factors, while not illegal, can be just as damaging to the health of your unit.

Is doing what you did ever right?

Although you should evaluate your workers solely in terms of their performance, there *are* factors that you can consider that may not obviously be a part of "performance," but there's always some danger.

You can consider how well a worker's style meshes with yours and that of other team members. If your work requires very close interaction among group members and one person tends toward brainstorming and "what if's" while the rest of the group is very linear and goal-oriented in its approach, the worker with the more global style may not fit with the rest of the group. BUT, he may be your most creative worker and add more by his differences than he would by being just like everyone else.

If your job requires lots of face-to-face contact with strangers and you have a worker who's not comfortable in unfamiliar social situations, you might be prone to give her less interesting assignments. BUT, while her interaction style might be different from the glad-handers in the rest of the group, she may win others' confidence in a quiet and unobtrusive way that is just as effective as that of the others—or even more effective.

So while you *can* consider factors other than demonstrated performance in deciding which workers should get greater support, almost any decision that's not based on performance has the potential to harm as well as help you and your unit. Sometimes the harm is so subtle that you'll never be conscious of it, but diversity of thought, of approach, of style, really can enhance the workgroup.

A tip for mistake-free managing:

Sometimes, particularly when there's a conflict between workers, you'll be caught in a situation where you can't escape favoring one over the other. But to draw the best performance possible from your group, your best approach is to support *everyone* in the group and avoid favoritism. We've talked earlier about the need to recognize that each worker is different from every other worker, with different "hot buttons" and different values. But you can accommodate a lot of different styles and still let every worker know that you support him or her as much as you do every other worker. People respond much better when they know they're appreciated.

1-3 The Mistake: Continuing to deal as a co-worker with people you now manage

The situation: You overhear this conversation in the hall:

"I just don't understand what's with Karen these days. Just Tuesday, she went out with us for a while after work—laughing and joking like she always has. Then today she called me into her office and I felt like I was being reprimanded for putting in a bid that was too high for the Step-athon job. One minute she wants to be my friend, the next she wants to be my boss. I sure never thought she'd turn on us like that when she got this promotion. It's a real disappointment."

Why was it a mistake?

The roles of manager and of worker are very distinct. One of the least pleasant aspects of being a manager is that you sometimes have to correct your workers. And even when the work is going well, you will occasionally be called upon to make decisions that are unpopular from workers' point of view—even though they may be best for the organization. Unless you work in a "leaderless team" environment, some differences will remain between worker and leader. And if you try to fill both roles, you'll fill neither of them well. Workers will resent your "two-faced" approach, and your managers will find you ineffective. So you'll lose on both fronts.

How can you recover from it quickly?

If you've been promoted from worker to manager in the same unit, so that the people you now manage used to be your co-workers, you're in a tough situation. Even though promoting from within is a sound management practice, it puts the new manager under additional pressures. Ideally, you will have taken steps already to make sure your staff understands your new relationship. If not, you can remedy the problem quickly.

Call your staff together for a general meeting. This doesn't have to be a special event; you can have the discussion as part of a regular staff meeting. But as part of the discussion, talk with them specifically about your relationship with them as manager to worker.

"I think that there are some real advantages to having been chosen as manager of this group from among the people working here. It means I'm familiar with the work that goes on here—my own former job as well as your work. It means I know all the people and how we work together and what we do well and not so well.

"But it also means that, as manager of the unit now, I'm expected to handle things differently from the way I did when I was at working level. It means that sometimes I'm going to have to make decisions that some of you won't like. It means that sometimes I'll have to talk to you about performance or your vacation requests or new policies or requirements that won't be very popular. And I'll have to support upper-management decisions even when I don't agree with them, because I'm part of management. There will be times when that won't be easy for either of us because we've worked side by side for so long.

"I hope that my being a part of the unit will be more of a plus for you and for the organization than a minus. But I think it's important to put on the table the way things have changed, so that we can all make the adjustment."

How can you consistently do it right from now on?

The most important thing you can do is to be aware that people who used to be your co-workers will look at you differently once you become a manager. That doesn't necessarily mean that you can't have social relationships with those people any more (but be aware that it might if neither of you are comfortable with the relationship in your changed roles). Here are some "do's and don't's:"

Don't be a part of the office gossip any more, since your role now is to support everyone on the team.

Don't join any longer in the periodic "boss-bashing" that goes on in most offices, partly because you're part of the management group now and partly because you may sometimes be the boss who's being bashed!

Do use your continuing relationship with the workgroup as an opportunity to be open and honest about your reaction to upper-management policies—even when you don't think they're good for the group. Because you know your workers so well, you can say, "I see some real problems with this decision, but we'll just have to stick together and tough it out." And since you can identify closely with the people you manage, they may have more trust in you when you have to lead them in a direction they're not comfortable with.

Do bring your experience with the group and the work to management meetings, not as an employee advocate, but as a manager who can see the impact of management decisions on the day-to-day workings of the unit.

Don't take your new role to the opposite extreme and separate yourself more than necessary from your former co-workers. Don't wear your position on your sleeve and don't project the attitude that you're better than your former co-workers because you're in management now. Not only will you lose all the advantages that promotion from within can give you, but you'll create distance and distrust between yourself and the workgroup.

Is doing what you did ever right?

There's a fine line between socializing with your workgroup and trying to be "one of the guys (or girls)." It is never fair to your workers to confuse your roles. It is always right to be warm and friendly and caring.

A tip for mistake-free managing:

One of your most important tasks as a manager is to earn the trust and confidence of your workers. When you move from a worker position to management, even though your workgroup may have trusted you implicitly as a co-worker, they will need time to test how well they can trust you in your new role as manager. You're going to make some mistakes in your new job; that's inevitable. How you handle those mistakes—whether you admit when you're wrong and try to correct it or try to hide what you don't know or what you've done poorly—has a lot of impact on the level of trust others have in you.

If you have trouble at first separating your roles as manager and co-worker, it's not fatal. It's seriously damaging and potentially fatal *only* if you fail to admit to the group that your role has changed and if you fail to take on your new role appropriately.

1-4 The Mistake: Talking about a worker's personal issues with others

The situation:

"I know you don't want to have to be out of town three weeks in a row, Jean," you admit, "and this is a lot to ask on such short notice. But Grace's son, Kyle, is very sick, maybe terminally ill, and I just can't ask her to be gone right now."

Reluctantly, Jean agrees. Not long after, Grace enters your office, visibly upset.

"I thought I could trust you," she accuses, "but Jean just came to my desk to get the paperwork for next week's trip and said she was sorry my son was so sick. If I had wanted anyone else to know about Kyle I would have told them myself. I certainly don't need you telling my business to everyone in the office."

Why was it a mistake?

Workers want information kept confidential for any of a plethora of reasons. They may find the topic embarrassing; they may consider personal information something that's nobody else's business; they may be too distraught to deal with others' inquiries and sympathy. And it really doesn't matter why they want to keep certain information confidential. It's their call to make.

Chances are that many of those workers weren't that happy even that they had to share the information with you. They recognize that, as the boss, you need to know personal details to explain their absences or requests for accommodation. But the only reason you have the information is that the worker saw no other way to make important arrangements to juggle both work and personal demands.

If the worker did share the information with you willingly, it was because she trusted your judgment and discretion. She expected that you would not broadcast her personal details around the office without her express permission.

You've violated a trust. That's why this was a mistake, well-meaning though you may have been. Your relationship with Grace is seriously damaged because you either ignored her request to keep the information confidential or because you weren't sensitive enough to even realize that what she'd told you wasn't to be shared. Once that trusting relationship is damaged, Grace will have a very difficult time confiding in you again.

Maybe that doesn't seem very important to you. Maybe you think that personal matters should be left at home. But that's not the way the world works anymore, and losing a worker's trust and confidence is a serious mistake—with long lasting consequences.

How can you recover from it quickly?

You can't. The best you can do is to apologize to Grace: "I'm very sorry I broke a confidence. I didn't realize that you wanted to keep your son's illness just between the two of us, and I misjudged the situation. Please understand that I was not trying to hurt you or Kyle. I was trying to help. I hope you'll forgive my blundering, and I promise I'll never divulge details about your personal life again."

How can you consistently do it right from now on?

This is actually a little trickier than our scenario might have implied. Some workers don't mind having you tell other members of the staff about their personal situations. In fact, some people will have told you things *because* they think it would be less awkward if other members of the staff heard the news from you rather than from them personally.

Divorce presents a common dilemma. If Grace and her husband get divorced, she may prefer that no one in the office knows about it. If someone finds out through other sources, she'll deal with it, but she's a very private person and would rather keep all the details of her personal life out of the office.

Jean might prefer that others in the office know she's getting a divorce, particularly if she needs to ask for some special treatment for a while, but she also might prefer not to be the one to tell them. She sees your role as her supervisor to act as a go-between, sensitively letting the rest of the staff know what's going on without bothering her. If other staff members approach her to offer support, she'll be happy to talk to them, but she feels awkward about making the announcement.

Another worker might want the other members of the staff to know that she's getting a divorce, but wants to tell them herself so she can be sure that her side of the story is heard. She may be concerned that staff members who know both her and her husband will "take sides," and she wants to influence which side they'll be on. So she'd rather you didn't tell anyone, although she'll tell lots of people herself.

The variations are endless. So how do you know what each person wants and expects who shares a personal confidence with you? You can't use your own instincts and reactions as a guide, because this is such an individual preference.

What's a good rule of thumb?

We've found that the best rule is to assume that a worker who shares personal information with you intends that you keep it confidential. It doesn't matter what the information is. It may be that her husband has been indicted for rape and murder and is likely to be sentenced to prison for the rest of his life. It may be that her son's babysitter has quit and she needs some time off. At either extreme, personal information is personal. And without express permission to share the information, the best choice is not to share it at all.

- *What if you think it's important for the worker's benefit that others know of her situation?*

What if Grace's son is likely to be in and out of the hospital for several months, and you'd like to ask someone in the office to be a backup for her in case she has to make a last minute cancellation of a business trip? It would be a lot easier to get a volunteer, and you wouldn't have to deal with others' resentment of Grace's "special treatment" if you could explain why a backup is so necessary.

In that case, tell Grace why you would like to discreetly share the information she's given you and *ask her permission*. At worst, she'll say, "Well, of course you can tell other people. Why wouldn't you?" More likely, she'll appreciate the fact that you've been considerate and sensitive enough to ask—and she'll be more willing to trust you with confidential information in the future.

- *What if it's important for the* company's *benefit that others know of her personal situation?*

What if Grace confides to you that her husband has been fired for selling his company's trade secrets to their competitors? You know the story is likely to get out. It may even be reported in the local media. Isn't Grace likely to be tarred with the same brush, even though you're convinced that she's completely loyal to your company? Could Grace's husband's indictment reflect badly on the reputation of your own company? Doesn't your boss need to know what's going on?

When an employee confides information to you that you believe *needs* to be shared with others in the company, it's not appropriate to ask her permission to share it. You already know what you intend to do, and it really doesn't matter whether Grace agrees or not. Your loyalty to your boss and to the company demand that you pass on what you've learned.

Here, you should simply tell the worker that you need to share the information. Tell her exactly what you intend to share and to whom you intend to talk. If you can pass the information in a way that is less harmful to the employee's confidence, do it. If you can limit the number of people who will be given the information, do it. But be absolutely honest with your employee about what you need to do with the information she's given you. Don't lie, and don't hide your intentions. She may not be happy about having given you the information, and she may be reluctant to share confidences in the future, but you *will* have maintained her trust and your own integrity. That itself is a lot.

Is doing what you did ever right?

No. You should *always* assume that personal information is not to be shared—with anyone—without the employee's agreement, or at least her knowledge.

A tip for mistake-free managing:

Although there are many situations in which sharing personal information may seem to be in the best interests of the employee, making the decision on your own smacks of paternalism. Maybe if other people knew about Grace's son being ill they would volunteer to help out with some of her assignments, take some trips so she can stay home, even offer to help with his care or to take on some of her household chores so she can spend time with him. But the choice is Grace's. It's equally possible that she doesn't want help from anyone else. Work assignments may help take her mind off her son's problems; occasional travel may provide a respite from the demands of home and family; household chores may offer an opportunity for her to keep an eye on her son at home without seeming to be hovering.

People's reactions to difficult times are highly personal and individual. There is no right or wrong reaction, and many times there's really nothing anyone else can do to ease the burden. So the best way for you to help your worker who's going through tough times is simply to:

1. Offer your support, but don't be offended if she declines, and

2. Keep your own counsel, unless she requests otherwise.

1-5 The Mistake: Taking workers for granted

The situation:

"Steve, this is just too much. This is the third time in a row you've asked me to do these inspection visits, and nobody else here has done any for months. It's not fair."

"But, Juanita, I thought you were the one person in the group I could count on. No one else does the visits as well, and you've always been available before. What's happened?"

"I just don't like the idea of you sticking me with this stuff all the time. Sure, I want you to know you can depend on me—I just don't want to be treated like a door-mat you can step on whenever you want to!"

Why was it a mistake?

Just as Juanita told Steve: Workers want their managers to know they're dependable, but they don't want to be doormats. Most workers know that there are lots of thankless tasks to be done in any job. But when you keep coming back to the same people over and over, without any recognition of their special dedication, those workers get burned out and turned off.

All workers need to be recognized both for their talents and for their willingness to stick with the job until its done. It doesn't take a lot of time or resources, but the paybacks are tremendous.

How can you recover from it quickly?

Go back to Juanita right away and let her know that you are concerned that she not feel she is being taken advantage of.

You could explore options for other people to become proficient in performing the work: "I think maybe I'll ask Tricia to go with you on this trip. Then, after you've shown her the ropes, and maybe worked with her back here in the office to get up to speed, she can begin taking over some of the load."

You can discuss with her shifts in her other work to allow her to carry the burden of this assignment without being overwhelmed: "Let's talk about the work you're doing on the quality management system. I really need you on the inspection visits, but we could probably hand some of the system planning work over to Tim."

And if you're really in a bind and need Juanita to do this job plus the other work she's normally assigned, let her know that this is only a temporary need and you'll figure out some other way to cover everything after this crisis is over.

How can you consistently do it right from now on?

There are several things you can do to keep your workers from feeling they're being taken for granted. You can do just one or (preferably) all of these together:

• *Thank your workers* whenever they take on extra work or expend extra effort on an assignment. Most people will be happy to do more for a manager who appreciates what they've done and recognizes their contributions.

• *Support your workers* in your dealings with other managers or other organizations. You don't *have* to volunteer your unit for every assignment—especially if there are other units that are not as busy. Balance your concern for the well-being of your workforce with the need to be a team player in the larger organization.

• *Don't give orders; make requests.* There's a big difference between making a pronouncement that Juanita will make the inspection visits and asking her to work them into her assignment. If you ask her to take on the assignment, and if you have a mutually trusting relationship with her, she will most likely tell you if she's feeling overwhelmed. Then you can negotiate out how best to get everything accomplished:

"Let's see if Corinne can take over the reports this month" or "We can let the deadline slip for the systems design project to give you time to squeeze in these visits."

And as we discussed in the recovery techniques above, even an explanation about why you need to ask for superhuman efforts in this case can help to get Juanita's buy-in.

• *Whenever possible, let your workers "self-assign" tasks.* If you have several people who could do the work, even if you already know that one or two of them are swamped, give the assignment to the workgroup as a whole and let them decide how to manage it. Maybe they'll negotiate out a swap in assignments. Maybe they'll propose some changes in deadlines or priorities. And maybe they'll even come up with the same solution you did. But it will be *their* solution.

You're not giving up control. Everyone recognizes that you're still in charge and will have the last word. But if your workers have a say in how the work is distributed, they'll be less likely to resent your piling more on them; they'll be more accepting of the final decision; and they may be able to distribute it even more efficiently than you could because they're closer to it.

Is doing what you did ever right?

Doing what you did is never the best way to get the work of your unit accomplished. If you only occasionally take your workers for granted, and only when there's a crisis looming, you probably won't have done much damage.

But the problem is keeping the practice to occasional crises. It's very easy to fall into the trap of considering everything a crisis, especially if that's the environment in which your company operates (and it often is these days). Soon your employees will become burned out and resentful of your disregard for them. At that point, productivity in even "normal" periods is likely to fall—which creates a crisis, which calls for emergency responses, which lures you into taking for granted their cooperation again, and on . . . and on . . . and on.

A tip for mistake-free managing:

Although it's important to reward workers who do a good job, effective motivation involves both *recognition* and rewards. Workers know that it's not always possible for you to give them monetary awards or even to formally recognize their accomplishments. In many organizations, those formal award mechanisms are controlled at much higher levels than yours.

But a "thank you" for a job well done costs nothing and reaps great benefits. Even in our generally nonauthoritarian culture, many people are "pleasers" who get their greatest satisfaction in knowing that they have fulfilled, or exceeded, your expectations of them. Let them know when they do—in simple words, without a lot of fanfare, just a simple "Thanks, I really appreciated that"—but *often*.

1-6 The Mistake: Criticizing without complimenting

The situation: "Lucinda, it was not a good idea for you to try to cover two stations at once. Cleo could have taken a break some other time, and she certainly didn't need to run errands right at the busiest time of the day. Your helping her out just encourages her to be gone longer. And then you couldn't keep up anyway. So now we've got a whole slew of unhappy customers and who-knows-how-many mistakes to correct."

"So maybe it wasn't the best judgment I could have made," Lucinda answers, "but I was trying to help you get the work done and not have to listen to her complain later. Surely I deserve some credit for that, not just blame."

Why was it a mistake?

When responsible employees make a mistake in the work or make an error in judgment, they almost always do it with the best intentions. When you criticize an employee without also complimenting, or at least acknowledging, what she did right, she becomes resentful and in time may come to believe that there's nothing she can do to please you.

It's important to note, though, that this is an area where there's a lot of disagreement about the right thing to do. Some managers believe that when you link a criticism with a compliment, you dilute the force of the criticism and your workers won't understand just how serious the criticism is. There probably are times when a compliment isn't appropriate (and we'll discuss those below). But for the most part, you need to let your workers know that, although you disagree with a specific action or decision, you still value them and appreciate their good efforts.

How can you recover from it quickly?

This is a mistake you can't recover from immediately. The damage has been done. But you can begin at least to recover soon, the very next time you have a specific "good deed" to discuss with Lucinda. That's an opportunity to take her aside and say:

"I know we had a difference of approach before, but I want to make sure you know how important you are to this team. What you did just now to make that customer go away happy is one of your real strengths. Thanks."

Again, you can't take back the words you said before. And you should make it clear to Lucinda that you're not being patronizing or condescending when you tell her how well she's doing in other areas. What you want to get across effectively is that there's praise to be given, not just criticism. She needs to hear both.

How can you consistently do it right from now on?

Whenever you need to criticize a worker, stop for a minute before you begin—to collect your thoughts and decide how best to approach the subject. Go over the incident or the pattern of incidents you want to discuss with the person. Identify

• What you wanted to have happen that didn't happen: Here, the problem is that you don't want Lucinda to take on more work than she can reasonably handle, because then she will end up satisfying no one.

• What behavior you didn't want: Here, Lucinda volunteered to cover for Cleo when Cleo needed to take care of her own workload. And then, after Cleo left on her break, Lucinda tried to cover both workstations at once.

• What the worker should have done instead: Here, Lucinda should have told Cleo that she was too busy to cover for her right at that time. Then, if Cleo left anyway, Lucinda should have worked both sets of customers into place at her workstation rather than trying to handle both workstations separately.

• What the worker did that was right and should be continued: Even though her methods weren't very efficient, Lucinda's attempt to compensate for her co-worker's absence was just what you needed for her to do.

Then, when you sit down with the worker, you can present a much more balanced and informative picture of what should have been done. Praising the good work along with criticizing the parts that need correction will keep your workers motivated at the same time they learn how to do the job better.

Of course, this is a simple example and sometimes it's a lot harder to identify something worth complimenting. Maybe one of your workers just spent three hours in a pleasant conversation with a dissatisfied customer but failed to get any useful information at all or to negotiate a resolution to the dissatisfaction. Maybe the report you absolutely needed last Wednesday was submitted right on time but was such a superficial analysis that it might as well not have been done at all. In those cases, you may really have to dig to find something to *genuinely* praise.

But the purpose of all criticism is to help improve your workers' performance. Remember that, and you'll be able to stay focused on trying both to correct the mistake and reinforce what the worker has done well.

Is doing what you did ever right?

Yes. There will occasionally be times when a worker does something so egregious or with such severe consequences that you need to shock her into accepting the need for *immediate* change. If a worker is rude to a customer or a supplier, if a worker has lied, if a worker publicly refuses to follow your direction, these are all cases when you must act swiftly and decisively. No compliments, no subtleties, just firm correction.

Every manager will have at least a few such incidents once in a while. But most of what you need to counsel or criticize employees about is neither so dire nor so urgent.

A tip for mistake-free managing:

People know when you're not being genuine. The formula we've described here won't work if you mechanically choose a compliment that's not sincere or doesn't fit the situation, just to have something nice to say. If you can't *honestly* identify something about each worker that is worth reinforcing, there's a real problem, either with you or your worker. And if you throw out compliments meaninglessly, workers soon won't know whether to trust anything you tell them.

1-7 The Mistake: Being too lax with your workgroup

The situation: "I see Bill's just getting back from lunch, and it's 2 o'clock already. He's over two days behind in getting those specifications to me, and it doesn't look like he's too worked up about it. I sure would like to *get* him worked up!

"But the minute I say something, he'll start whining that Chris was late coming in yesterday morning, and

Josef left early, and on and on and on. It's just not worth the hassle. I think I'll let it go this time. Next time though . . ."

Why was it a mistake?

Failing to deal with the problems that arise in your unit, whether they're performance or conduct issues, is a mistake on two counts:

First, your workers won't know what's expected of them if you don't tell them. Failing to let them know that there's a problem that needs to be corrected means that it *won't* be. And you'll end up living with it from now on.

Second, while you may believe you're being kindhearted not to push the issue, that's not the message your workers will get. They're going to believe you really don't care what happens in your workgroup. And the natural response is, "If the boss doesn't care, why should I?"

How can you recover from it quickly?

If your lackadaisical response to issues is one you've practiced over time, you can't recover quickly. If you've been letting things go, putting them off, hoping they'll take care of themselves, any attempt to correct course quickly is going to make you look like a tyrant. And that only creates another problem.

But if you've let things slide only a few times and haven't really developed a pattern of behavior, you can recover immediately and simply: Take action.

What happens if you challenge Bill about his long lunches: "Hello, Bill; I noticed you were pretty late getting back from lunch today. That seems to be happening quite a bit lately. Is there some problem?"

Either Bill does have some problem that means he has to be gone longer at lunchtime than the usual company practice would allow, or he doesn't: "No, there's no problem. I've been trying to squeeze in some errands along with a quick lunch, and I guess the time just got away from me. I'll have to watch it a little closer."

And, assuming that Bill is as good as his word, that's probably the end of it.

How can you consistently do it right from now on?

Decide in advance what you will accept and what you won't. This is a first step only. The purpose of this exercise is to help you set out for yourself what behavior is tolerable and what isn't. Then when you're tempted to blow off something, you can look back on this little list and remind yourself what your limits are.

We're not talking here about establishing a rigid or comprehensive set of rules, but rather a short set of guidelines in key areas. You'll want to cover things like attendance and lunch breaks, timeliness of assignments, customer relations, and just one or two other areas in which the worker can control what he does or doesn't do.

Some things will already be covered by company policy, and you just need to list the area and know what the policy is. If your company has a rule against accepting favors from prospective suppliers, you don't need your own guideline—the company has already established one.

You also don't need to try to cover every situation. These are guides for you, at least initially, to help you shape your own decisions. So, in the case of long lunches, you may decide an occasional two-hour lunch is okay, if it happens only rarely, but you won't go along with a worker's consistently coming back from lunch 15 to 20 minutes late.

Use your list to help decide when to act and when to lay back. If Bill seems to be coming back from lunch on time for a couple of weeks and then begins his "extended" lunch pattern again, you've decided in advance about when you need to step in. It's going to be harder to temporize or procrastinate, because you've told yourself already whether it's time to act.

Act. When Bill crosses the line, talk to him—in just the way we described above. Use a straightforward, matter of fact approach:

1. Explain what happened that shouldn't have (or what didn't happen that should)

2. Identify what should (or shouldn't) happen in the future

3. If Bill doesn't offer on his own, ask for his commitment to change

Practice, practice, practice. Use your guidelines to deal with each situation that arises, over and over and over again, until it's such a consistent response that you can throw the list away.

Is doing what you did ever right?

Without a doubt, there are times when you need to cut your workers some slack. Deadline pressures, personal issues, a particularly demanding customer all temper your decision to correct or not to correct. You don't make a mistake when you use your best judgment to decide that one situation needs to be dealt with one way and another needs to be dealt with differently. (That's exactly what you're *supposed* to do!) You make a mistake when you establish a pattern that consistently fails to deal with problems, so that your workers come to expect that they can get away with almost anything.

A tip for mistake-free managing:

Two of the most important skills managers need to develop are knowing when to step in and knowing when to step out. And one of the most important times to step *out* is when workers come to you to resolve differences between them. "Do I have to stay late to cover the phones this evening or can Linda stay?" "I think the cover of this report should be blue, but Charlie insists on making it green." "Marcus doesn't want to mention the contract review project when we pitch to this customer, but I thought it was a really good selling point."

Unless the issues really have serious significance, your only response should be, "Work it out yourselves."

Unlike the failure to correct problems that arise, refusing to arbitrate these petty disputes is not laxity, it's empowerment. You want your workers to make their own decisions; you want them to take risks and try new ideas for improvement. Your job is step *in* to coach and mentor and lead them, to the point that you can step *out* and let them take over on their own.

1-8 The Mistake: Being too strict with your workgroup

The situation: "So, Randy, just what was the idea of your not calling in this morning to let me know you were going over to the Stony Brook office before you came in here? Don't you realize that I need to know where you are? What if something had come up?"

"Wait a minute, Boss. I've worked here for five years for a lot of different managers, and I have *never* not been somewhere I was supposed to be. I go over to Stony Brook every few days to look over the new claims and talk to the examiners. I've never had to report every move to any other manager, and I don't know why I should report every minute to you."

Why was it a mistake?

Being too strict with the members of your workgroup causes several problems.

• *It restricts their ability to make decisions on their own.* You can't make all the decisions or do all the work that has to be done in your unit. That's why you have a staff. But to use the staff efficiently, you need to "leverage your resources"—to let the staff do as much as they can without intervention so that you can multiply the amount of work that gets done.

• *It sends the message that you don't trust them.* When you require your workgroup to report to you on every single event of their days, to ask permission before they do anything, to call them to task for every deviation from *your* norms, they get the idea that you don't trust their actions or their motives. And you create a self-fulfilling prophecy: Treat people as though you don't trust them, and they will begin to act in untrustworthy ways. Watch the clock to see when people get in after lunch, and they'll start playing games to see how much they can get away with. Check every detail of every single piece of work your staff produces, and they'll stop worrying about the details on their own—because they know you'll catch the mistakes.

• *It demotivates your staff.* We know a (true) story of a manager who used to call in her staff every morning to tell her what they planned to do that day, and who had them write reports at the end of every day to tell her what they'd accomplished. You can imagine how fast people bolted from that unit! And the people who were stuck did less and less work—until they eventually spent a good part of each day just writing their accomplishment reports, but producing almost nothing. How would you feel?

How can you recover from it quickly?

This is one of those cases where the best recovery is an apology, as in: "I'm sorry, Randy, I do trust you to manage your own time. I was concerned that you weren't going to make it to our 10:30 meeting. And you were a key player in that discussion. I just overreacted."

How can you consistently do it right from now on?

• *Plan your responses rather than reacting on the spot.* This is another case (like the manager who's too lax, discussed above) where it's very useful to work out in advance which things are important enough to warrant some intervention and which things are best left alone. Then stick to your plan and use it as a touch-stone to evaluate other situations that come up.

• *Get to know your workers, strong points and their weaknesses.* There's no single formula that will be effective with every person. It's a mistake to treat all workers alike. Some people need to be prodded and work best in a structured envi-ronment. Those people will benefit from set rules and some enforcement, and it's worth playing to those preferences, at least in the short run. Most people work best when they have some autonomy, and they then require much less direction or enforcement. But more autonomous workers may respond to closer supervision in some areas. It's up to you to figure out what works best.

• *Set up regular staff meetings to keep in touch with what everyone's doing.* Many staff meetings turn into weekly sermons from the boss on any of a number of (often irrelevant) topics. Your staff meetings will be different. Instead of your speaking for half an hour or forty-five minutes on the topic of the day, use your staff meetings as an opportunity for the whole group to share with each other what's going on in the unit. Encourage workers to bring up troublesome cases so that the group can brainstorm on how to solve them. This might be tough at first. Not many workers will want to admit to you and their peers that "I just can't fig-ure out how much we're bound by this letter of intent to Crystal Club." So start by "planting" some workers who'll talk about one of their problem cases, and how they solved it. Once the ice is broken and people see how they can learn from one another, they'll be happy to participate in these group problem-solving sessions.

And how does that cure your tendency to be too strict with the group? In sev-eral ways.

First, you don't have to be an "enforcer," demanding to know what's going on all the time in your unit, because you'll find out on a regular basis. Second, by solving problems as a group rather than through your efforts alone, you'll not only get the benefit of many ideas, but you'll be able to guide the staff by adopting other people's suggestions (not always by your pronouncements). This approach still ensures that you set the direction for the unit, but softens your authoritarian image with a more participative style.

Is doing what you did ever right?

It might be. We suggested before that you need to get to know your workers—to recognize who works best with very little direction and who needs more help. Unfortunately, many workers, especially those who don't have a lot of job experience, come to us with limited self-management skills. Many haven't even learned the most essential basics, like the need to show up on time, to put in a full shift, not to spend company time gossiping on the telephone. Those workers need more coaching.

If Randy is one of those workers who's not reliable, then checking up on him is appropriate, at least until he learns what's expected of him and begins to deliver.

A tip for mistake-free managing:

One of your goals as a manager should be to develop your unit to the point that you don't need to play "enforcer" anymore. Even in working with those employees whose self-management skills are weak, you should plan to spend only a limited time reinforcing your message.

Let your employees know what you expect of them. Tell them up front: "This is how we work here. This is what I expect." Coach, remind, reinforce, and remind again—but not forever. At some point, we expect our workers to take responsibility for performing to expectations. Some very bright and competent workers are just more trouble than they're worth, and you'll reach the point where it's time to part company.

1-9 The Mistake: Not keeping your workers fully trained

The situation: "I just don't understand what's wrong with you, Don. It seems as if you're in here every other week wanting to go to this class or that class, or some seminar or conference. You went to that cost-accounting session a couple of years ago when we changed our system. Nothing all that earth-shattering has happened in the office since then. So why do you keep bugging me about going to training?"

Why was it a mistake?

We're assuming that all of your new employees do get the training they need to take on their new assignments, whether in a classroom, or through video or computer-based training, or by sitting with a senior worker to learn the ropes.

But what about the people who've been with you for two or three or four years? With shrinking budgets and a shrinking workforce, it's very easy to conclude that you can't afford to provide additional training for workers who already know how to do the job.

Big mistake!

If you have workers who haven't received any training in the last two years, they've already fallen behind. Workers need training not only to learn new skills, but also to refresh the skills they already have. Even the best of workers can't keep up in technologically advanced fields without regular exposure to new ideas and practices. But the need for periodic updates isn't limited to just high-tech work. Business practices change; workers get comfortable (and stale) in the same old rut; people lose skills in areas where they don't get a lot of opportunity to exercise their abilities. All of those are compelling reasons for making sure your staff (even your senior, most experienced people) get the chance to interact and learn from others in their fields.

How can you recover from it quickly?

This is one of those times when quick recovery isn't as important as making a consistent change in your behavior. Sure, sending everyone off to a conference some time this year will help. But what happens in six months, or next year, or the year after? Will you deny the next round of training requests, figuring that once everyone's gotten recharged you won't need to worry about continued training for another year or two?

How can you consistently do it right from now on?

• *Talk to all of your workers about how they can improve their skills.* That's not going to be the same for each person. Some workers would benefit from college courses that will expand their skills. Others would be helped more by opportunities to interact with others who work in similar fields to share ideas and exchange "best practices."

Tie your training discussions to the specific job each person performs. When Don, who keeps the accounts straight for the office, decides he wants to attend a computer graphics workshop, you need to ask him how he plans to use his enhanced skills on the job. If he tells you it's so he can design better presentations for your monthly reports to the company president, that might be a great idea. But if he can't tie his request to current or reasonably foreseeable job demands, it's probably not an investment your company will want to make.

• *Keep everyone on the alert for training opportunities.* Keep a folder in your office of seminars, conferences, and skill-building classes that apply to the kinds of work your staff performs. As advertisements and announcements come in (and they arrive nearly every day—unless you've coached your secretary to weed them out before they reach your desk), flip through them to see if they are likely matches for any of the training needs you've identified with your workers. Let your workers review the folder occasionally too. They may spot something worthwhile that you've missed.

• *Look for alternative ways to update your workers' skills.* Formal training is not the only way to keep your workers at the cutting edge. You can have an in-house conference in which people throughout your company share their knowledge and skills with one another. Maybe every couple of months a staff meeting could be devoted to a review of some new business practice or idea. Workers could volunteer to read particular periodicals and newsletters, then report back to the rest of the staff. When you send someone to a training event, make it a practice to have him share what he's learned when he returns.

Ask your staff to help generate ideas for enhancing their skills without spending thousands of dollars. Once they recognize that you're serious about training, you'll all be attuned to ways to increase competence without draining resources.

Is doing what you did ever right?

Certainly we're not advocating that you grant every worker's request to attend training. You need to exercise your discretion in deciding which training will enhance the skills of your unit and which is just "nice to have."

But it's never appropriate to dismiss your workers' requirements for continuing skills development. The rest of the business world keeps moving ahead, whether you're with it or not. And, if you're not, you'll soon be left behind.

A tip for mistake-free managing:

Take a break from the day-to-day routine once in while to ask yourself, "What do I think this office should be doing two or three years from now that it's not doing today?" Then followup by asking, "And whom do I have on my staff that's capable of doing that work?"

If the answer is "no one," you've got a training need.

Begin to think of training as an investment in the future—the future of your company. Many companies over the past few years have made training issues a part of the strategic goals of the organization. Those companies recognize that, while it's great to have a vision for where they want to be, they'll never get there without skilled and knowledgeable workers to carry out the vision.

1-10 The Mistake: Not encouraging your workers to improve

The situation:
Jessica caught you in the hall early this morning, as you were dripping with rain and trying futilely to wipe your briefing notes dry.

"I wanted to explain about that report I gave you yesterday," she began. "I felt like I could have done so much better if I knew a little bit more about statistics or research design, and, even though I did my best, I don't think I covered all the bases very well."

"No problem," you fibbed, smudging the briefing notes even more with your damp scarf. "I just asked Rita to look it over and spruce it up a little bit. Nobody expects you to be an expert on something you get stuck with only a few times a year. And besides, we've already got a couple of research people on the staff. You just worry about making sure the numbers add up, and we'll let Rita worry about explaining them."

Why was it a mistake?

Jessica has shown some initiative in wanting to improve her skills. If she's a good worker already, she can become even more valuable by developing further.

The real problem, though, is that when you limit Jessica's development, she'll not only fail to advance, but she's likely to lose interest even in the areas where she's already skilled.

Good workers need to grow. In some ways, workers are like flowers. If you try to reduce the amount of sun or water a flower gets so that it won't outgrow the pot it's planted in, it just doesn't work. Instead of staying the same size, it becomes less robust; it droops; its leaves and petals wither and fall away. In just the same way, when you stifle the growth of your workers, their performance doesn't remain the same. It, too, deteriorates from lack of attention and stimulation.

How can you recover from it quickly?

If you can without missing an important deadline, retrieve Jessica's report from Rita. Take it back to Jessica, explaining, "I know you did the best you could with this, Jessica, so I didn't want to make you feel bad this morning about not having done as well as you would have liked. But if you're really interested in developing your skills, let's have you work with Rita as she interprets the data you've pulled together."

The quality of the work will still be high since you'll have your senior analyst working on it, but Jessica will get a chance to see how the work is done. Then you and Jessica, perhaps with Rita as another resource, can decide later whether Jessica has the aptitude to do the work and how best to learn it.

How can you consistently do it right from now on?

• *Make sure that at least two people in your unit know how to do every job.* One of the most natural ways to expand your workers' skills is to cross-train them in the functions you're already performing. That's good not only for your staff but for you too. We've been caught before in situations where we were only "one deep" with no backup, had a worker with an emergency and a critical deadline, and had to call in reinforcements from an entirely different office. It's both embarrassing and traumatic.

Assign job "buddies" to cover for each other during absences and peak periods. Buddies can be workers who have similar responsibilities, or they might be workers with different kinds of jobs who want to explore other lines of work. You can give your staff an opportunity to expand their horizons at the same time you strengthen the unit itself.

• *Listen carefully when workers tell you they want to "get ahead."* Do you hear your staff making comments like: "I'm looking for something a little more challenging." "This routine is getting a little dull; maybe it's time to look for greener pastures."

How do you react? Do you immediately assume that means "I want a promotion?"

Maybe it does. But often, especially in today's environment where people know that promotions are few and far between, it means just what the words say: "I've got this job down pat now, and I want to do something more interesting."

Jump on those opportunities as fast as you can. What kinds of skills do your workers already have? Could your unit perform better if your people had better or more varied skills? Are there new markets you could conquer or new functions you could handle that are close to what you're doing now, but require just a little "plussing-up" of your skills? When your workers come to you looking for something new and exciting, have some of those ideas in your hip pocket. Then challenge your staff to find ways to develop the skills and make themselves even more indispensable to the company.

• *Make it a habit to encourage your staff*: "Good work, Jessica. It looks like you're really picking up on these statistics." "Thanks for finding those mistakes in our performance report, Rita. You really saved us that time."

Let your good workers know that you notice what they do and appreciate it. You don't need to look for new challenges all the time. If people know that they're in an environment that encourages growth, they'll respond.

Is doing what you did ever right?

Once again, you have to know your workers.

If Jessica is someone who's made a career of beating herself up over things she can't control (and looks for confirmation of her own poor opinion of herself), your instincts were correct. This first discussion of her project was *not* the time to talk to her about how she could improve her skills. On the other hand, if Jessica is a consistently positive and confident worker who's genuinely interested in improving, you should take advantage of every opportunity to encourage her to improve her skills.

In either case, your overall goal needs to be to keep your workers challenged and interested, both so they'll develop new skills and so they'll maintain a keen edge on the skills they already possess.

A tip for mistake-free managing:

Remember the last time you got so wrapped up in a project that you became oblivious to everything around you and just charged through the work? While much of the work we do isn't likely to be that engrossing, those peak experiences, demanding and exhausting though they may be, are the events that keep us charged up and motivated.

The next time a new project comes up that you think is just a stretch beyond what one of your staff can handle, think about assigning it to her anyway. The demand to stretch and improve is also an opportunity to grow.

1-11   The Mistake: Permitting workers who need to work together to compete

The situation: "We could have done a much better job on that training package," Tommy complained, "but Kristen just wouldn't cooperate. So she did her part and I did my part, and the final product reflects it—looks just like two people did two pieces of work and stuck them together."

"Kristen has always seemed like a pleasant sort of person to me," you reply, "and the parts of the project she showed me were excellent. What do you think happened?"

"Oh, I know exactly what happened," countered Tommy. "It's exactly as you said, Kristen wanted to come in and show you personally what she'd done. This wasn't a chance for us to work together to put together a great piece of work. It was a chance for her to show you how much better she is. A star performer, but a rotten project. And what's worse is she got away with it!"

Why was it a mistake?

Tommy hit the nail squarely on the head. By allowing Kristen to compete with Tommy rather than cooperate to complete an important project, you may have identified a stellar performer, but you've ended up with a rotten project.

You've also sent the message to Kristen (and anyone else who was watching) that it's not important to cooperate with other members of the staff. If much of the work of your unit requires teamwork, the lack of cooperation will have significant effects on the quality of much of the work you produce.

How can you recover from it quickly?

You probably can't. The environment in a work unit doesn't develop overnight, and it won't change overnight. If you haven't structured the work of your unit in such a way that cooperation is more rewarding than competition, it's going to take some time to turn the situation around. But you can begin the change immediately.

Review the product Tommy and Kristen developed. Is Tommy right? Does it look as if two different people did two pieces of work and then stuck them together, whether they fit or not? If so, that's not a quality product. And neither of the people who worked on the project are "star" performers if the product as a whole isn't stellar.

So call Tommy and Kristen both in and let them know the results of your review: "Tommy gave me your finished training package, and I have some concerns about its quality. You both did excellent individual work, but the final product is disjointed and doesn't always make sense because the different parts aren't coordinated. The two of you need to get together and make sure this thing meshes."

Focus on the product, not on Kristen's behavior. If she's as good as you think she is, she'll make the connection herself.

How can you consistently do it right from now on?

• *Talk to your workgroup about the problems caused by lack of cooperation.* As with your immediate response to Tommy and Kristen, focus on the performance deficiencies that arise when team projects become competitive efforts. Try to find several examples of work over the past few months (not just Tommy and Kristen's project) where the work was either especially good because the staff did cooperate or where there were problems in the final product because they competed with one another.

• *Arrange with your training department to find or develop some classes to help your staff learn cooperative skills.* If you haven't asked them to cooperate before, they might not know how. American schools, and many workplaces until fairly recently, stressed competition among individuals and groups as the way to motivate people. Cooperation isn't just an attitude; it's a skill. And, like any other skill, it has to be both learned (often through formal training) and practiced.

• *Identify some assignments which require your employees to work in small groups.* Workers need an opportunity to try out the cooperative skills they've learned. Tie in these projects as closely as you can to the training, so the group gets a chance to practice what they're learning as soon as possible. Your group projects don't have to be production-type assignments. If you must, create group projects such as designing a peer feedback system or developing a customer satisfaction assessment tool or reviewing some of your key work processes. The goal here is to identify some meaningful project that requires cooperative efforts.

• *Examine your performance appraisal and reward structure.* This is probably the most significant action you need to take to ensure that the focus *stays* on cooperation rather than competition. Take a long, hard look at what the rewards really are in your unit. Are the individual stars the ones who're selected for promotions? Do pay increases depend solely on individual performance? If you have a formal appraisal system, are there any elements that focus on teamwork?

If you need cooperation, reward cooperation. Review and revise your reward structure as necessary so it pays for cooperation. Recognize workers who help others get their jobs done. Give awards to teams, not to individuals. If workers are usually assigned to work with the same group of people consistently (rather than moving from one team to another), consider giving group appraisals to the whole team. Or have the team appraise its own members.

However you choose to structure your appraisal and reward system, make sure that cooperative efforts are valued at least as highly as individual efforts.

Is doing what you did ever right?

If the work of your unit does not usually demand cooperation, then your permitting Kristen to compete with Tommy in accomplishing the work isn't nearly as harmful as it could have been. But work environments have changed tremendously over the past ten years or so, and it's a rare job that doesn't require team effort at least part of the time.

A tip for mistake-free managing:

How much do the people in your unit know about what everyone else is involved in? Workers don't have to be formally assigned to projects to be able to help out or offer ideas. If you use your staff meetings for workers to share information about projects and problems, everyone in your unit can profit from the group's insights and expertise. Sometimes the suggestions your staff members offer one another won't be of much help because they're not all involved in the details of specific assignments. But often that outside, detached view is just what you need to slice through the forest of details and find a solution.

1-12   The Mistake: Holding on to workers when they want to leave

The situation:

"What's this I hear about your wanting to go work for Fred in the marketing department, Rhonda? You've been a very valuable employee here and I'm sure we can do something to make you want to stay."

"That's kind of hard to imagine," Rhonda replies. "Fred's going to give me an assignment designing all kinds of print materials. You know, brochures, and catalogs, and posters—maybe even some advertisements for the newspaper or local magazines. I'm really looking forward to getting the chance to use my art and design degree. And I just don't see those kinds of possibilities while I'm here in production."

"Well, now," you respond thoughtfully, "Just because we have a big marketing department for the whole company doesn't mean we can't do a little specialized marketing out of my department. What if I gave you some collateral assignments—say, design some of the cover pieces for our appliances. Wouldn't that exercise your artistic skills?"

Rhonda admits, "I really would rather keep working for you. I've heard that Fred can be a real ogre when workload gets heavy, and during last year's media blitz some of his folks were working 70- and 80-hour weeks. Maybe we can work something out."

Why was it a mistake?

After all, you've retained the services of a valuable worker. Why shouldn't you do what you can to keep a good person longer? There are a couple of reasons why this was a mistake:

1. You've had to make some bizarre changes in the assignments in your unit to accommodate Rhonda's preferences. Your unit probably doesn't normally design the covers for the appliances you manufacture. That's probably done by some other unit. Now, you've either caused friction with that other unit by stepping on their toes or you've given Rhonda an assignment that has no real meaning because her designs will never be used.

There are other contortions you might have had to undergo to accommodate Rhonda. Maybe she's leaving for a salary increase, so now you'll have to raise her salary out of line with others in your unit. Or maybe she doesn't like working for a particular supervisor or in a particular team. Are you going to change the assignments in the whole unit just to keep Rhonda? No matter how good Rhonda is, it's probably not worth disrupting the entire unit just to keep her from leaving.

2. Rhonda probably won't be satisfied for long and will leave anyway. The chances are good that the accommodations you make won't be sufficient either to overcome Rhonda's basic dissatisfactions or to compete effectively with the enticements she was offered elsewhere. Then one of two things will happen: Either she'll feel obligated to you because of your efforts to accommodate her (and eventually resent being stuck in your unit) or she'll leave regardless of the accommodations you've made. In any case, you'll lose.

How can you recover from it quickly?

Go to Rhonda and explain that you're very sorry she's leaving. But then replay the rest of the conversation. Instead of, "I'm sure we can do something to make you want to stay," express your appreciation for what she's contributed to the unit and your regret that she's leaving: "You've been a very valuable employee, and I wish we could do something to make you want to stay. But I can't see any way to use your art and design skills that's not out of sync with what the rest of the unit is involved in. I'm just glad that you'll still be a part of the company. And if you ever decide you'd rather be working over here, just let me know. I'll do what I can to get you back."

Rhonda knows that she's appreciated and that you're not trying to push her out the door. But you've been honest about the limitations on your ability to accommodate her interests. At the same time, you've let her know (without making any commitments you might not be able to fulfill) that she's welcome back in the unit if her career should lead that way again.

How can you consistently do it right from now on?

When one of your better workers comes to tell you that she's accepted another job, your conversation should follow these line.

• *Express regret that she's leaving, and, if you don't already know, ask why she's accepted the new job.* Make sure Rhonda knows that you're truly sorry to lose such a valuable employee and that you're concerned about her reasons for leaving.

If she's leaving to pursue opportunities that aren't available in your organization, you should be pleased for her sake and wish her well.

If she's leaving because of dissatisfaction with your organization (even if that's only part of the reason), follow up with questions to identify the specific cause of the dissatisfaction, whether it's something that's within your control, and whether it's a problem that can be corrected or a necessary condition of the work.

• *Don't make any commitments.* No matter what the reasons for Rhonda's departure, this is not the time to commit to any changes in the work environment or her specific situation. You need time to investigate the possibilities before you make a decision.

Especially if she's leaving because of problems in the work environment, the one commitment you *should* make is that you'll check out the situation.

You can even let her know that you'll look to see how well you can accommodate her, if that might induce her to stay. But any problem or dissatisfaction that's serious enough to induce a good worker to leave is also serious enough that it shouldn't be resolved with a snap decision.

Later, after this conversation, decide how you want to react to Rhonda's notice.

• *Review the options.* Look at the work your unit does, your salary structure, your organization and potential for promotion to see what you can realistically do to accommodate Rhonda.

• *Offer Rhonda only those incentives to stay that are good for the* whole *unit.* If you can make her an offer that won't disrupt the work of the rest of the unit, that's fine. Decide how far you can bend to make the accommodation and negotiate with Rhonda. You may not want to make your greatest accommodation your opening offer: "You said you needed to be able to arrange your work schedule around your child care arrangements, since your husband's new job requires a lot more travel. There are some specific times you need to be at work, but we could probably negotiate some flexibility in your starting and stopping times. Would that give you the leeway you need?"

If your opening offer isn't sufficient to induce Rhonda to stay, you can make one or two progressively more generous offers. But more than a couple of changes in position in this kind of negotiation is likely to give her the impression that you're so desperate to keep her that you'll give up anything. She, in turn, may be tempted then to ask for more than she'd really be willing to settle for—because you appear to be such an easy mark. Instead, signal your final offer: "I'm afraid the best we could do would be to let you come in as late as 9:30 and leave as early as 3:30, but somehow during the week you'd have to get your forty hours in. Any more flexibility than that is going to seriously impact our customer service."

At this point, Rhonda will either accept your "best and final offer" or she won't. But you will have been true to your primary loyalty, which is ensuring that the work of the unit is performed effectively.

• *If accommodations aren't appropriate, don't offer them.* Tell Rhonda that you've looked at the organization carefully, but there's just no way you can make the kinds of changes that would be likely to induce her to stay. Let her know that you appreciate her contributions and you'll miss her, but don't offer something that's not appropriate.

You can still let Rhonda know that she's welcome back later—again, without making a specific job commitment that you might not later be in a position to honor.

Is doing what you did ever right?

There are situations in which workers have skills so unique that it might take you months to replace them. If a worker with such sought-after skills leaves for another job in the middle of an important project, it could be devastating. In that case, it may be critical to the organization to make whatever accommodation is necessary to retain that worker.

But even in this situation, you should not consider yourself "home free" just because the worker has agreed to stay for the duration of the project. Whatever it was that drew her to the other organization (or drove her away from yours) is not likely to be fixed easily. So the chances are very good that she eventually will decide again to find another job.

A tip for mistake-free managing:

Workers perform best when they feel valued for the contributions they make to the organization. We've discussed in an earlier chapter the importance of praising your staff for their good work. Making a fuss over a worker who's leaving won't make up for lack of feedback that's extended over months or years. If you want your good workers to stay, you need to tell them often how valuable they are and thank them for specific contributions they make.

Especially if you find several of your better workers leaving the organization at nearly the same time, you should ask yourself whether they felt appreciated when they were with you. If you suspect that the answer is "no," then it's time to examine your feedback system to find ways to praise good work *clearly* and *regularly*.

CHAPTER *2*

MISTAKES IN DEALING WITH PERFORMANCE

2-1 The Mistake: Not having clear objectives

The situation: "OK, Saundra, let's look at your sales performance these last two months. You and I agreed that you were going to make some real improvements, right?"

"We did, but I thought we weren't going to look at what I'd done until the end of the quarter. Anyway, I think I made some pretty good improvements."

"Well, your total sales seem to be up a little bit, but most of them seem to be coming from smaller accounts."

"I tried not to ignore any of our large accounts, but I thought the best way to build up my sales was by working some of the middle-level accounts. It may not have been great, but it worked."

"Well, somewhat—but I still need everyone focusing on the large accounts. Just a small volume there could lead to real dollar increases."

"Oh—was it dollar volume I was supposed to go after? I thought that I was going to start by increasing the number of lines I sold individual customers and go from there."

"Number of lines is OK, but it's still not dollar volume."

"You mean all this work I did didn't amount to anything?!"

Why was it a mistake?

Unless objectives are clear and relatively specific, it's easy for them to hide serious disagreement. The worker meets the objective as she sees it, only to find that it's not what the manager wanted. In this case, Saundra was focusing on the volume of sales, and particularly the number of lines sold to individual customers, while her manager wanted increases in the dollar volume.

Objectives are important for improvement, but they're just as critical for regular, ongoing work. Objectives lay the groundwork for everything else that happens on that piece of work. When objectives are clear, workers have clear targets and can focus their energies on providing just what they, the manager, and their customers expect. And it always takes more time, effort, and money to correct problems that come up while the work is being done than it does to prevent them by effective planning.

How can you recover from it quickly?

Saundra is getting frustrated; perhaps you are, too. But you can turn the mistake into a productive discussion quickly if you change the focus of the conversation. Let's pick up with Saundra's last statement and see how you might do this:

> "You mean all this work I did didn't amount to anything?!"

> "Not at all. I can see now that you and I thought you were going to get different results when you improved. I was concentrating on dollar volume, while you were looking at number of sales. Neither of us was wrong; both of these are important. And I appreciate the time and effort you put in increasing your sales.

> "Good—I was beginning to wonder."

> "No, those were real improvements from how you were looking at the objective. I'd like to talk now about how you might improve even more over the next quarter, and we'll both make sure we're looking at these improvements the same way. . . ."

The real disagreement between Saundra and her manager wasn't over her performance but over the objectives each of them thought she was shooting for. The manager has redirected the discussion to help them set realistic objectives they both can agree on, so that next time they'll both be looking at the results she gets from the same perspective.

How can you consistently do it right from now on?

A good objective describes what the desired result will look like and when it will be produced. It will include one or more clear standards that describe the characteristics of a successful product (the next case goes into this in detail). If the project is extensive a good objective also contains subobjectives and milestones for when these subobjectives will be reached. It describes any interim status reports desired. And unless the project is simple and straightforward, it is reduced to writing and at least initialed by everyone concerned. Using the example that began this case, let's look at each of these in turn:

• *Good objectives describe what the result will look like and when it will be produced.* You can easily get trapped in the minutiae of an objective—who will do just what by just when, and so forth. They may be important, but not unless everyone is clear about the desired result. Look at Saundra: She pursued the objective as she understood it and then found she'd largely wasted her time. Suppose she and her manager were in headquarters and the project had been an important new directive for field salespeople? The misunderstanding would have been even more serious. Notice, too, that there was a misunderstanding over *when* Saundra would have produced the improvement. All of this interferes with successful performance. Before anything else happens, everyone concerned needs to have the same understanding of what the result will be and when it will be delivered. It may take time, but it's time well spent.

• *They include one or more clear standards that describe success.* This case and the next one are really a matched pair. The next case deals with the importance of standards and how to set them.

• *If the project is extensive, the objectives are supported by subobjectives and milestones for these subobjectives.* The more people who are involved in the project, the more they have to depend on one another, and the less experienced they are, the more important it is to have clear subobjectives and milestones. Large projects can get into trouble quickly and easily, often before anyone realizes it. When many people are working however, they may get out of sync with one another or misunderstand what others need. And individuals not used to working on large projects can get in over their heads without ever realizing it. Saundra and her manager might not have ended up so far apart if their first milestone had been to review her performance after a month.

• *The objectives describe any interim status reports desired.* Interim subobjectives and milestones need always to be linked to interim reports, whether these are written or oral. But even if the project isn't extensive enough to have subobjectives, a manager may want one or more interim meetings to check on progress. This is particularly true if the workers involved aren't experienced in working on projects or on projects in this particular area and/or the manager isn't accustomed to working with them. This would have been another reason for Saundra and her manager to discuss her progress after a month.

• *If it's at all complex, the objective is reduced to writing and is at least initialed by everyone concerned.* Handshakes have sealed many multimillion-dollar deals in Texas, but attempting to achieve anything but the simplest objective on the basis of a purely oral understanding is asking for trouble. Written objectives might or might not have helped Saundra and her boss, but their lack certainly didn't help them.

Is doing what you did ever right?

In one circumstance (and it has to do with those multimillion-dollar handshakes). If everyone on the project is experienced at working with everyone else and with this type of project, and if everyone knows he or she can trust everyone else, the manager may be better off by keeping the objectives as clear and basic as possible and then limiting the agreement to a brief oral review at the end.

How often are you in that situation? That's how often you might come out ahead, and notice that even then the overall objectives must be clear. For that, there is never a substitute.

A tip for mistake-free managing:

Objectives have many uses. When workers are new, or new to a particular kind of work, detailed objectives keep them from wasting time. They can also help them learn quickly what the work involved is and what its priorities are. More experienced workers can use clear objectives as the basis for their own planning and for parceling out responsibilities. So ensure that the objectives are tailored not only to the job to be done but to the experience and capabilities of the workers who will do it and the strength of the relationships among them.

2-2 The Mistake: Not having clear standards

The situation: "OK, Larry, let's look at your sales performance this last quarter. You and I agreed that you were going to make some real improvements, right?"

"We sure did—and I think I made them pretty well."

"Well, your total sales seem to be up a little bit."

"Six and seven tenths percent, to be exact. I'm pretty proud of that."

"Certainly it's an improvement, Larry, but I was really expecting something more like a 15 to 20% improvement—10 percent at the least."

"Ten percent? Do you know how hard I had to work to get what I got?!"

"OK, let's let that ride for the moment. [Pause] I see you made a few more calls on new customers."

"I didn't quite make it, but I tried to do a new call each week."

"I was thinking more in terms of two or three a week."

"Two or three?—I had a problem trying to get in just one more! . . ."

Why was it a mistake?

Workers need clear objectives, to ensure that they do what the manager expects them to do. (The last case pointed out how important this is.) But workers also need clear standards—they need to know what the manager's expectations are for a successful result. Look at the disagreement between Larry and his manager, not because he didn't perform but because they each had a different standard for what would be successful performance.

Sometimes measurements need to be very exact. A workgroup that produces spare parts for machinery needs to know (as an example) the tolerances and the tensile strength that the customer needs. It can err by producing parts that fail to meet these tolerances and strength requirements. It can err just as easily by wasting time creating closer tolerances and higher tensile strength than the customer needs.

Even workers in white-collar or knowledge-work jobs need clear standards, although they may not be as exact as those used in manufacturing. In fact, they may have to be quick-and-dirty standards, something that the manager and the worker can agree to that keep them both looking for the same range of results.

How can you recover from it quickly?

Not only is the discussion between you and Larry getting nowhere fast, but it's playing havoc with his attempt to improve his performance. However, you can turn the situation around immediately, and make it a productive session between the two of you. Let's begin with Larry's last statement:

> "Two or three?—I had a problem trying to get in just one more! . . ."

> "OK, I hear how frustrated you're getting. We had really different ideas of what you were going to do, and I can't blame you for that. But I do appreciate the improvements you've made—I really do."

> "I'm glad. I was beginning to worry for a moment. It really felt like you weren't happy at all with what I did."

> "I am happy with it. But I think you're an extremely talented person who could be producing at a much higher level. Let's talk about how much improvement we might get over the next quarter."

Notice how quickly and effectively the manager deals with Larry's frustration and then refocuses the conversation back on improvement.

How can you consistently do it right from now on?

• *Recognize that standards are not arbitrary measures placed on workers but measures of successful performance.* Because of the history of labor-management conflict over "engineered standards," most workers look on standards as a burden forced on them by managers—a way of forcing them to produce more than they would on their own. A manager can use standards that way if necessary, but it is never their fundamental use. Standards are statements of the conditions, quantitative if possible, that define successful completion of a task or objective.

White-collar workers often complain that their work can't be measured quantitatively. It's more accurate to say that it can't be measured easily. If a manager and worker can describe the results desired, they can find some way to measure these results. Again, the standard they arrive at is first and foremost a definition of what successful results will look like. Look how much trouble Larry and his manager would have saved if they had agreed on standards for improvement when they set the improvement objectives.

• *Don't expect standards to be easy or complete.* Most of the time, unless the job is repetitive, you will have to settle for "ballpark" standards that catch the heart of successful performance.

• *But do them.* That sounds easy to say, but how do you actually do it? Here's a quick four-step process that will get you started:

• *Step 1.* Be very clear about the objectives (see the preceding case if you need help).

• *Step 2.* Identify the critical elements of a successful result. In Larry's case, this would be a certain percentage improvement in total sales and new calls made. For an accountant, it might be when end-of-the-month reports are produced and their accuracy rate. For a college recruiter, it might be the percentage of acceptances received from the organization's top picks. Milestones should always be treated as standards if meeting them is critical for the success of the job or project. Always pick elements that are critical for success; *never* choose an element simply because it's easy to measure. (Example: Firm after firm set a standard for its customer-service representatives of at least so many calls handled in an hour. Then they found customer dissatisfaction rose sharply because meeting the standard resulted in curt and perfunctory service by these representatives.)

• *Step 3.* Put together preliminary standards based on the critical elements. If nothing else works, take a good guess. Larry and his manager might be able to agree on 10 percent improvement in sales and one new call a week. The accounting group might be willing to commit to completing preliminary reports with 95 percent+ accuracy by the fourth workday after the end of the month, and final reports, with less than .5 percent errors, by the tenth workday.

• *Step 4.* Keep working with and improving the standards. For instance, Larry might find that when he contacted new customers was more important for results than how many of them he contacted. His standard might then change to something like: Larry will contact at least one new customer each two weeks at prime selling time for that customer. Or it might be something completely different. Just keep refining the standards. When one doesn't work well, pick it apart to see why. Learn!

Is doing what you did ever right?

Unfortunately, especially when organizations, managers, and workers aren't used to working with standards, there may not be time to develop them for a specific project. Even when this seems true, treat it as an aberration. Always try to develop at least one standard that you and the worker(s) can use to judge the success of the results. The more you and your workgroup get into the habit of this and work on it, the easier it will become to develop effective standards.

A tip for mistake-free managing:

Whenever it's possible, there's always one effective standard: customer satisfaction. If your workgroup produces a product or service for identified customers, always look to them for the basic standard. How do you do this?

• *Create a standard form to survey customers at the completion of every project or job.* If your work doesn't flow that way, survey them at regular intervals.

• *Have workers visit customers to get their reactions.* If necessary, provide workers with a structured set of questions to ask. (This can be particularly helpful when they're new at the visits.)

• *Call customers yourself, on a random basis or on a regular schedule.* Use a structured set of questions if necessary.

• *Hold periodic focus groups with customers*, preferably conducted by individuals who have no connection with you and your workgroup.

If you use the techniques that are relevant for you, you'll begin to accumulate solid data on customer expectations, requirements, and reactions. These can then become the raw material for a solid set of standards.

2-3 The Mistake: Not arranging for feedback

The situation:

"Well, boss, we finished that self-paced training package for the department two days early," Rafael said smiling.

"That's good—but if you'd just given them what they wanted it would be even better."

"What?! We followed the agreement we made with them last September to the letter. I can show you chapter and verse."

"Maybe, but something's gone wrong. Augustine Mills just called from the chief's office, and he's not pleased at all. He wants to see you and me in his office first thing tomorrow morning."

Why was it a mistake?

When work is routine, feedback can be standardized. Do ten publicity releases a month, hold missed discounts under 3 percent. But not all work is routine; Rafael's wasn't. Projects get arranged, and then there's often a significant period of time before the final result is delivered. You can take this to the bank: *If much time goes by between the initiation of the project and its completion, the customer's requirements will have changed.* Is that the way you want it? Of course not. But that's the way you'll get it.

And if it is a long-term project, the workers who perform it will either get continuing feedback on the customer's evaluation of their work in progress or they will almost certainly fail to meet the customer's expectations. It's not a lot more complicated than that.

How can you recover from it quickly?

You can't—except by being as responsive as possible to the department chief's comments. Though they're very late in the game, they're at least valid feedback. If the project can be "fixed" with relatively little work, use this feedback and make revising the project a top priority.

By the way, unless Rafael deliberately refused to get and accept feedback, don't let him be the fall guy. This truly was a managerial and workgroup mistake.

How can you consistently do it right from now on?

Projects of any length usually permit, and often require, continuing contact with the customer. Turn these contacts into opportunities to get feedback. How do you do this?

• *Make sure the opportunities exist; if they don't, create them.* The longer the time that passes between contacts, the more your workers and their customers are likely to get out of sync with one another. If you don't have scheduled contacts often enough, invent reasons for them. "Hey, we've got the outline done for the course you want. How about looking at it with me on Thursday?" "I've got to be in your building on the twelfth; could we get together for a few minutes so I can get your candid opinion of what we've produced so far?"

• *Always ask the customer for her response to anything you show her—and pay close attention to the response.* All too many writers and consultants talk as though all you have to do to get clear, objective feedback from customers is ask them. *This is not true.* Customers very often have little stake in giving you feedback; after all, aren't you supposed to know what you're doing? And they don't want to make you mad, so they stick to saying nice things. And on and on. You will get feedback only if you ask for it and clearly listen to it.

• *Do not* ever *react negatively to criticism, no matter what you think of it.* That's not a terribly bad rule for life in general, and it's an absolute necessity if you want useful feedback. Do you agree with the criticism? Who knows? You listen to it, carefully. You ask questions, so you know exactly what's being said. Then you make a reasonable response. The response can range anywhere from "I had no idea—we'll fix it immediately" to "I understand why you're so upset, but let me explain what I think is really happening here." But you can't make a reasonable response until you understand the criticism completely. And only if you listen to it, understand it, and respond it will you get any negative feedback in the future.

• *Arrange for the feedback to come to the workers, not to you or other managers. Don't* ask a customer to call you if anything happens she doesn't like. Then all the feedback the workers will get is what you choose (or remember) to tell them. Even worse, it cuts down the interactions between your people and their customers. Make it clear to your workers that they are to satisfy the customer, then make that same point clear to the customer. You stay out of the relationship unless and until you have reason to believe that something is going really wrong. How will you know this? Through regular progress reports in which your workers give you feedback on how they're doing on the project.

Is doing what you did ever right?

There's no right or wrong here, but trying to successfully complete an extensive project without in-process feedback is extraordinarily difficult. If the customer's completely satisfied with the final product, you can chalk it up as much to luck as to your workgroup's performance.

In other words, no.

A tip for mistake-free managing:

Workers can make in-course corrections and improve their performance only if they get prompt, direct, usable feedback. If the feedback is delayed, filtered through levels of management or staff offices, or in a form that is difficult to use,

workers have great difficulty translating it into desirable performance improvements.

The Quality movement stressed making feedback a part of the operation of
every process. Workers should be able to see how well the process is functioning
in real time—say, by using process-control charts. They can then take the feedback from the process and use it to improve operations immediately—not a week
or a month later. In most cases, the process is a routine process and the feedback
is generated routinely. If you have any similar processes, whether mechanical or
clerical, you should have feedback built into them.

But most of your work may not be so routine. You can still see that there's
effective feedback. Talk with your workgroup. Ensure that they understand the
importance of feedback. Work with them on specific projects to see that they
develop effective methods to get feedback. If need be, help them interpret and use
the feedback. Focus yourself and everyone else on getting and using feedback.
You'll be amazed how your operations will improve.

2-4 The Mistake: Praising without knowing the facts

The situation: "Tim, this was a really great job—one of the best I've
                          seen in months. You're a first-rate worker, and I think you
                          can count on some recognition for this."

                          "Gosh, thanks, boss. It was a lot of hard work, but I
                          enjoyed it. Besides, I always try to do my best for you."

                          Everything was rosy until just after lunch, when you
                          happened to hear Whitney and Astrid talking.

                          "Can you believe Tim taking credit for that job?! If
                          we hadn't held his hand through it he'd still be wander-
                          ing around trying to find where to start."

                          "That's bad enough, but from what I can tell he has
                          the boss convinced he's the greatest thing since sliced
                          bread. Well, at least if he got promoted out of here we'd
                          be rid of him!"

Why was it a mistake?

This one doesn't take a lot of explanation. The manager has caught himself
in a real bind. It feels good to be able to tell someone they've done a great job

without waiting for the facts, but the hangover lasts a lot longer than the feel-goods.

How can you recover from it quickly?

You can recover quickly only if you're willing to confront Tim with what he's done. Are Whitney and Astrid credible sources? Will they talk with you at greater length and level with you? If so, you have just the excuse you need to deal with the situation. Arrange a private discussion with Tim and present him with the information you've learned—that Whitney and Astrid were instrumental in the project's successful completion. Tim will almost certainly acknowledge his co-workers' contributions (and if he doesn't you've got a more serious problem on your hands). At the same time, you've begun to get yourself off the hook—a hook you should never have put yourself on in the first place.

How can you consistently do it right from now on?

First, you can always follow the basic rule: Get the facts before you act. It doesn't matter whether the situation appears to call for praise or blame—get the facts. If you make this a practice, you'll soon discover that all too much of the time the first account you get of a situation is seriously flawed.

Second, unless there's some compelling reason for quick action, *think about what you know before you act.* Even with enough facts, you may be tempted to react automatically, rather than to make the best response. Consider the difference between these two approaches:

> *Automatic reaction:* "Tim, I just found out that you hogged all the credit for the project you gave me a few days ago but that other people had to show you how to do most of the work. I want you to stop this way of doing things, and I want you to stop it right now!"

> *Thought-out response:* "Tim, I'm really disappointed in something I heard. When you showed me the Ames project, you made it sound as if you did it all yourself, but now I hear that you got some really substantial help that you didn't mention."

Note that the first reaction slams the door on any further discussion. In addition, it will almost certainly make Tim angry at whomever squealed on him. In the second example, a reasoned response, Tim has the chance to say whatever he wants. Since the discussion didn't open as explosively as the other one, it creates the possibility for Tim to present his side—which may have more merit than you knew—and or the two of you to really look at his behavior.

Get the facts, think about the facts, then take the action that seems best. If you'll do that consistently, you'll avoid most instances of foot-in-mouth disease.

Is doing what you did ever right?

Some workers are so solid that you know they did what they claim to have done. When you deal with them, you can have the luxury of taking their word and reacting accordingly.

Remember this, though. Every time you react automatically with praise, you're helping create the habit of doing so. And most of us would rather react on the spot than postpone a response until we've gotten additional facts. Don't let your natural inclinations here lead you back into a bad habit.

A tip for mistake-free managing:

It feels good to praise workers. If we could all do that all the time, life would be so much more pleasant. In fact, if your work is done well, you should spend far more time praising workgroup members than criticizing them. But keep these tips in mind:

• *Remember that you're praising (and criticizing) behavior, not individuals or their characters.* "I really appreciate how you always get your projects in on time" is far more effective than "You certainly are a good worker."

• *It's at least as important to praise the right people as it is to criticize the right people.* Whenever you praise someone, you encourage them to repeat the behavior that earned the praise. You also encourage others to imitate the behavior. If Tim's tendency to hog the credit gets him praised, other workgroup members may well conclude that they will best earn your praise if they also hog all of the credit they can.

• *Praise only when you can sincerely do so.* Phony praise sounds like just what it is—phoney.

2-5   The Mistake: Not noticing good work

The situation: As you walk down the hall, this is what you hear:

"Bea, am I imagining things or did we do a really first-rate job on that last application we developed?" Paulo asks.

"Let's see—we finished a week early, and the branch folks said they loved it. I'd say that amounts to a first-rate job."

"Yeah—and would you believe that *she* hasn't mentioned a word about it? I know she's a demanding boss, and she expects really first-rate work from all of us, but she could at least notice when she gets it."

"She may not have said anything to *us*, but I'll bet *her* boss knows all about it—at least all about how her superb management produced it."

It's all too clear who "she" is, isn't it?

Why was it a mistake?

This one was a double mistake. First of all, when workers produce consistently high-caliber work and the boss never seems to notice, they can easily conclude that they don't really need to work quite so hard. They don't need to commit themselves to the work quite so much. They can settle for slightly lower quality. (After all, the application didn't really need to be finished a week early, did it?) And so, slowly, almost invisibly, performance starts to decline.

The second mistake is at least as bad. The workers are beginning to believe that the boss takes all of the credit for their good work. If she noticed the work and praised them for it, they might believe that she praised them to her boss. As it is, the easiest thing to believe is that, since she doesn't mention their good performance to them, she doesn't mention it on up the line.

How can you recover from it quickly?

You can't recover from something like this in a hurry. But you can get started. Assuming it's true, you might make a remark at an appropriate point in a staff meeting: "Mr. Norris asked me to thank each of you for the tremendous job you're doing. He recognizes how really well you perform and how important you are to the organization."

This doesn't change the problem with noticing good performance, but it does make it clear that you're not trying to hog all the credit. (Remember, though, don't ever say something like this unless it is completely true. Try to fudge, and it may come back to haunt you.)

Now, what about recognizing good performance? That's easy—start doing it. The next section has some tips on how.

How can you consistently do it right from now on?

Many managers have the idea that it's harmful to praise workers too much. After all, they might get swelled heads and start slacking off. That's an interesting theory, but if you praise appropriately you can prove for yourself how wrong the theory is. How do you do it right?

• *Notice good work.* You might end up nominating someone for an award, or giving him a bonus, or formally recognizing him in some way. But noticing good work is very different from that. Noticing good work means exactly that— keeping your eyes open for good work, so that you see it when it happens. This sounds ridiculously simple, and it is, but you may not do it. How many times a day does someone do something well—perhaps just answering the phone in an extremely courteous way—and it just passes by you? Don't let it. Notice it.

• *Praise it as specifically as possible.* What does this sound like? Perhaps like one of these:

> "Tabitha, I'll bet the person on the other end of that call really believed that you cared about him. Thank you."

> "Ron, your summary of the problems we need to overcome was masterful. You didn't downplay any of them, but you made it clear that we could lick them. Thank you."

> "Bea, I couldn't wait to get back here to tell you how much the branch liked the application you did. And they couldn't believe you got it to them a week early. Performance like this makes the workgroup look like heroes, and I really appreciate it. When you see Paulo, would you ask him to drop in for a moment? I want to thank him in person, too."

• *Use noticing as the basis for formal recognition.* It takes away from the value of a bonus or award or other formal recognition for continual high-level performance if the recognition comes weeks or months after the performance. Many times, though, the organization's recognition system imposes this delay. Either the award has to come on a preset cycle or it has to be written up in detail and approved by all too many managers.

Don't wait for the formal recognition; notice good performance and recognize it in the workgroup. It might be as simple as, "Hey, I think all of you ought to pat each other on the back for the job we just finished" or "Bea and Paulo did a really great job with that application, and I know several of you were really helpful to them. Thank you all."

But don't stop there. If your workers know they're good—and they do, because you've told them so—they'll feel that they deserve their share of the goodies of the formal recognition program. Don't be lazy; see that they get them. If you take notes whenever you notice high-level performance, you'll have the recognition half written when you start. Then, when they get the recognition, it won't come as a surprise even if it's three months after the fact. "I know you all remember when Bea and Paulo got that application done so professionally a couple of months ago, and now the organization has recognized how good a job they did. All of you keep up the good work, and we'll have the department convinced this is the most productive workgroup they have."

Is doing what you did ever right?

No. Don't ever just expect high-level work from workers and ignore it when you get it. Notice it. Rejoice in it. Help them rejoice in it. Don't ever let them believe that you just take their performance for granted.

A tip for mistake-free managing:

Tom Peters has said that one of the top jobs of a manager is to be a cheerleader. By that, he means that a manager should be the first to notice the good work of his people and praise them for it. It's good advice.

Now, how are you at accepting praise? When your boss or one of your workgroup tells you he or she appreciates the job you've done, do you accept it as a sincere compliment? Or do you shrug it off or otherwise devalue it, as so many of us do? Stop. When you get sincere praise, enjoy it. Savor it. Thank the person for it. Give a responding compliment if it's appropriate, but only if it's appropriate.

Do you want a healthy work environment? Then help create one in which you and each member of your workgroup are continually grateful for the contributions you make to one another's work and success.

2-6 The Mistake: Not dealing with substandard work

The situation:	You look through the contract that Wanda just finished and laid on your desk. It doesn't take a degree in rocket science to write a contract for office equipment, but Wanda somehow managed to make several noticeable errors. She didn't follow the standard format in several places. There's an obvious math mistake. Most of all, the prices seem somewhat higher than they ought to be. You think briefly about discussing the mistakes, but then decide not to. Wanda doesn't take criticism well. You pull out your pen, sign it, and toss it into your out basket.

Why was it a mistake?

If you want consistently high performance from your workgroup, you cannot simply look the other way when you get mediocre performance, much less when you end up with substandard work. That sends a clear message to the others in the workgroup: If you want to slack off, take it a little easier, and produce so-so work, it's OK. You don't ever want to send messages like that. The short-term stress you save yourself will buy you only real long-term worry.

How can you recover from it quickly?

The contract is still in your out basket. Nothing stops you from pulling it back out and asking Wanda to join you to discuss it. If you want to get the conversation off to a dramatic and pointed start, ask her to take a seat, show her the page of the contract with your signature on it, and then: "Wanda, I really wanted to sign off on this. In fact, I did. But I shouldn't have. This isn't good work, and we need to talk about it." At that point, you clearly scratch over your signature and say, "Let's start with item four on page six."

How can you consistently do it right from now on?

Dealing with substandard performance takes a five-step procedure, which we'll get to in a moment. But if you've let an individual's performance slide, so that you end up with a product that has a number of errors, you have an additional step. It's probably overkill to try to deal with all the problems at once. You have to decide which errors to concentrate on.

In Wanda's case, do you worry about the format, the math error (or errors—there may be more), or the high price? The latter is most important, but the first two are clearer. You'll often find that this is the choice: between important but not-so-clear errors or less important errors that are easier to spot and define.

Which do you do? We can't tell you. But we can suggest that you focus on one or two errors, or a few more if they are all similar to each other. You're going to expect Wanda to change, so don't overwhelm her. There'll be time to correct the other problems later.

Now, what are the steps for any performance correction?

• *Step 1*. Clearly define the problem. "Wanda, the prices we've agreed to in this are higher then I'd expect. How many different stores did you contact to get bids?"

• *Step 2*. Give the worker a chance to respond and ask questions. Do not accept defensiveness, excuses, or attempts to bring up unrelated matters.

• *Step 3*. Insist that the worker focus on the problem. She may continue to evade responsibility through additional excuses or red herrings. However the conversation goes, keep it focused on the problem. If you're lucky, she'll finally recognize it. If not, you simply insist that it's a problem and hope that she accepts it after the conversation is over.

• *Step 4*. Develop a "get-well" plan with the worker. Be specific about what the worker will improve and when the improvement will be completed. Set dates for review of his or her improvement.

• *Step 5*. Don't leave the situation alone until the improvement has occurred—*all* of the improvement. Don't accept partial improvement; if the Wandas of the world see that they can get away with less than they agreed to, they'll do it. And then, when they make an error, they'll remind you that you never insisted that they really change, so they didn't think it was important.

Is doing what you did ever right?

Of course. Wanda may be a few weeks away from retirement or from separation. She may have gotten a job elsewhere and just be putting in her last few days. Then there are the iffier situations: Perhaps she's just won a discrimination complaint against you and is just aching for the chance to yell reprisal. Be careful, though. Insisting on high performance is the normal course of action. Anything else is an exception, and needs to be thought over carefully.

A tip for mistake-free managing:

Now, suppose that Wanda is the opposite of what we pictured here. She tries ever so hard. She listens to every word of criticism and takes it seriously. She takes notes. She promises to correct her mistakes, and she does. But she makes them again, or makes a new set of mistakes. How do you deal with these Wandas?

Look at the case just before this one, on noticing and praising good work. You should be doing that constantly. Notice Wanda's efforts and praise her for them. Notice when she corrects her errors and praise her for that. Notice when she doesn't repeat an error and praise her for that. (Are you uncomfortable with all that praising? Then thank her each time, genuinely.) When you notice what she does right, it will be much easier for her to focus on and correct her mistakes without getting overly upset about them. And, in the long run, she will make fewer and fewer mistakes.

2-7　The Mistake: Not allowing workers to make their own mistakes

The situation:　　"Oh, look, Glenda, here's a whole stack of folders that need to be sent over for scanning. You can't start reviewing payment histories until you've done that. Otherwise, the file won't be established in the system by the time you're ready to key in the rest of the data elements."

"But, I thought if I reviewed the payment histories now it would save time later on when the data are ready for input. There always seems to be some downtime in this process while we're waiting for the scanning anyway."

"No, Glenda. That's not the way we do it. Just do what I say, and everything will run smoothly."

"Well, I will if that's the way you want it, but I'd really like a chance to try out my idea."

"Maybe some other time," you conclude, as you walk away, knowing full well that "some other time" will never come—at least not on your watch.

Why was it a mistake?

It's always a mistake to deny someone the opportunity to learn from his or her own errors. Remember when you learned to ride a bike? Or the first time you tried to bake a cake on your own? Or even when you first became a supervisor? We'll bet there was a lot of trial and error, and many mistakes, but that's how you learned what worked and what didn't.

There are two important reasons why workers should be allowed to make mistakes, at least occasionally:

1. When a worker makes a mistake, she can see for herself the consequences of her actions. She knows firsthand what happens as a result of a step she took. This is a much more powerful way to learn than simply being told what the consequences are.

2. Making mistakes allows a worker to test the limits of the process she's using. In any process, some steps are more important than others. Likewise, some steps must be accomplished exactly according to plan, while others can be shortened or varied without significant detriment to the overall process. But unless the worker can test those limits, she'll have no idea when she can bend the process rules and when she can't.

How can you recover from it quickly?

Return to Glenda and revisit your earlier conversation. "You know, Glenda, I've been thinking about your suggestion. You're right, we do always seem to run into some down time. Let's try an experiment: Set aside maybe 20 or 30 of the folders you're working on, and we'll try it your way. Then we can compare them with the rest of the group you're working on."

Glenda won't get horrendously behind in the process, but she'll have a chance to give her idea a workout. If it works, you'll have a process improvement. If it doesn't, she will have still gained a better insight into how the process flows.

How can you consistently do it right from now on?

• *Know when to step in and when to stand by.* There are some mistakes that you must avoid. There are also times when you need to minimize the possible damage as much as possible, but, within certain limits, workers can be free to experiment. And there are mistakes that workers can make because there's also ample opportunity to correct them before serious damage is done. It's part of the fine art of managing to recognize the difference, and act accordingly.

• *Encourage your workers to bring their ideas to you.* One way to avoid mistakes without stifling innovation and creativity is to encourage the open exchange of ideas and suggestions among your staff. You might ask staff members to identify processes or steps that aren't working well and then assemble teams to work out solutions to present to the rest of the group. You might institute an in-unit suggestion program, apart from the more formal company program (that most of your people probably don't participate in anyway). You might simply ask workers to present their ideas at staff meetings or by leaving you notes or work samples to review. But, regardless of the procedure you choose, soliciting your workers' good ideas will encourage them to challenge the system and improve it in the process.

• *Review work to identify mistakes that are made frequently, and let your workers learn from each other.* Obviously, not all mistakes are the result of attempts to innovate and improve. Many mistakes arise because people don't know how to do the work correctly or because they've become so accustomed to the tasks that they become inattentive. These mistakes *do* require remediation, and prevention if possible.

One way to reduce these kinds of mistakes is to periodically review the work of your unit to see what kinds of errors are being made most frequently. Then discuss them with the people who do the work. Perhaps some workers have found ways to consistently do things right and avoid the errors that plague the rest of the group. Ask them to share their "secrets of success." Perhaps the process is flawed and there are changes that need to be made. Let your staff work through those process problems and devise solutions. If the mistakes are frequently made by just one or two workers, but not the group as a whole, deal with these as you would other substandard work. The preceding case can give you some ideas.

Is doing what you did ever right?

Yes. There are times when it's not only right to prevent workers from making mistakes—it's absolutely necessary. Particularly if the safety of workers is involved, you must step in and prevent the mistake from happening. There are other times, as well, when the mistake is too costly or too disruptive to permit. Whenever you see a mistake in the making, you need to evaluate the potential consequences before deciding whether to intervene.

A tip for mistake-free managing:

When workers operate under rigid systems and processes, some will be likely to chafe at the bit, become resentful and impatient, and look for opportunities to "work" the system. Others will give in to the process, do just as much as is necessary to get by, and lose whatever initiative they possessed when you first hired them. Neither result is desirable.

Initiative and experimentation are healthy. They allow workers to "own" their own processes and encourage them to look for improvements. But, any change, no matter how positive and foolproof it may appear, always entails risk— the risk of failure. Things will never get better unless you also allow them occasionally to get worse. And sometimes things have to get worse *before* they can get better. This is all healthy and useful. As long as you don't let the situation get out of control—to the point where there is a serious degradation in performance or service to your customers—encourage your workers to try new ideas. Most times, the worst that will happen is that the idea won't work, and you may have a little cleanup to do.

2-8 The Mistake: Rewarding safe mediocrity

The situation: "I called you all together today because Greg is getting a much-deserved award—the Employee of the Quarter Award and the check that goes along with it. As all of you know, Greg is always dependable and always available to lend a hand. He's very thorough in his work, and I never get anything from him with a misspelled word or a comma out of place. And you know that he's a team player with a good, positive attitude. For all these reasons, I want you all to give him a big hand."

Why was it a mistake?

Suppose you were just a little bit cynical, as many workers are. You might hear the speech this way: "As all of you know, Greg never really produces anything outstanding, but he's dependable. Since his workload isn't that heavy, he's always available to lend a hand. He doesn't come up with new ideas, but at least when I get anything from him I know I won't have to worry about the details. Maybe most important of all, he never disagrees with anything I say or wants to do something a different way. In other words, I don't get much out of him but he doesn't cause me much trouble, either."

Now, if that's the only significant recognition anyone in that workgroup has gotten during the last six months or so, exactly what kind of performance expectation is the manager communicating to the rest of the workgroup?

How can you recover from it quickly?

You can't. You've made your statement, and you're going to be living with it for a while.

How can you consistently do it right from now on?

You begin by seriously asking yourself what your true values are where your workforce is concerned.

1. Do you say, "I want you to be innovative and forward looking," but then reward workers for doing what they're told and not causing problems?

2. Do you say, "If you don't think the way I want you to do things is the best way, come tell me and we'll work it out," but then respond each of the few times it happens with a patient explanation of why your way really is the best way?

3. Do you say, "I want you to take initiative," but then chew out workers any time they do anything that your boss questions?

Now let's say that you've looked at your values and they don't really add up to strong performance and high initiative. Do you really want to change? Are you willing to change your approach and reward the kind of behaviors that produce high performance? If so, follow these suggestions:

• *Pick one behavior that supports the performance you want, one that workers won't see as too dangerous.* For instance, it's better not to start with "I want all of you to begin telling me when you think I'm wrong." Your workgroup probably won't believe you mean it, and you probably won't. Start with something like "We really need some new ideas on how to use our computers. I know some of you've been thinking about this, so please share your ideas with me."

• *Notice specifically whenever any worker does what you've said you wanted.* If Vicky casually remarks that you could use your spreadsheet to track projects, notice it immediately with a comment such as: "Vicky, thanks for my request for suggestions about new ways to use the computer. Tell me more about your idea."

• *Do not reject what the worker says or does, no matter what your initial reaction is to it.* If you said you wanted more initiative and Shelly went off into left field to get some new ideas, don't chew him out for it. He did what you wanted. Notice that and thank him for it. The problem is that he didn't do it competently, and you'll want to discuss that with him. If you've been rejecting real initiative in your workgroup for years, people aren't going to be very competent at exercising it. Help them learn.

• *Make an example of anyone who successfully does what you asked.* If Vicky's idea is worthwhile, make sure everyone knows it was her idea and you approve of it. If Shelly learned from your discussion and comes up with a much more usable idea, make sure the group knows about that. And make sure the workers get the credit, not you.

• *When workers really begin to take you at your word and start doing what you've asked for, select another behavior you want and make it clear that it's important.* Then follow all of the suggestions above. You'll probably find that workers respond more quickly and positively, now that they've seen that you meant the first statement. After several successful instances where they see you really are serious, you might be able to say, "I want all of you to begin telling me when you think I'm wrong" and have at least a few workers believe you enough to try it.

Is doing what you did ever right?

Yes, if—and that's a big "if." If you routinely notice, recognize, and reward high performance, it doesn't hurt to recognize a performer who's not a star occasionally. You want to be sure that the workgroup likes the individual and, you'll hope that they respect him or her. You also want to be sure that you can mean what you say, hollow recognition is far worse than no recognition at all.

A tip for mistake-free managing:

Do you understand each of your workers, what each contributes and their strong and weak points? Why ask that question in a case of mediocre performance? Because different workers contribute to an organization in different ways. Greg might not be a great performer individually, but his positive attitude, his willingness to pitch in and help, his desire to be a team player—these may make a real contribution to the team. On the other hand, Ken may be a tremendous individual performer who constantly irritates other team members—he may also make a real contribution.

The moral: The better you understand each group member's individual strengths and weaknesses, the easier it will be to identify what he or she is contributing and then to recognize and reward the person for it. We can promise you that the more specifically you understand and notice an individual's core contributions, the more the individual will treasure—yes, *treasure*—that recognition.

2-9 The Mistake: Using "only one can win" rewards

The situation:

"And," you end your short speech, "I know that each one of you will want to join me in giving a warm round applause to Gennie for being selected as the Employee of the Month for the department." And everyone did applaud.

As you were talking with Paul Wonders, you overheard Nancy Grayson say to Emory Hill, "What made her so special? I know she does a good job, but no better than you or me. You think she's got something going with the boss?"

That was bad enough, but before you and Paul finished your conversation Gennie drifted by, obviously wanting to talk with you. You tactfully ended the discussion with Paul, then turned to Gennie.

"I really wish you had asked me about this," she stammered. "Now everyone in the group's going to be angry with me, and I can't get my job done without their help!" Then she turned and walked quickly away.

Why was it a mistake?

Whenever only one performer can win a particular award or recognition, you guarantee that most individuals will be losers. Every once in a while, one individual stands so far above the rest that no one begrudges him or her the recognition. But not usually. Instead, the manager must select one person from among a number of very good performers, with a real possibility that the others will be angered, and that their performance may drop.

Many managers solve the problem by rotating awards. They do their best to see that everyone gets at least some recognition over a particular period of time. The issue then becomes not "Who was the best performer?" but "Who's turn is it this time?"

How can you recover from it quickly?

You can't. If you've let yourself get sucked into using only formal "only one can win" awards, you've already established the precedents and created the expectations with your workgroup. Once the award is given, it's given. You can't take it back.

What you can do is to switch immediately to a more effective way of recognizing and rewarding your workgroup.

How can you consistently do it right from now on?

• *First, recognize good performance when it happens.* Don't wait for some award cycle. Employees (like managers) sometimes enjoy big, flashy recognition. Day in and day out, though, what they really value is knowing that their manager notices and appreciates their work. They value a well-placed word, a note of thanks, or other small tokens that send the message that you're paying attention.

• *Encourage workers to recognize each other's performance.* Recognition means just as much, and sometimes more, coming from a peer rather than from a manager. (Doing both, of course, is best.) You probably don't want to make a formal program of it, but encourage all of your workers to recognize one another. Then, when you hear one employee noticing what another has done and thanking him or her for it, you have a ready-made recognition.

• *Set up and/or encourage the organization to set up programs that recognize everyone who meets or exceeds a certain standard.* Are you familiar with your local United Way? If you are, you know that they have just this kind of recognition. If you give a certain amount or percentage, you get a certain pin or certificate. Or perhaps you've read those bumper stickers: "My child is on the Honor Roll at Midlands Elementary School." In both cases, there's no limit on how many individuals can get a given recognition.

There are individuals who focus on winning: Either they're first or nothing matters. Don't build a recognition program for them. Instead, build it for individuals who believe in setting their own goals and achieving them. They don't care that much whether they had the lowest error rate in the branch—but they may care very much that their error rate was under 1 percent. And that you noticed this and thanked them for it.

You can create a system like this, whether the organization wants to be part of it or not. Perhaps you create a "Circle of Honor." Every month or quarter, every worker who met a certain standard—perhaps one that the workgroup created— gets to be in the Circle. Perhaps each member gets a coffee cup or a free lunch for it. Then, perhaps, that person is responsible for mentoring one or more other members who didn't make the Circle, to help them make it the next quarter. If that doesn't sound like a winner, develop your own. But don't make it a competition.

Is doing what you did ever right?

As the "Why was it a mistake?" section noted, something like this can be appropriate for a genuine star performer, one whom other employees recognize as the best. And sometimes you have to submit nominees for awards like this just so your workers get their share of the limelight. If you do that, make it clear to the workgroup that this is what you're doing. Perhaps the workgroup might even decide who will be the nominee. (Their reasoning might surprise you.)

On the whole, though, don't use awards like this until after you've made sure that you and all your workgroup members recognize all the good work that happens. That's the cake; awards like Employee of the Quarter aren't ever anything more than the icing.

A tip for mistake-free managing:

Unless you're in a very unusual situation, you don't want to encourage your workers to compete with one another. "Only one can win" awards do just that. Instead of promoting cooperation, they can easily lead workers to withhold information and help from one another. ("Why should I help her? That'll just make her look good and won't do anything for me.")

If you have to give lip service to Employee of the Quarter awards, by all means do so. And make sure your workgroup gets at least its share of recognition. Just don't put much faith in this kind of award. Put your time and attention into the daily, informal recognition that notices and recognizes good performance on the spot. Then if you want to create a "Circle of Honor" type of award that potentially everyone can win, you will have laid a solid foundation for it.

A final thought. Many organization impose a strict quota on the most widely used form of recognition: performance appraisals. Somehow, it's supposed to be helpful to someone if you strictly limit the number of high ratings. What a copout! What you really want to do is to define a high standard, one that takes real commitment to reach and then do your best to see that everyone reaches that standard. Then you can say "Sure, my folks are arranged along a normal distribution—they're just all distributed in the Outstanding quadrant."

2-10   The Mistake: Expecting the annual performance review to improve performance

The situation:

"All right, Melanie, it's time for your annual performance review. Let me just ask you—how do you feel about your performance this past year?"

"Well, I really feel pretty good about it. I've been getting more of my projects finished on time, haven't I?"

"You have, and I want you to know I appreciate that. I've also noticed that your summaries are more concise and to the point and that the number of grammatical errors is down."

"Yes, I've been working on those," Melanie replied, smiling, "so I'm glad that I've gotten better."

"On the other hand, I have had to ask you to redo several of the reports you've handed in because you hadn't done as much research as I thought you needed to."

"I'm sorry about that, and I've been working on it. Don't you think I've done better later?"

"I really haven't noticed, but I promise I'll pay particular attention to the next one or two and let you know. And there's one other thing—I've noticed you've been away from the work area a number of times in the last few weeks. I just need to make sure that you're spending the time on business."

"That's mostly the Retro project," Melanie answered. "I won't be running around on it much longer."

"I'm glad to hear that. Now let's see—if we sum up the pluses and the minuses I think we come out with just about what you got last year. Does that sound fair to you?"

Melanie paused for a moment, then answered: "Yes, sure."

Why was it a mistake?

Look again at the conversation with Melanie. It's been shortened tremendously, of course, but it has in it most of what you probably learned in your supervisory course on giving performance reviews. The manager gave Melanie plenty of chances to speak, and he began with two positives. He presented the negatives nonjudgmentally and gave her a chance to comment on them, too. Then he ended with her performance rating, which she accepted.

Now, what will the result be? Melanie will probably continue to do more concise summaries, and they'll be grammatically correct. She'll try to do better research, but can't be sure her manager will help her much on this. She'll continue to be away from the work area, whatever the reason, quite possibly until the manager says something again. And she'll be disappointed in her rating, because she believes she's improved over her last rating.

Now, how much performance improvement does that add up to? Zero.

How can you recover from it quickly?

You can't, and you shouldn't waste time trying. Annual performance reviews are ritual events that satisfy almost no one, but almost every organization requires them. They don't improve performance, and they weren't designed to improve performance—period. So do what your organization requires for a review, do it conscientiously, and then depend on other ways to get actual performance improvement.

How can you consistently do it right from now on?

• *When you see good performance, recognize it then and there.* Waiting for the appraisal cycle to tell someone they're doing a good job never works, except as a summary of all the little recognitions you've given throughout the year. Notice and recognize good work whenever and wherever it occurs.

• *Deal with poor performance when it occurs.* The manager in this case should have been working continually with Melanie to improve her summaries and her research abilities. If he was concerned about her being gone from the area too much, he should have asked her about it as soon as he got concerned. Both he and Melanie should know specifically where any problems are and what progress she's making in overcoming them.

• *Use the annual review as a quick summary of what you and the worker already know, then put the proper rating on his or her performance and go from there.* Suppose that Melanie's manager had recognized her good performance and dealt with her poor performance throughout the year. This is what a perfectly adequate performance review might sound like:

> "All right, Melanie, it's time for your annual performance review. I think you've been a valuable contributor during this past year. Have I communicated that to you?"

> "Yes, you really have. I feel good about what I've done."

> "Excellent, because you ought to. Do we agree, though, that there've been some problems? As I understand it, you've completely licked the problem with your summaries and you're doing much better research now. Is that how you see it?"

> "Yes," Melanie responded, "I think I'm coming along with the research, and the next report should show you that."

> "Great! Now, last year you got an Above Satisfactory rating. You've certainly improved this year, but I have a question. Do you think you've improved enough to deserve an Outstanding rating?"

Melanie paused, then shook her head. "If you want to give me one, feel free, but I think I need to get that research down pat to really deserve it. Go ahead with the Above Average again, but if I improve on my research I'm going to be expecting Outstanding next year." She grinned, stood up, and stuck out her hand.

Is doing what you did ever right?

It's not whether it's right or wrong. If you expect even the best annual review to really improve performance, you're almost certainly going to be disappointed.

A tip for mistake-free managing:

Many managers solicit input from their workers for the annual review. Some even go so far as to ask them to write up in detail what they've done and suggest the rating they should get. This doesn't solve the basic problem, but it does at least get some specifics onto the table.

One caution: There is often an inverse correlation between the expertise of workers and the ratings they would give themselves. Really good workers are often very demanding of themselves; they see all too clearly how far they fall short of their ideals. Poor workers, on the other hand, narrow their goals and their vision; and they know how hard they've worked to produce what they have. Thus a powerhouse worker may rate himself or herself even lower than a mediocre worker's self-rating. This doesn't mean don't use self-ratings. Just be prepared to balance them out to reflect performance as you see it.

A final note. Many organizations are trying 360-degree ratings—in which an individual is rated by his or her boss, peers, and subordinates. These may or may not be an improvement, but you should know one characteristic of these ratings. In general, you will get your highest ratings from your workers, the next highest from your boss, and the lowest from your peers.

2-11   The Mistake: Not using appropriate competition with other workgroups as a motivator

The situation:

"Boss, I think we need to set up a sort of three-way competition with the A and B units," Sam said emphatically. "It doesn't have to be a big deal, but I think we can out-produce either of them."

"I don't think so, Sam—after all, we're expected to be one big happy family here, and I don't think it's appropriate for us to be competing with one another."

"Aw, come on. It would be good for us—keep us on our toes. I think we can do better most of the time than either A or B, but we'll have to push ourselves to do it."

"No, it's just not appropriate. Everyone here knows what he or she's supposed to do, and I expect everyone to do the best job possible. I think trying to compete would just distract us. But thanks for sharing the idea with me."

Why was it a mistake?

Appropriate competition can increase a workgroup's performance. By refusing to let his workgroup compete, this manager is turning his back on what could be a real positive motivator. All this assumes that the circumstances are right for competition, and we'll look at what that requires in the second section below.

How can you recover from it quickly?

Fortunately, you can recover quickly. Wait a few hours or a day, then go find Sam. Tell him you've been thinking about what he said and you may have answered too quickly. Ask him to go over the idea with you again.

What do you do then? Look at the next section.

How can you consistently do it right from now on?

You should consider friendly competition with other workgroups whenever the following conditions are met:

• *None of the groups involved should be dependent on another as a supplier or have another as a customer.* When work units stand in a customer-supplier relationship with each other, no matter which side you may be on, they're part of a single process. They must cooperate for the process to work effectively. If the two groups compete with one another, one may be tempted to cooperate just a little less to help itself pull ahead in the competition.

In this case, the three units work independently of one another. None of them is part of a process that includes the other. Competition will probably work.

• *Most of the workers in the groups concerned are at least willing to give competition a try.* For any of a variety of reasons, workers may be afraid of competition. They may be unsure about their abilities, or fear that other workgroups will take advantage of them. Like the manager in the example at the start of this case, they may simply think it's wrong for two workgroups in the same organization to compete. Or they may think it's just one more hassle to worry about, one they don't need.

If a number of workers really don't want to compete, it's probably better to let it be for now. If others who want to compete volunteer to convince those who are reluctant, let them try. Then look at the idea again. But if most workgroup members are at least willing to give it a try, competition may be well worth it.

• *The groups can keep the competition friendly.* Of course, you can't answer this for sure until you get into the situation. If you see that some of your workers have an ax to grind or a point to prove, be cautious. Rabid competition can be truly distracting. Even more, it can actually harm production—as individuals find ways to take short-cuts and doctor the statistics to make their groups look good. No one has yet found a measurement system, especially when it's used as the basis of serious competition, that workers and their managers couldn't subvert if they were sufficiently motivated.

But if the competition is for no more than bragging rights, and perhaps a steak luncheon, workers will probably put about the right amount of energy into it. And it might not hurt you to set up your own competition with the managers of the other workgroups, so that you have a little extra at stake yourself.

Is doing what you did ever right?

Certainly. If all three of the conditions in the section just above aren't met, competition will probably do more harm than good. Go ahead and turn it down for now with a clear conscience. But keep the idea on a back burner somewhere; things may change, and competition may become a viable alternative.

A tip for mistake-free managing:

Every manager needs to know when to opt for competition and when to stress cooperation. Neither works all the time.

Remember that the critical element is the work flow. No individuals or units in the same work flow with one another should ever compete, simply because it will give them a clear motive to disrupt the flow as a way of making themselves look good.

Perhaps the most important point to keep in mind, though, is what happens when the competition is fiercely serious. Perhaps jobs are at stake, or promotions. In these circumstances, it's a perfectly rational response for managers and workers to "game" the system, to distort the figures in ways that make them look good. Often the best gameplayers, not the best performers, win. And don't kid yourself that "these are a bunch of straight shooters; it won't happen here." Provide a large enough difference between winning and losing, and it *will* happen here.

CHAPTER 3

MISTAKES IN MAKING ASSIGNMENTS

3-1 The Mistake: Giving assignments that aren't clear

The situation: "Jan, what have you done here? I asked you a couple of weeks ago to see if you could make sense of these pricing computations. I didn't say I wanted a full-blown presentation on overhead allocations and support service outsourcing and market competition. How did you get such a simple assignment so blown out of proportion?"

        "I just did what I thought you asked for, Ms. Poydras. You said you had a presentation this week and wanted to be able to sound like you knew what you were talking about on pricing policies. I only wanted to make sure that I outlined all the factors we take into consideration when we set prices, in case something came up about why we charge the way we do. How was I to know any different?"

Why was it a mistake?

In this case, it's pretty obvious that Jan spent (and wasted) a lot of time putting together much more information than you wanted or needed. On another occasion, the problem may not be wasted labor; it may be that you get caught *without* information or a product you need because you weren't clear about your assignments. Either way, you haven't made very efficient use of your staff, and you didn't get what you needed.

How can you recover from it quickly?

If this is as simple an assignment as you believed it was, and if you still have a day or two before your pricing presentation, take the assignment back to Jan. But this time, make your request a little differently.

"Jan, it looks to me as if we have two or three different ways of computing prices, depending on what products and services we're selling. Could you look over these figures for me and outline what our basic charges are and how they differ from one product line to another? Sometime in the future, I may want to look at whether we really need several different pricing systems, but for right now, I just want to be sure I understand what all of them are."

You've asked some of the same questions, but you've taken one additional step. You've *limited* the problem. You've told Jan what kinds of things you *don't* need to know, as well as what you do need. Now she'll be in a much better position to focus her answer.

How can you consistently do it right from now on?

Follow these four steps whenever you give an assignment:

First, *state the problem.* "Jan, I have to make a pricing presentation in a couple of weeks and I can't make heads or tails of these computations. Could you translate these pricing methods into plain English for me?"

Then, *identify what outcome you're looking for.* The outcome might be a report, or an explanation, or a set of briefing charts, or even a single number (like the dollar value of your capital assets or the number of people you expect to hire in the next six months). Be as clear as possible about what you expect.

"I need just a few paragraphs explaining what our different pricing approaches are (like "per unit" or "per hour") and which products and services use which approach. If there seems to be some obvious pattern to which products use which pricing methods, you can tell me that too."

Next, *limit your request.* As in the example above, explain to Jan what you *don't* need (such as an analysis of whether pricing policies are consistent across product lines). Obviously, you can't give Jan an exhaustive list of everything you aren't looking for. But take a few seconds before you speak to Jan to think about how your request would sound if you were on the receiving end. As a talented, ambitious worker, what related avenues might *you* be tempted to follow? If some of those avenues are really blind alleys, make sure Jan knows not to pursue them.

Finally, before you end your discussion with Jan, *ask her to tell you what she expects to give you and when.* This may seem as if you're belaboring the assignment, but it can be an important check to see that you've communicated clearly and that she's understood your request. For some workers, after a while, you may be able to dispense with this step. But while you're concentrating on trying to make your assignments clearer and more definitive, asking workers to identify what they perceive your request to be will give you some very useful feedback.

Is doing what you did ever right?

Sure. Sometimes you may not know exactly what it is you're looking for. You may know something is wrong somewhere, or you may just detect the odor of something "fishy" going on, but you can't really identify where or why. In such cases, your assignments will necessarily be ambiguous.

"Jan, these pricing methods look awfully haphazard to me. I can't tell for sure, but it looks as if we may be charging one way for some products and an entirely different way for things that are really very close. And I'm not sure that I can explain to the director, or to customers, what the differences are. Could you see if you can make sense of all this?"

If all you have is incomplete information or a vague sense of unease, sketchy assignments are the best you can give. But they're not a very efficient way to manage day to day.

A tip for mistake-free managing:

Sometimes workers aren't very clear in giving information to their managers either. How many times has someone walked into your office and launched into a long and detailed explanation about something, and you're not even sure what the conversation is about? We all tend to speak (and write) as if we assumed that the person we're addressing already knows everything we do about the subject.

When you're dealing with an employee who starts conversations or correspondence in the middle, rather than at the beginning, have her step into the shoes of her listener. Make sure she answers the basic "newspaper" questions: who, what, when, where, why, how? That simple formula clears away a lot of fog.

3-2 The Mistake: Always delegating to the same few workers

The situation: "Roy, I need some help on this customer survey. Could you do a literature search and see what kinds of questions seem to give the most useful feedback?"

"Wait a minute," Roy objects. "Sheila's been sitting around for the last couple of weeks waiting for a callback on some account she's courting. She's got plenty of time. Julio and I always seem to be the ones who get these 'special' requests. Why not share the wealth a little?"

Why was it a mistake?

There are a couple of problems with giving assignments to the same workers over and over again. First, your best workers are likely to get burned out. Everyone in the unit knows who works and who doesn't. Good workers want challenge, but they also become resentful of others who aren't carrying their share of the load.

Second, your mediocre workers, the ones who don't get many new assignments, don't get a chance to improve their skills and don't get an opportunity to show what they're really capable of doing. Some people take longer to pick up new skills than others, and, by focusing on your fast learners, you deprive others of the chance to grow.

Finally, you deprive yourself of opportunities to fairly assess the capabilities of your staff and lose the chance to deal productively with whatever problem performers you have.

How can you recover from it quickly?

Respond immediately to Roy's concern. Maybe he's right, and you should ask Sheila, or some other underutilized member of your staff, to do the research. Especially in a project such as this one, a brief time delay while Sheila gets familiar with research sources and wades through the material won't be fatal.

Or maybe this project requires skills that no other members of your staff possess. Consider having Sheila help Roy do the research. He can identify possible sources and tell Sheila how to find them, then she can look up the information herself and summarize her findings, and Roy and Sheila together can recommend changes to the customer satisfaction questionnaire.

How can you consistently do it right from now on?

• *Review the assignments of everyone in your unit.* See if you do have imbalances in staff assignments. Are most of your workers at the same level, or do you have a mix of technical specialists and support staff at various levels? Are work-load differences reasonable, given differences in skill and pay levels? Or are you loading up your best people, while your less capable or less productive workers skate by with fewer requirements?

Even if the amount of work assigned to each of your staff members is about the same, what about the difficulty of that work? Do just a few people carry most of the tough assignments, or do all workers at the same pay level have about the same mix of demanding and routine work?

And what about new or "special" assignments? Are there certain staff members whom you call on to do a little extra—over and over and over again? Or do you distribute the short-suspense, one-time chores to the same few people? Those incidental assignments are a lot harder to keep track of. You may think you're being fair, but when you sit down and list all the extras you've given over the past few months, you're likely to find that they've usually gone to a chosen few.

• *Set up a "task distribution" system.* If most of the people in your unit do the same kind of work, set up a rotating list of workers to whom new assignments will be given. For example, in a unit in which nearly everyone processes payment vouchers, you can probably give reconciliation assignments to everyone inter-changeably. Let the staff know what you intend to do and how assignments will be given.

"I've reviewed all our current work, and I've decided to institute a new system for additional work coming in. From now on, I'm going to put together a set of file folders with your names on them and keep them in a central place. When new assignments arrive, I'll just slip them into your folders in turn—first to Roy, then to Sheila, then to Julio, then to Chris . . . and then starting over again with Roy. That way, everyone will get a chance to work on all the different kinds of problems we get hit with, and we'll expand our expertise."

Then stick with the system. Don't cheat! If an assignment comes in that you'd really rather give to Roy, but you know Chris ought to be able to do it and it's her turn—give it to Chris! Sure, it's tempting to have Roy take care of it. You know he will, and without any bother to you, but you won't have helped Chris improve and you won't have made her accountable for her own performance.

If the work of your unit is specialized, so that only one or two people have the expertise to solve specific kinds of problems, assignment distribution isn't as simple.

1. List the kinds of skills each worker has developed, and also identify skills each worker *could* develop given the opportunity.

2. Develop a rotation system like the one we described above to whatever extent you can, given the specialization of your staff.

3. Identify opportunities for cross-training. It's seldom wise management practice to allow your unit to be only "one-deep" in any skill area. Review your staff's qualifications and training to see what areas they might be able to learn effectively. Even if additional training or education is necessary, the advantages of having a backup system, as well as the ability to distribute work more equitably, make the investment worthwhile.

• *Take the actions necessary to correct poor performance.* If you're consistently delegating work to the same few people because there are others on your staff whom you can't trust to get the job done right, then you're avoiding a problem—not correcting it. Allowing performance problems to continue not only results in further deterioration of the poor performer's work, but also exacerbates your other workers' resentment and feelings of being taken advantage of. To deal effectively with poor performance, you need to follow these steps:

1. Identify which duties your poor performer accomplishes satisfactorily and which she needs to work on.

2. Counsel her on her poor performance. Case 3–2 gives you some tips on how to conduct the performance discussion.

3. Determine whether your worker needs additional training to perform adequately or whether she would benefit from working more intensely with a senior member of the staff who could mentor her in the tasks she needs help with.

4. Set up a "get well" plan with your worker. Identify what she needs to do to improve and how soon you expect to see progress.

5. Keep monitoring your worker's performance. If she's making improvements, be sure to praise her for her accomplishments and encourage her to keep up the good work. If she continues to perform unsatisfactorily, discuss with her the alternatives to continuing in her current position. You may be able to assign her to other work that she is capable of performing (perhaps at a lower salary), but you may have no alternative but to separate her.

6. If a new job assignment or termination is necessary, be sure to consult with your human resources department to find out what specific procedures your company follows in taking these actions.

Is doing what you did ever right?

It is never good practice to habitually delegate tasks to the same few workers over and over again. But there will occasionally be periods of time when the work that comes in just happens all to fall within one specialty area or when you're short-staffed and have to rely on the people who are available to shoulder more than their normal share of the work. As long as those periods are occasional and not routine practice, your workers will generally understand and gladly cooperate. When they begin to see a consistent pattern that some people get most of the assignments, while others carry a much lighter load, you've made a significant mistake.

A tip for mistake-free managing:

There are many jobs in which workload isn't even from day to day. Work may come in batches, or there may be peaks and valleys in the distribution of work. Multi-functional workers, who can perform several different kinds of tasks, can be a real boon in dealing with these workload fluctuations. Workers who aren't busy with their regular assignments will be able to help others who are over-loaded. Conversely, when staff members are out sick or on vacation, you'll have a ready-made system of backups in place.

As long as each worker gets an occasional opportunity to use the full range of her skills, you'll find that it's almost always an advantage to spread knowledge and skills throughout your unit.

3-3   The Mistake: Keeping the most challenging work for yourself

---

The situation:

Ben was ending the meeting. "OK, everyone understands what he's doing?"

"Sure," Carrie answered, "but who's going to pull the report together and finalize it?"

"I'm going to do that," Ben responded. "I'm more familiar than anyone else with the operation, so I can pull it together faster than anyone else."

"Shucks," Weldon exclaimed, "That's the only part of the whole project that's interesting. What we're doing is just the grunt work!"

Why was it a mistake?

Why do most of us get promoted to managers? In part, it's because we're recognized as experts in our line of work—as really effective production controllers, accountants, claim processors, or programmers. From the point of view of higher management, this means that we understand our business and can prevent serious mistakes. It also means that we can intelligently review the work of our workgroup and train new members.

It's fine for managers to be technical experts. Unfortunately, it also presents all of us with a fatal temptation—the temptation to do the work instead of delegating it to our workgroup. Most managers learn that they have to delegate most of the work; if they didn't, it wouldn't get done. Then the temptation becomes to delegate everything but the most demanding, most interesting work. Like Ben, we justify keeping it for ourselves because we have more technical expertise. Or because we don't want to get stale. In reality, though, we often keep it because it's interesting—the kind of work we enjoy doing.

No matter the reason for keeping the most interesting work, it's wrong for at least three reasons:

• *The job of a manager is to delegate all of the work of the workgroup.* If this doesn't happen, the "manager" is really a team leader or a senior worker. And as this incident makes clear, it puts the manager into competition with the rest of his or her workgroup. *Managers should never, under any circumstances, compete with the individuals that they manage.* Period. Workers resent it when it happens, because the deck is stacked against them. (Does your boss occasionally keep the really interesting work for himself/herself? If so, how do you feel about that? If it disappoints you or makes you angry, would you expect your workers to react differently?)

• *You keep your workers from learning.* Stop and think about this for a moment. You want very competent, highly motivated workers. That means you want workers who are constantly learning, because competent, motivated workers *always* want to learn. They want to increase their skills, and they can't accomplish this unless they get a chance at different, more difficult, challenging work. When you keep the really challenging work for yourself, what do you do to them? You turn them off. You decrease their motivation. Some just give up and become good, solid, *mediocre* performers. The really good ones start looking for another place to work. Either way, you, the workgroup, and the organization lose.

• *You tie yourself down to technical work when you should be doing managerial work*, which is very different. Here are a couple of "f'r instances":

• You want your workers to perform independently, but you also have to train new workers and help those who are having problems. How can you do this if you're tied up with a project? Even when it means that you're not busy all of the time, you need to be available to support your workers.

• Suppose your boss has a hot project, one you'd love to do. And suppose that you're performing a project in your workgroup and that you've not developed anyone else to do work at this level. You have two choices. You can do your boss's project and let yours go. Or you can do your project and let someone else do the higher-level project. Do you like either choice?

How can you recover from it quickly?

• *If this is the first or second time you've made this mistake.* You decide who can best perform the work and then meet with the individual and delegate it to him or her. What if you're not sure you can depend on him or her to complete it effectively? Break it into segments, then have the individual perform each segment and then discuss it with you. For instance, if the project is a report (as in the example), you might ask the individual to first develop an outline and then discuss the outline with you. The two of you make any changes necessary, then you assign the next step—perhaps writing the first section or two. You review that, make changes as you have to, and go from there. (You can find more ideas on how to delegate in other cases in this chapter.)

• *If you've consistently been making this mistake.* If you've been doing all of the most challenging and interesting work for some time, you can be sure that no one in your workgroup has the competence to do it. You can't just suddenly delegate the work and expect it to be done without your help. You can take one of two approaches.

1. You can use the approach in the section just above, where you delegate the work in discrete segments and ensure that each segment is done correctly before the next one is performed.

2. Or you can ask one or two members of the workgroup to work with you. You keep the overall control, but delegate as many of the specific tasks as possible to the individual(s) helping you. Be careful, though, that you don't just give them the simplest work. Give them the hardest tasks that you believe they can perform. After all, you're overseeing the project, so you can help them past any mistakes they may make.

Remember, whatever you do, your goal is to develop your workgroup to the point that it can perform even the most challenging work with little or no oversight by you.

How can you consistently do it right from now on?

Follow these steps:

Make clear to all of your workers, and to new workers when they join your workgroup, that you expect them to reach the point where they can do the most difficult work independently. If they *expect* to do the work, it will be far easier to assign it to them successfully.

Actually, you need to start the process at an even earlier step. If you intend to develop as many workers as possible to do the most challenging work, you need to hire workers capable of doing this work. So you spend all the time you must to find and hire effective workers.

As we have emphasized many times, you must create a trusting learning environment. You already know that there's little learning in the second kick of a mule, so you deal with repeated mistakes as performance problems. But the first mistake is always a learning opportunity, and no one gets criticized for it.

Remember that you will have a range of capabilities in your workgroup, no matter how hard you work to develop everyone. Some workers will be better at one type of task than another; for instance, one may handle numbers really well while another writes well. You want to develop each worker, but you don't want to force individuals to do work they're not good at (and probably don't like because they're not good). You *do* want to encourage them to work on their weaknesses, and you want to give them opportunities to do so.

Is doing what you did ever right?

You might keep the most challenging work for yourself if

1. Most of the workgroup is new and untrained and the work has to get out quickly. (If you find yourself using this reason often, you need to reevaluate what your goals really are.)

2. Everyone capable of doing the challenging work is busy with challenging work of their own. (What if they're busy with routine work? Most of the time, you take on some of the routine work so they can perform more challenging tasks.)

A tip for mistake-free managing:

What if you take over a workgroup whose previous manager did keep all of the interesting work for himself or herself? You have a dual problem. First, the workers don't know how to do the challenging work. Second, they think that this work is "manager work" and may resent your trying to assign it to them. How do you change this? Patiently. Use all of the suggestions in this case. Don't push hard or try to force workers. But keep the pressure on, recognize each worker who accepts the challenging work, then recognize the individual again for doing it well. You have a basic psychological fact on your side: Most of us really do prefer challenging work. Just take your time, keep encouraging, and wait for your workers' natural desire to do challenging work to take over.

3-4 The Mistake: Delegating without controls

The situation: You've been waiting for several days to get Bob's input for the quarterly report, quietly fuming all the while. Finally, in exasperation, you jump him in the hall one afternoon: "I'm still waiting for your accomplishments report," you begin.

"Hold on," Bob interrupts, equally irked, "I finished that report over a week ago and sent it on up to the front office. Didn't you get your copy?"

"Not only did I not get a copy, I never told you to send it up to the director without going through me. Don't you know how sensitive he is about those reports? That's where he gets the information for his board meetings—and now you've gone around me and sent something up I've never even seen."

Now Bob is worried. He knows he didn't handle this assignment the way you wanted him to, but he's not sure what went wrong. "You know, I did what I thought you wanted from me. I thought you were making me responsible for the report. If you weren't, you really should have told me."

Why was it a mistake?

Obviously, your delegation to Bob was faulty because, by failing to impose some controls on your delegation, you didn't communicate effectively—and you've upset a valuable worker. But the consequences could have been even worse. Imagine what would have happened if this were a really critical delegation and Bob were a less conscientious worker.

1. What if you had asked Bob to get together with a representative of another company to explore the possibility of contracting for some support services and instead he actually negotiated the contract?

2. What if you had asked him to get some price estimates on a new piece of machinery that you had an option to buy from a specific dealer and he committed you to buy from someone else?

In all these cases, your assignment to Bob may have been very clear. But if he didn't know the limits of his authority or you didn't impose controls on the delegation to be sure that he did what was expected, and only what was expected, when it was expected, you could have a real mess on your hands.

How can you recover from it quickly?

Since Bob's report has already been sent to the director's office, there's not much you can do to correct the problem this time. The most you can accomplish is an after-the-fact review, hoping to catch any significant gaffes. But if in the future you find yourself delegating authority without imposing adequate controls, you can usually correct the mistake by clarifying your delegation even after it's been given.

The problem with failing to provide controls at the same time you delegate is that you won't always be able to impose controls effectively later. In the examples above, failing to tell Bob that his report is to be given to you first is probably correctable (at least until he's already sent it out), and you also can usually correct a failure to designate priorities clearly. But if you asked Bob to explore some option for you, but didn't clearly tell him how far to pursue that option, he may very quickly over commit himself and the company. In that case, there's not much you can do to correct the delegation if you failed to impose adequate controls from the beginning.

How can you consistently do it right from now on?

• *Be as clear as possible in describing the delegation.* As with any assignment, you need to be sure your worker knows exactly what it is you're asking him to do. Are you asking Bob to attend transition management team meetings as a "fly on the wall," or are you asking him to participate as a voting member? Are you giving Bob the authority to enter into a contract or are you asking him to research options and make a recommendation?

• *Limit your delegation, with a concise explanation of the limits.* Tell your worker what he's not empowered to do as well as what he is—and *why*!

In the scenario we described, you might have told Bob, "I'd like you to compile all the information for our quarterly report. But this isn't just for internal use anymore, so I'll need to review the report before it goes to the director."

There's no implication that you don't trust Bob's ability to prepare the report accurately or to phrase it sensitively. Instead, you've explained that this isn't the routine assignment it used to be, so you'll need to see it before it goes forward. Most employees understand that, as the supervisor, you're going to be held responsible for the work of the unit, whether you're involved in its production or not. So they won't resist controls—as long as they understand them.

• *Plan for gradual lessening of controls.* As Bob becomes more comfortable with the delegation you've given him and as you become more comfortable with the decisions he makes in exercising that delegation, you should plan to gradually give more and more responsibility and authority to him to carry out the work on his own. There are several different levels of delegation.

1. You can ask Bob to make recommendations (or a draft submission), but run each one past you for approval before it's sent on.

2. You can ask Bob to prepare the report in final form, but to be sure to clear certain kinds of issues with you before he releases it. Those issues should be ones that you know are particularly sensitive or are of particular concern to the people who'll use the report.

3. You can ask Bob to prepare a final report and release it without any clearance from you, with the understanding that he'll deal with any sticky issues and let you know later (or elevate to you those things he knows he's not empowered to deal with).

For most assignments, for most workers, the last level of delegation is the one that you should be working toward. But many assignments require a progression of controls while the worker is learning what the stickiest areas are and while you're learning how far you can trust your worker's judgment in that specific area.

Is doing what you did ever right?

If you are in the enviable, and unusual, situation of delegating to a worker in whom you have absolute trust in all areas of responsibility—to the point that there's nothing you believe your review could possibly add, then there's no problem at all in delegating freely and without controls. If you have workers of that caliber in your organization and you've worked with them long enough to have established that level of mutual trust and respect, you're fortunate indeed.

For the rest, and larger segment, of your workforce, delegation should *always* be accompanied by controls, even if those controls will be in place only as long as it takes for the workers to demonstrate that they don't need them.

A tip for mistake-free managing:

Managing is always more of an art than a science. Knowing what level of control is appropriate is largely a matter of experience and gut instinct. Other cases in this book can help you figure out the appropriate balance of freedom and control for individual delegations.

3-5 The Mistake: Delegating the wrong things

The situation: "Katrina, you've got to tell George Munica to get his boss off the dime," you explain to your division assistant. "He can't delay installation of this system any longer, and if he can't do the work, I've got just the person who can."

"That's really not fair to ask of George," counters Katrina. "You're putting him in the position of telling his own boss that he's not performing. That's just not something subordinates should be expected to do. If you put somebody new in the job, George will be blamed for it. And if you end up not naming a replacement, George will be paying for his apparent disloyalty for a long time to come."

Why was it a mistake?

There are some areas that just aren't appropriate for delegation, areas that require you as the boss to exercise full authority and responsibility. When you delegate those chores to others you send a message to others that the tasks aren't significant enough to require your personal attention. That message, in turn, can insult important clients, irritate your boss, or let your staff know that you don't take the matter too seriously. In the wrong situation, any of those messages and outcomes can be fatal.

How can you recover from it quickly?

You can immediately retract your direction to Katrina to have George talk to his boss and instead make an appointment to talk to him yourself. In that meeting, you should be prepared to explain exactly what the problems are with the way he's handling the installation of the new system and that you're prepared to replace him if you can't gain the cooperation you need.

How can you consistently do it right from now on?

• *Put yourself in the place of your subordinates.* Whenever you decide to delegate a particularly unpleasant chore (and most of the matters that aren't appropriate for delegation are not in the "fun to do" category), ask yourself how you would react if your boss asked you to take on the same task? If this is a job you would feel awkward performing for your boss, then it's not something you should be asking one of your staff to perform either.

• *Use this checklist to determine whether this is a "nondelegation" item:*

  1. Does the issue require the presence of someone at a particular level within your organization?

  There are times when a relatively routine or even trivial issue requires the personal involvement of someone at a particular level—usually because of the level of the other people involved in the transaction. When you're dealing with an important or influential client, when you're working with someone at a relatively high level within your own company, when you're working out a problem with a manager at one of your suppliers, when you're dealing with members of the media—these are all times when you need to be involved just because you're the supervisor.

In cases like these, your personal involvement lets the other parties know that you consider them to be of sufficient stature that you will attend to them personally. Is this an issue of status, and even ego? Almost certainly. But no matter how egalitarian you may be in your own internal management, it's also critical to acknowledge status and stature elsewhere. This isn't bald flattery or toadying; it's a mark of interest and respect for the other person's position and importance to your success.

2. *Does the item pose substantial risk to the organization or to the person who handles it?*

When you're making a proposal you know won't be popular to your management group, when you're giving bad news to your boss, when you're promising results you're not sure your group can deliver, when you're mending fences with a client for whom you failed to perform—these are situations when you need to be the one who takes the heat personally.

Part of a manager's job is to provide an environment for her unit that's sheltered enough that workers aren't afraid to take risks. Any attempt to improve your products or your work processes involves some risk, and, without an environment that encourages reasonable risks, you'll never improve anything. But to create a safe haven for your unit you need to be prepared to deflect criticism and fight battles for your workgroup. When you delegate the higher risk work to your staff, you're like the generals who stay well behind the danger zone, well protected and safe from harm, while your troops struggle to hold the line. Instead, you should be leading the charge—never sending your unit into a battle you wouldn't fight yourself.

3. *Does the item involve giving direction to a member of your immediate staff?*

Your staff members look to you for guidance, not only on what to do, but also on priorities and commitments. When you send messages to your staff through an intermediary, you're telling them that you don't consider them very important or don't consider the message very important. And criticism of your staff members must come from you. Criticism that comes through other channels isn't likely to be taken very seriously. Further, the person you're criticizing should have the opportunity to ask you for an explanation and guidance, and he should be able to question your decision to correct him. Those opportunities aren't available when you delegate the chore to someone else.

These are the kinds of situations in which it's not appropriate to delegate to your staff. At first, you may need to analyze every situation to see whether it meets these criteria or whether your instincts tell you it's not something you would want your own boss to delegate to you. But after a while, you'll develop an easy familiarity with the areas that require your personal attention and you'll hold on to them naturally.

Is doing what you did ever right?

We won't go so far as to say, "Absolutely not." But there are very few times when you can delegate the kinds of issues we've discussed here without hurting yourself or your unit's performance.

A tip for mistake-free managing:

You'll notice that the first action we suggest for delegating the right things consistently is for you to measure your own internal reactions. Although it's not foolproof, there are many times when the best test of whether a decision is good or bad is your own "gut instinct." All the management training you obtain and all the advice we give you here can help you develop those instincts, but there are no formulas and no recipes for being a manager. The best we can do is give you basic guidance and touchstones to measure your decisions.

Over and over again you'll find that the problems you encounter fall somewhere between all the situations you've been taught about. When you've developed your instincts to the point that you can feel the trill of exhilaration when you've made a good decision or the clenching in the pit of your stomach when you're about to make a bad one, then you'll know you're on your way to becoming a *really* good manager.

3-6 The Mistake: Making overdetailed assignments

The situation:　　　　"Now, Clem," you begin your instructions, "you'll be responsible for monitoring our balance sheets to make sure the unit's not overspending its budget. So when you see this column over $130,000 or this column over $27,000 or when the two of these added together is more than this one over here . . ."

　　　　And an hour and fifteen minutes later you've finished explaining to Clem every single column on the balance sheet and what it measures and what he needs to look for (or what he can ignore) and who uses the information and what the formulas are for deriving certain figures, and on, and on, and on—when all Clem really needs to do is match a few column totals against a few others when the monthly report comes out and then let you know if things aren't matching.

Why was it a mistake?

Seems odd, doesn't it, that in so many cases we're advising you to spend time with your workers to make sure they understand everything they need to know about assignments, and the work, and the unit's relation to other units—and now we're cautioning you against giving too much detail? But the problem with overdetailed assignments is twofold.

1. Too much detail will obscure the real point of the assignment. When you leave Clem's desk, will he know whether he's supposed to monitor the entire accounting system or just some of the expense data?

2. Too much detail is also overwhelming, and it's likely that Clem won't have absorbed much of the information you've tried to give him. As a result, he'll have an incomplete understanding of even the relatively small piece of the system he's responsible for.

How can you recover from it quickly?

Stop yourself before you launch into your explanation and follow the steps we've outlined below.

How can you consistently do it right from now on?

Break the assignment down into a succession of instructions, "bite-sized pieces" that can be digested individually before you offer the next piece.

• *Stage one. Give the essential features of the assignment.*

Answer these questions for your worker:

1. *"What's the goal of this assignment? What's the final outcome you're looking for?"*

   In this case, you want Clem to let you know when your unit is spending too much money and will run over budget.

2. *"What information do I need to meet this goal?"*

   This is the *basic* information that Clem must have access to—the information contained on the monthly accounting system reports. And it's not *all* the information on those reports, but only a few key figures.

3. *"What do I need to know to process or evaluate that information?"*

   He doesn't need to know all the ins and outs of the accounting process. At least initially, he needs only to know about the specific columns his information comes from—what they mean and, perhaps, what's included in the computation.

4. *"Why does this assignment need to be done?"*

   Again, Clem doesn't need to know all the people who will see the information he gives you or what they'll do with it. He just needs to know on a superficial level that you'll use his review to decide whether to adjust your spending in the unit.

• *Stage two. Fill in some gaps.*

After your worker has performed the assignment for a while, problems or questions may arise that he can't resolve with just the basic information you gave him initially. *Now* it may be useful to provide some of the details or background of the assignment that will help him put it into perspective.

1. Explain where the information comes from that goes into the report he sees. More important, try to identify the sources of errors or mischaracterizations of information that may distort what's available to him.

For instance, if there's a significant lagtime between when you spend money and when it shows up on the accounting reports, it may appear that there's more money left in your budget than there really is. As Clem becomes more familiar with the reports and tries to make the status reports to you better, he needs to know what the lagtime is and how it affects the currency of the accounting system information.

2. Explain in more detail what impact his assignment has on other operations (either the functioning of your own unit or the performance of work for customers).

If Clem's monitoring is intended only to give you a ballpark idea of where you are financially (kind of like an early-warning system), he needs to know that greater precision is neither necessary or even desirable. But if you're relying on Clem's monitoring to make fine adjustments in your spending, it will be helpful for him to know how you'll use the information he gives you.

• *Stage three. Have your worker become the expert.*

Eventually, you can reasonably expect Clem's knowledge to surpass yours. You may want to send him to formal training if the assignment is sufficiently complex or important. You might decide to have him work with the people in the accounting system to find out how they do their work and how they collect and compile the information he gets from them.

At this stage, the detail and level of proficiency you can expect of Clem is substantial. But note that this is the level where you *started* when you made the mistake we illustrated above. Good management practice would have this be the point at which you *end*, when Clem becomes the expert rather than you.

Is doing what you did ever right?

Sometimes. If you're adding to an assignment that your worker has already taken on, so that he's already familiar with the work, piling on more detail may not be necessary, but it's not much of a problem either. As a general rule, though, excessive detail usually confuses and seldom enlightens.

A tip for mistake-free managing:

The four areas we asked you to address in giving your initial assignment are good guideposts for any assignment. In order to perform effectively, workers need to know what you want (the goal of the assignment), where to get the information (or tools) they need to perform, the knowledge or skills they need to use the information or tools, and the reason the work needs to be done (or how it fits into a larger context). Once you've provided that information, your worker has everything he needs to get started on the assignment for you.

3-7 The Mistake: Giving poorly done work to someone else to complete

The situation: Papers in hand, you begin this dialogue with a little flattery: "Tito, I know you know how to do these trend forecasts better than anyone else in the section." Then the kicker: "I just got these from Christian, and I think he must have used some bad numbers or made some computation errors because they just don't make sense. Could you look over his work and fix it?"

Why was it a mistake?

First, it's not very efficient to ask Tito to correct Christian's work when he has no idea how Christian computed his trends in the first place. Tito will now have to make independent computations and then try to back into Christian's numbers to figure out what went wrong.

Second, and more important, when Tito reworks Christian's product, Christian has no opportunity to improve his performance—and may not even know that there was a problem. He has no chance to learn how to do the work better and no motivation to improve since he knows that Tito will be there to bail him out whenever he prepares a substandard product.

How can you recover from it quickly?

Go back to Tito and retrieve Christian's papers. Take them to Christian and explain your concerns about the accuracy of his work. Then ask him to work with Tito to review his sources and computations to be sure he's figuring the trends appropriately.

How can you consistently do it right from now on?

• *Make sure Christian knows that he will be held accountable for the quality of his own work.* When you make the assignment, instruct Christian to give his findings directly to you.

If he protests, "But I really don't know how to do those forecasts very well," let him know that you understand that he's still learning. At the same time, tell him that you'll help him identify any corrections that need to be made in the product he submits.

This puts the onus squarely on Christian. He'll understand up front that he's expected to do the work, and that he's responsible for its quality.

• *If the assignment needs rework, give it back to Christian.* If Christian is inexperienced in this area, identify for him what corrections need to be made and, if necessary, how he should make the corrections. But if he knows how to do the work and just hasn't done it well, no explanation should be necessary:

"Christian, this trend line isn't going the way I would have expected from the numbers I gave you. I need for you either to give me an explanation or rework the figures."

Christian is not going to like this. He will want you at least to identify the problems— and the solution too. But when you fix Christian's problems for him, he has no motivation to fix them himself or to do the work right the first time.

(We once had a clerk in our office who consistently typed memos with numerous mistakes in spelling and punctuation. Contrary to our previous practice, we stopped circling and identifying her mistakes; we just gave her back the memos and told her to "fix them." At first, she was angry and accused us of not cooperating. But it wasn't very long before those memos began coming in picture-perfect the first time through.)

Our clerk was right in one important respect: We weren't cooperating. We weren't cooperating with her attempt to slough off responsibility for her own quality control on us. And when we placed that responsibility back firmly on her shoulders, her performance changed markedly.

• *If Christian needs coaching, assign him to an experienced worker—but only for advice.* Christian may not know how to recognize his own mistakes and correct them, especially if he's not very experienced or talented in performing the assignment. But, even then, it's necessary for him to rework the product himself so he can learn how to monitor his own quality independently.

The worker you assign to help Christian should be someone who is willing to point out mistakes or suspicious results, to help *Christian* work through the cause of the error and its solution, and to review the results of his rework. It's fine to offer hints and suggestions: "I think you may have inverted this ratio, so your trend line is going in the wrong direction."

But it's not appropriate for the worker to make the correction herself: "See here how you inverted this ratio. I'll just reverse the numbers, and see how the trend line rights itself?"

People learn by *doing* much better than simply by observing others. Christian's performance will not improve significantly until he gets a chance to learn from his own mistakes.

Is doing what you did ever right?

No. At least hardly ever. Obviously, if you have an immovable deadline to meet and the work has to be absolutely correct, you may have to ask another worker to make quick corrections. But, even in that case, you should give the work back to the person who performed it and ask for complete corrections.

A tip for mistake-free managing:

Improving performance is just like any other change workers are asked to make: They are not likely to change if there's no payoff. The payoff may be a negative one, like not losing a job or not having to listen to your criticisms, or it may be more positive, like recognition for a job well done or a customer who's especially pleased.

Both the carrot and the stick are important components of a motivational system. Avoiding negative consequences (like getting work back to correct over and over again until it's finally right) can be a powerful motivator to change. But for long-lasting change, positive reinforcement is more effective. When your worker begins to improve, be sure to recognize his improvement and give him a pat on the back. He'll be more likely to keep up the good work.

3-8 The Mistake: Letting a worker delegate back to you

The situation: "Tricia, we need to make the arrangements for our meeting with Consolidated Cartage for next month. We'll
need to arrange a meeting space and caterers and let our
folks know and get in touch with the CC group, and probably a lot of other things I haven't thought of yet."

"No problem," Tricia responds. "How about if you
take care of the contacts with CC and letting our own
folks know, and I'll handle all the facilities and food
stuff?"

"Sounds fair to me," you agree. "Let's get back
together next week and figure out where we are."

Why was it a mistake?

On a practical level, you can't do all the work assigned to your unit. That's
why you have a staff of people working for you. When you allow your workers to
delegate back to you, you cause two problems.

1. You don't make use of the staff you have to accomplish more work. The
work performed by the unit becomes limited by the amount of work you yourself
can perform.

2. You vest the decision-making authority in your staff, rather than retaining
it yourself. It's not bad to delegate some decisions to your workers. Certainly there
are areas where their specialized expertise makes it more efficient and effective
for them to make decisions. But when you allow your workers to delegate to you,
you reverse the decision-making structure. You become the worker; your workers
become the boss.

How can you recover from it quickly?

Go back to the scenario we described above. At the point where Tricia
responds, "How about if you take care of . . . ," you say, "Wait." Then explain:

"I've asked you to take care of all these arrangements because I've already
decided what I need to do, like work out an agenda and figure out if there are other
guests or speakers we need to invite. That's why I need for you to handle your
part, so we can get everything done to make a good meeting."

Tricia may not be thrilled to have to do the work herself, and she may try to recruit someone else on the staff to help her, but you will have made a successful delegation.

How can you consistently do it right from now on?

• *Be vigilant.* Some of the workers who are most skilled at upward delegation are also among the most pleasant and apparently cooperative people on your staff. There are many ways workers will try to delegate back to you. They may be direct like Tricia: "How about if you take care of . . ."

Or they may be much more subtle: "I was thinking that maybe Consolidated Cartage would rather be contacted by you than by someone at my level." "I'm having a hard time getting the people at the caterers to return my calls. Could you call and throw your weight around a little?"

Upward delegation may not even appear to be a request at all: "I just don't seem to be able to make contact with people at the right level at Consolidated Cartage. I'm afraid they're only going to send their project workers rather than real decisionmakers. That would be a waste of all our time."

At this point of course, the expectation is that you'll jump in and say, "Well, let me call. I'm sure I can get the right people to show up." This is the mark of a real master of upward delegation. You haven't just accepted an assignment from one of your subordinates, you've *volunteered* for it!

Of course, any of these requests or hints *could* be real concerns or problems that legitimately require your intervention. With a little experience and knowledge of the working habits of the people on your staff, you'll be able to sort out the wheat from the chaff of upward delegation.

• *Politely, but firmly, refuse the delegation.* Just as with the "quick recovery" we described, calmly turn the delegation back to Tricia. Even with subtle requests that you've identified as part of a pattern of upward delegation, you can explain that you're really depending on Tricia to perform.

One way to parry the attempted upward delegation is to suggest another way of fixing the problem Tricia's identified—one that doesn't require your intervention: "Why don't you call Roy Stump at Consolidated Cartage and let him know why we need to have this get-together. You can use my name, if you think it'll help. But I'm sure he'll see that the right people show up."

Or you can suggest another worker who might help Tricia: "If you can't get the caterers to return your calls, maybe they're not that interested in our business.

Ask Gertie to go through the phone book and make some calls to see if there's someone else she can line up."

You will have successfully resisted the upward delegation, but helped solve Tricia's real dilemma at the same time.

Is doing what you did ever right?

Of course. There are times when it *is* necessary for you to make contacts because no one at a lower level can command an appropriate response. Your job is not only to resist inappropriate upward delegations, but also to correctly distinguish between upward delegation and genuine cries for help.

A tip for mistake-free managing:

Workers who are consistently given the opportunity to successfully handle a complete project are much less likely to try to delegate back to you than are workers who are handed only the uninteresting details to attend to. Completion of a whole project, or a substantial segment, gives your staff a sense of accomplishment and pride in a job well done.

No one wants to handle the "grunt work." After all, isn't that part of why *you* delegated it to someone else? But when the messy details are a part of an overall project, they're much more palatable and their relevance to the whole is much more apparent.

3-9 The Mistake: Letting workers play "that's not my job"

The situation: "Tom, could you do the graphics for this class Denise is teaching next week? Kaye was going to handle them, but she's out sick and I'm not sure she'll get back to work in time to finish before class starts."

"I don't mind," Tom replies, "but Billy's been sitting around for the last few days with nothing to do. He could do the graphics as well as I could—probably better. And anyway, I'm a teacher just like Denise. Doing graphics isn't part of my job."

Disappointed, you retreat. "Billy's going to be starting another project, and I really need to keep him available. But I guess I could try to get him to squeeze it into his workload."

And during this entire exchange, you're seething. What's this "it isn't part of my job" stuff anyway? Helping out is helping out. It's part of *everybody's* job.

Why was it a mistake?

It's a mistake for just the reason you named: Everybody is expected to pull together and help out wherever there's a need. There are lots of jobs that come up from time to time that fall between the lines of "official" job descriptions. That doesn't mean they don't have to be done.

When workers are allowed to pick and choose which work they'll do and which they won't, you have no control over the production of the unit. Important tasks may not be accomplished because they don't fall within any particular person's scope of responsibility. Or you may end up having to do all those chores yourself. Or you may have to resort to calling on the same tried-and-true workers over and over again—who will eventually feel they're being taken advantage of.

Enough reasons?

How can you recover from it quickly?

Nip it in the bud. When Tom replies that doing graphics isn't part of his job, you return: "Helping out when we're in a crunch is part of everybody's job. I'd appreciate it if you'd talk to Denise this afternoon to find out what she needs."

How can you consistently do it right from now on?

• *Make sure that your staff knows that their jobs aren't limited to what's on their official job descriptions.* In a staff meeting or a policy statement, announce to your staff that everyone is expected to contribute whatever skills he or she has to the unit's production. Give some examples of situations where duties aren't assigned to a specific job, but workers still are expected to pitch in. These might be cases like helping new workers learn the job, starting up a new project, or taking on work that's been transferred from another unit, as well as the day-to-day "fill in" jobs that inevitably arise.

• *Demonstrate your own flexibility in helping others.* Show your staff that you're willing to step in and take on some of the load when the volume of work becomes overwhelming.

When your staff is working long hours to complete a project, do you stay late to help review work or assist with some of the report writing?

When tasks are transferred from another unit, do you roll up your shirt sleeves and help your staff work through how to divide up the chores and see that they get accomplished?

• *Reward workers who go outside their assigned duties to help out.* Show your staff that a willingness to go beyond their formal job descriptions does reap its own rewards.

Give some time off to a worker who stayed late or came in on weekends to help a colleague finish an important project.

If Bob volunteers to help others with graphics work, make sure he gets some kind of recognition—either kudos in a staff meeting or even a small bonus.

Make cooperation and willingness to assume additional assignments one of your criteria for deciding who gets promoted to higher level positions.

• *Don't take "no" for an answer.* Whenever a worker tries to avoid an assignment by saying "it's not my job," answer the objection, but refuse to be sidetracked. As the supervisor of your unit, you can expect everyone in the unit to perform any task that is reasonably related to the unit's mission. You probably can't ask computer analysts to do the janitorial work, and you obviously can't ask workers to perform tasks that they're physically incapable of doing. But you can certainly ask your analysts to make out their own supply requests, and you can ask clerks to change their own printer ribbons, and you can expect an instructor with graphics development skills to help out another instructor.

Is doing what you did ever right?

It is entirely appropriate to consider a worker's legitimate objection to accepting an assignment. Problems such as lack of skill, other pressing deadlines, even suggestions that another worker has more time or ability in an assignment area are all serious considerations. You should give those objections weight when you decide whether to give an assignment.

"It's not my job" is an entirely different breed of objection, however. It's not based on any legitimate work-related consideration; it's a statement of an employee's personal wish not to be bothered. At its heart, the "it's not my job" objection is a thinly disguised power play. Do you make the assignments or does your worker? Who's the real manager here?

A tip for mistake-free managing:

When workers feel that they are part of a team working toward a shared vision and goals, they're much less likely to object to any assignment that contributes to the attainment of that vision and goals. A vision for your organization isn't created just by issuing a well-worded statement that describes a rosy future. It's created day to day as you demonstrate to your workers how their work contributes to the success of your company and the welfare of your customers. It's created as you recognize each member of the team for the contribution he or she makes to the effective functioning of the whole. When a unit shares such a vision, no one will object that an assignment "isn't my job." The job becomes the unit's successful performance—whatever it takes.

4-1   The Mistake: Ignoring customers

The situation: Boss, I keep telling you that the department is really unhappy with the multimedia training course we're developing for them."

"And I keep telling you, Ali, that you shouldn't be wasting energy on that. Tell me—did we interview them extensively when we started to find out what they wanted?"

"Yes, but . . . ."

"Did we spell out what we and they agreed to and did both organizations sign it?"

"Yes, but . . . ."

"And are you following the agreement exactly?"

"Well, sure, but . . . ."

"Ali, in this business people have to decide what they want and stick with it. The department told us what they want and I expect them to stick to it. You work on the course and let me worry about their reactions."

Why was it a mistake?

If your workgroup provides complex services or products to other parts of the organization, you can be sure of two things. First, you will have difficulty helping your customers decide exactly what they want. Second, if much time passes between the agreement and the final product what they want will change. This is true whether you provide a training course, computer programming, internal consulting—you name it.

It's one thing not to provide for ongoing contacts between projects (see Case 4-5). That's dangerous enough. But to deliberately ignore feedback from the customer during development verges on the suicidal. It creates a situation in which the product you deliver is not what they currently want, and they will simply not use it.

How can you recover from it quickly?

This is difficult, particularly if you've set a clear precedent that you don't want to hear what customers have to say. If you're determined to change, though, there's one positive step you can take. Call the manager of the customer organization and offer to come talk with him or her about the problem. When the two of you talk, this is a likely scenario:

> "Adrienne, Ali keeps telling me that you're dissatisfied with that multimedia project we're doing for you. He's said it so many times I thought I'd better pay some attention and come talk to you."

> "It's about time!" Adrienne leans forward on her elbows." When we agreed on the project, we thought your folks understood what we were looking for. But what they're doing is clunky and slow—not even close to what we need!"

> "I understand. But we're all getting on the new system in a few weeks. Won't it run OK on that?"

> "First of all, about half the people who need the training won't be on the new system for another year or so. Second, most programs like the one you're doing for us will run the same on the new system. Clunky now, clunky then!"

> "But it will run on it. And after all, we did agree that . . . ."

> Adrienne leans even further forward. "I don't give a damn what we 'agreed to.' Your folks didn't understand what my folks were trying to tell them, and they're screwing things up. Dammit, I want something that does us some good!"

That will probably get your attention, and you'll probably decide you'd better stop ignoring what the department is trying to tell you.

How can you consistently do it right from now on?

Follow these suggestions:

• *Never assume that the agreement has everything the way the customer wants it.* Agreements sound so solid and concrete on paper. We do this, they do that, and everyone goes home happy. Not often. Your people have one specialty, your customer has another, which means that words and phrases often have very different meanings to each of you. The people who gave you the information have one idea of how something should be, but the people who will evaluate your product will have another. Something important changed two weeks after the agreement was written.

Any agreement for a complex product or service (and for a number of simpler ones) is a working document. The more of it that you can follow, the better. Assume, though, that the agreement will never be enough. Expect it to change, and plan accordingly.

• *Set up a system to ensure that your workers get constant feedback from the customer.* Case 2-3 can give you some suggestions.

• *Be prepared to listen and negotiate at any point.* If your customer comes to you with changes early on in the project, they can often be incorporated without great strain. But what if the changes surface later on? If a major change comes up halfway through? Then you and your customer both have a problem, because the change will probably create a significant workload over and above what you planned.

Here is where good listening skills *and* good negotiating skills are invaluable. Your workers need to listen closely and ensure that they understand just what's involved. Perhaps if they understand the core concern, they can give the customer what he or she wants. If not, this is where the negotiating skills come in handy. You don't want your people to agree to anything that isn't reasonable. They need to be able to identify the customer's needs, lay out their own case—being as responsive as possible to the customer—and then expect the customer to join them in finding a solution that a reasonable alternative for both the customer and them.

• *Remember, it's not over 'til it's over.* Translation: The project's not done until it's been delivered and the customer is completely satisfied.

Is doing what you did ever right?

To ignore a customer? Never.

A tip for mistake-free managing:

The more complex the product or service you provide a customer, the more the customer must be a part of the process of designing and developing it. As helpful as Total Quality Management (TQM) is, it has been somewhat misleading in this area. TQM was designed to improve the quality of manufactured products, on the assumption that they were produced in response to clearly articulated customer needs by routine processes. In this environment, TQM has helped any number of firms.

But the rationale falls apart when processes are nonroutine and products and services are complex and often one-of-a-kind. You still need a solid agreement up front and effective processes for all of the routine activities that support the design and development effort. But the critical element in a successful result is the involvement of the customer at every stage. Not that you dump your responsibilities on the customer (they resent that) or schedule endless meetings and in-process reviews. Instead, you schedule interactions with the customer as necessary for him or her to see the direction of the project and suggest any in-process corrections necessary.

4-2 The Mistake: Substituting your judgment for that of your customers

The situation: "Maintenance just called," Barb said, dropping into a chair. "They'd like us to give more weight to experience in the promotion plan we're developing for them."

"How much weight does the plan we're working on have now?"

"Experience is about 40 percent of the total value, and we give credit for up to three years at the journeyman level."

"Barb, that sounds like a lot of weight to me, particularly when Corporate is stressing the need for competencies these days. What do you think?"

"Well, I think what we've got is enough. You know how conservative those guys are down in Maintenance. If we let them, they'd give all the points for promotion for years of experience."

"OK, call them and tell them we considered what they said but we just don't think it's in their best interest."

Why was it a mistake?

Did Barb bring Maintenance's concern to her manager's attention? Yes. Did they discuss Maintenance's concern before they reached a decision? Yes. Then where's the mistake? *Instead of making a decision* with *Maintenance, they made a decision* for *Maintenance.* No matter how carefully they considered the matter, because the customer (Maintenance) wasn't part of the discussion they effectively substituted their judgment for that of the customer. This virtually guarantees that at least some factors important to the customer were left out of the decision-making process.

How can you recover from it quickly?

Can the manager catch Barb before she calls Maintenance back? If so, the entire matter can be corrected. But suppose Barb has already called? Then the manager might call Maintenance and begin the conversation this way: "Ed, got a question for you. Barb tells me that you guys wanted to give more weight to experience in this new promotion plan. She and I discussed it, and I asked her to call back and tell you that we didn't think it was really in your best interest to do this. But I thought about it and decided to give you a call. Is this really an important item for you?"

The conversation goes on from there. The manager hasn't really had to backtrack, but he has reopened the issue. Suppose Maintenance says that, yes, it is an important issue. Then the manager needs to be responsive and he needs to make sure not to do it at his worker's expense. This is how he might do both: "OK, Ed, if it's that important we'll take a hard look at it. Barb's been carrying the project, and she understands these issues at least as well as I do. I'll tell her that I jumped a little too soon and that I want her to get together with your folks and go over it with them. Understand, though, that all I'm agreeing to do at the moment is talk about it. Barb will really have to be convincing to get me to change my mind."

Now everything is back on track and the customer will get to make his case.

How can you consistently do it right from now on?

• *Realize that you don't understand your customers' needs as well as you think you do.* The only way you can ever get close to understanding customer needs is by listening constantly to the customer. Organizations that don't do this quickly lose touch with what the customer wants. That's bad enough, but the organization typically doesn't recognize that this is happening. It still believes it understands the customer and continues to act as though it did. This is a self-defeating spiral, and before long the customer opts out of it.

• *To overcome this, stay in close touch with every customer.* Your workers should already be keeping in close touch with each customer for whom they're working on a project. But that's not enough. You need to stay in close touch with them when you're not working on something for them. You need to know what their day-in-day-out business concerns and issues are.

This will help you understand what's important to the customer, of course, but it has another benefit. If you know your customers' real concerns, you may be able to suggest to them additional ways that your workgroup can help them.

• *Educate your workers never to substitute their judgment for that of their customers.* Many occupations have internal standards of what makes a "good" product or service. Engineers do, as do accountants, instructional designers, attorneys, and a whole host of other professional and semi-professional fields. And many nonprofessional fields, such as human resources management, want to be thought of as professionals. The net result of all this is that they want to make the decisions on what is really "right" for the customer.

Don't permit this to happen. Professional standards are important; don't attempt to bypass them or water them down. But the customer's needs always come first, and the customer is always the final judge of the success of a product or service. By all means, act like a professional and encourage your people to do the same. But begin by taking professional pride in identifying and meeting the customer's needs and let everything else follow from that.

Is doing what you did ever right?

No. Assuming you know your customer's needs without asking him or her will always get you into trouble.

A tip for mistake-free managing:

Do you listen to all of your customers? Yes. Do you listen to them all in the same way? No. You listen to most customers to keep abreast of their needs and their business issues. But there are two very special kinds of customers. You listen to them in different ways and you listen to them very carefully:

1. *Your honest customers.* It's unfortunate, but most of your customers will tell you they're happy with your services even when they're barely satisfied. (We've had to deal with this for years.) But a few of them will level with you and tell you what they really think. Treasure them and listen to them. They will keep you honest, which means that they will keep you from convincing yourself that your products and services are uniformly wonderful (which they almost certainly are not).

2. *Your progressive customers.* An even smaller number of your customers will be genuinely forward looking—trying to see what their work environment will be in three, five, or ten years. If you listen carefully to them and ask the right questions, you'll get invaluable information on new directions for your own workgroup.

To return briefly to the theme that opened this case: If you substitute your judgment for your customers in general, you will do both them and yourself a major disservice. But if you substitute your judgment for that of your most honest and most forward-looking customers, you're inviting disaster.

4-3   The Mistake: Not letting workers deal with their customers

The situation:

"I know it's a problem, boss, but I can handle it."

"I really appreciate your willingness to take care of it, Jonathan, but I think I'd better deal with this one. From what you've said, Ambois: Accounting is pretty unhappy with us right now."

"They are," Jonathan replied earnestly, "but I understand the situation and the people involved. Let me work with them for a few days. If we don't have it resolved then, I'll come back and tell you and let you take over."

"Sorry, I just can't take the risk. I'm going to call Sven Hansen myself and see if we can't get the problem ironed out. If we can get the basics taken care of, I'll be happy for you to take it from there.

Why was it a mistake?

Depending on the exact situation, the manager has just communicated to Jonathan:

1. "I don't trust you to take care of the problem."

2. "When big problems come up, I don't think you're capable of dealing with them."

3. "I think perhaps you caused the problem, but I won't know for sure unless I look into it."

Now, what do you suppose Jonathan's reaction will be? The odds are that the next time a problem like this starts to develop he will either hide it and work on it until it gets clearly beyond his control or figure that he doesn't want the hassle and delegate it to you immediately. Either way, you lose.

You lose another way. By taking over the problem, you teach your customers that your workers can't handle anything serious. So they'll begin bypassing workers and bringing problems directly to you. Do you really need that extra workload?

How can you recover from it quickly?

Call Jonathan back in. Tell him you've thought it over and do want him to handle the problem. If you really have doubts about him, ask him how he'll approach it and if necessary suggest a better away. Agree with him on when he'll report back to you on his progress, making it clear that you won't necessarily take the problem over when he does. Tell him that you're available to help him at any point, but you prefer for him to resolve it by himself if he can.

How can you consistently do it right from now on?

• *Make it clear to your workers that their customers are* their *customers, not yours.* You will get the most and best work from your employees if they know their customers and believe it is *their* responsibility to take care of them. Are things going well? Fine. Are problems arising? Perhaps workers might sometimes want to ask your advice. That's fine, but both they and you should understand that it's only advice and that they are the ones who're expected to solve any problems.

Why is this so important? The more that workers see that their customers are really theirs, that they are responsible for satisfying them, the harder they will work to take care of these customers, the more they will truly be *their* customers. Like Jonathan in the example above, they will want to handle the problems that arise. Let them. Even more, encourage them. Not only do you get more highly effective workers but you save yourself the time you'd have to spend dealing with the customers. It's a double win.

• *Make it clear to your customers that your workers will take care of them.* It's tempting, isn't it, to jump in when things get sticky? A customer calls, upset over what one of your workers is doing. How easy to get sucked into taking over the problem and making the individual at the other end of the line *your* customer. What better way to keep from falling into this trap than to make it clear to all your customers that your workers are fully capable of handling any problem that arises?

Whenever a customer calls to complain about the way a project is going, make sure to direct him back to the worker who's actually involved. Sometimes that requires arranging a three-way meeting: the customer, the worker, and you. But never bypass your worker to deal with a customer yourself. That only encourages the customer to continue to insist on working with you.

Is doing what you did ever right?

Not unless the worker is just learning, consistently overestimates the kinds of problems he can solve, or is determined to solve all his customers' problems no matter what. Even in those circumstances, you may be better off having a thorough discussion of the situation with the individual and then letting him or her handle it.

A tip for mistake-free managing:

True experts can tell when they're getting in over their heads and go for help. You want a workgroup composed of this kind of true experts. You want them to be responsible for these customers, but you need assurance that they won't bite off more than they can chew and get both themselves and you in trouble. After all, their customers are your customers, too.

Here's a practical step you can take: Encourage your workers to discuss problems with you when they arise. Then fight your natural tendency either to take over the problem or to start telling the worker how to handle it. Listen, help the worker understand the situation, draw out his or her ideas of how to deal with it. If the worker's ideas aren't adequate, then—and only then—make recommendations on what the individual should do.

4-4   *The Mistake: Treating all of your customers as though they were alike*

The situation: "Winnie, what's this? I see that the materials for Supply went out before those for Marketing. Don't I remember that we got the request from Marketing before the one for Supply?"

"Yes, we did. But Supply called a few days ago and asked if it would be possible to expedite their package. I checked with Marketing, and they said it would be OK as long as we got their materials to them by Monday. So, we finished Supply's work, got it to them, and then had Marketing's to them by first thing Monday morning."

"I guess you were just trying to be helpful, but I don't really like this. One of our cardinal rules is that we treat everyone the same. We don't make exceptions for anyone; you know that I've turned down some pretty big wheels who were trying to get us to give them priority. Please don't do that again."

Why was it a mistake?

Any workgroup with clearly identified customers (that is, almost all workgroups) must walk a careful line between treating all its customers alike and responding to the valid differences among customers. In this case, the manager made the mistake of choosing uniformity as the important value, at the expense of individual service. Insisting on either one at the expense of the other all the time will create problems. And because all of us respond positively when we believe we're getting service tailored to us, the more individualized service your workgroup can provide, the happier your customers are going to be with you.

How can you recover from it quickly?

Since the way back from this one is simple and straightforward, let's assume that the manager realizes it immediately, before Winnie has made it out of his office. All he has to do is say: "Winnie, wait just a moment. I was a little too restrictive in what I just said. It sounds as if you probably did the right thing. Do me a favor, though. The next time someone asks for priority, don't take any action on it right then. Come talk to me and we'll see whether we can give them an exception without looking as if we're playing favorites."

That simple change allows the workgroup to balance the priorities the next time a problem comes up.

How can you consistently do it right from now on?

Providing individual service to each customer sounds like a good idea—and it is. It's the goal any organization or workgroup should strive for. But the same organization or workgroup has an obligation not to play favorites, not to be more responsive to customers it likes or those with organizational clout. In short, individual service needs to be based on customer need, not on customer likeableness or power.

So how do you do this? Here are some basic ideas:

• *Intend to provide the most individualized service you can.* If you begin with the intent to treat everyone alike, you will probably fall quickly into rigidity and a bureaucratic rut. Nothing inspires customers to ask for exceptions like dealing with an organization in this rut. Instead, begin with the intent that you will meet each customer's needs and that you will do this in a fair and equitable way. Just doing this and communicating to customers that these are the workgroup's priorities will probably eliminate at least half of the requests for special treatment.

• *Avoid even appearing to reward friendship, clout, or poor planning.* Traditionally, most customers try to get special treatment based on friendship with someone in the supplier organization, their own organizational clout, or because they planned inadequately and need someone else to disrupt their processes. None of these are good reasons for making exceptions.

But don't look at it in these negative terms. Put it positively: *Reward good customers.* Reward the customers who are clear about their needs, who do their planning and inform you of what they need quickly, who understand your limitations and will work with you to overcome problems. Never, ever punish a good customer by putting him or her on a back burner while you deal with the problems created by a poor customer. This may be difficult at first, but if you keep communicating what makes a good customer and how good customers get rewarded, well, you'll start to get more good customers.

• *The better you know your customers, the better you can anticipate their needs without having to make exceptions.* This makes the whole system work. When you know your customers, you can individualize the service you provide one without having to shortchange other customers. In the example above, Winnie might have been able to anticipate Supply's need for quick service and take it into account in the arrangements she made initially with Marketing. Or, because she knew Supply typically waited until the last minute to send in an order, she could have been prepared just to let them wait their turn.

Notice, though, that none of this can happen unless you understand your customers and are willing to balance responsiveness to the needs of each one of them with fairness to each one of them.

Is doing what you did ever right?

Sometimes an organization may get so mired in bureaucracy that a workgroup can survive only by stressing fairness and even-handedness at the expense of everything else. Otherwise, it would get mired in favoritism and power plays. If you're caught in that kind of situation, you may have to be rigidly impartial, at least in the beginning. But if you and your workers can get to know your customers, and vice versa, you may begin to develop the freedom to introduce some individualized service.

A tip for mistake-free managing:

The more complex the product or service your workgroup provides, the more difficult it becomes to "treat everyone the same." First of all, every customer wants something different from you. One may want a fast turnaround time on a quick-and-dirty fix for a pressing problem. Another may not care that much about the time frame involved but may be extremely concerned about the quality of the final deliverable. Second, customer requirements often keep changing, making it difficult to forecast just what resources will be needed when. And both you and customers get hit with unexpected events that foul up your best plans.

So what do you do? First, you make the most realistic agreements possible with your customers up front, at the same time realizing that they will almost certainly change. Second, have individual workers or subgroups responsible for individual customers, or even individual projects. If a customer wants special treatment that wasn't agreed on, the worker or group serving that customer has to defend its need for more resources.

Nothing works perfectly, but following these two principles will gain you some stability.

4-5   The Mistake: Not seeing your customers' changing needs

The situation: "Boss, Package Design just called and they need the order for the new software out of here by tomorrow."

"What do you mean, Mike? We've got it scheduled for week after next and they'll have it easily by the first of the month."

"Yeah—that's what I said to them. But they said it wouldn't do them any good then. Corporate's rushing to get the new line of valves out, and Package Design has to have this new software to meet their deadlines."

"When did all this happen? I guess it doesn't matter. Mike, you do what you have to and get their order out of here. I'll call Max Burnstein in Package Design and find out what's going on."

Why was it a mistake?

Because it caught the workgroup by surprise. First, it has to interrupt its normal operations and expedite Package Design's order. Expediting an order is always less efficient than handling the same order routinely. Second, the workgroup knows very little else about how circumstances have changed for Package Design—or for other customers. Is this just an aberration, or the tip of an iceberg? Is the pace changing for all of their customers?

The workgroup doesn't know, so it can't respond effectively to whatever the situation is.

How can you recover from it quickly?

The manager is taking the only step he can in the very short run—calling the manager of Package Design to find out all she can about the changes occurring there. Let's take a quick look at how that call might go:

> "Max, how're you doing?"
>
> "Rushed! Did Mike tell you we've got to have that new software ASAP?"
>
> "He did, and we're taking care of it. He said something about a rush job for a new line of valves?"
>
> "Yeah. Apparently, Acme is working overtime trying to beat us to market, and you can figure what the brass thinks of that. This is a real make-or-break job for us."
>
> "I understand, Max, and if we can help you any other way let me know. I've been slacking off and haven't encouraged Mike to spend some time with your folks to see what's happening in your world. OK if he drops over and spends a little time getting a feel for your operation?"
>
> "Sure, just make sure he calls first. We'll be glad to spend time with him, but we're all pretty pushed right now."
>
> "I think he and I both understand that. One last, quick question before I let you go. Do you think that this kind of thing is going to keep happening, or is the shoot-out with Acme just a blip on the screen?"
>
> "I don't know for sure, but it feels to me like this is just the beginning. . . ."

One phone call is barely a start, but look at what the manager learned. She now knows more about why Package Design is rushed, and she's laid the groundwork for the worker serving the organization to find out even more. Manufacturing is probably already rushing to get into production, and Distribution is gearing up. They'll probably need expedited service. And the manager now knows that this may be just the beginning of a trend; her workgroup may have to change its whole way of doing business. And, as we said, this is barely a start.

How can you consistently do it right from now on?

The basic answer is simple: Stay in close contact with your customers. How do you do that? If you look at the conversation between the manager and Max Burnstein, you'll see that she was concentrating on three points:

• *She wasn't thinking of her workgroup as providing goods or services, but as helping her customers be successful.* This may not sound like much, but if you take it seriously it is. You're there to serve your customers' needs, and these needs are generated by their attempt to accomplish their goals successfully. Corporate has established a tight deadline for Package Design, which needs to meet this deadline to succeed. To meet the deadline, they need the new software—and that's where you come in. If you get the software to them, you help make them successful. It's that simple.

• *She was going to have her workers spend time with their customers.* This should be happening constantly. How are you going to find out what your customers need to be successful if your workers don't spend time with them? The manager in the example knew she couldn't. She knew that she could do some of the contact work, but that most of it needed to be done with individual customers by the workers who serve them. She was going to make sure she got her workers out there, even if only for an hour a week, so they could find out what their customers' hot issues are and be prepared to respond to them.

• *She was committed to do whatever was necessary to keep up with the overall changes in the organization.* As effective as she was, the manager shouldn't have expected her workers to get all the information. There may be important organizations that workers don't have dealings with. And significant changes may be beginning at a level or two above the level where the workers' contacts are. So she needs to be in contact with managers throughout the organization, personally or by phone, and keeping up on the hot issues that will be affecting her customers.

(Just a note. If you attend a weekly staff meeting held by your department head or CEO, don't expect it to answer all of your questions about significant changes. Supplement it with one-on-one visits or calls to other managers, even if it's just to follow up on issues raised in the staff meeting.)

Is doing what you did ever right?

No. Make a practice of being out of touch with your customers, and your workgroup will always be running at top speed just to keep from losing ground.

A tip for mistake-free managing:

Take seriously the idea that your workgroup's job is to support your customers' success. It doesn't matter what the workgroup produces or how large it is or whether its customers are internal or external. Your workgroup's job is to help your customers succeed—and that is exactly how you and each worker should see it.

How does a workgroup act when it realizes this is its job? First of all, you and every worker realize that you have a genuine contribution to make. What the workgroup does matters, regardless of what it produces. But it can never take refuge in the idea that it did what it was told, because that's never enough. To really support customer success, both you and the workgroup must understand what the customer does with what you produce. You and your workgroup must also understand both how customers' needs are changing and how you can support these changes.

Then you and each worker will truly understand what your job is.

4-6   The Mistake: Refusing to work with your customers

The situation: "They want us to do what?!" Gina Simonetti was one of your best workers, but you couldn't help exploding at what she had just said.

"Don't forget about not killing the messenger," she said, pointing her finger at you. "Now, you heard me— Graphics wants us to completely change the way we install and maintain their software."

"Who in blazes do they think they are?! We have more work than we can possibly accomplish now. How do they expect us to find the time and people to do things differently for them? No! But I won't make you be the messenger twice; I'll call and give them the message myself. And thanks for telling me so promptly."

Why was it a mistake?

To begin with, for all the manager knows the new way may take less time and effort than the way the workgroup is handling software now. But that's not the important point. The workgroup has a customer who has asked for a change in the service it's being provided. When a customer asks for a change, the customer deserves to be listened to, even if the change appears at first sight to be quite disruptive. Whether your workgroup can provide the changed service is another question; you work that question *after* you listen to the request and understand it in detail.

How can you recover from it quickly?

Call Gina. Ask her to arrange an appointment in the office of the chief of Graphics for both you and her. And ask her to make it clear that the purpose of the meeting is to listen carefully to Graphics' request. You won't able to decide until later what if anything you can do to help them.

How can you consistently do it right from now on?

• *You must not only listen to your customers but* demonstrate *that you're listening to them.* Your words must show that you've heard and understood what your customers are saying. That may mean restating their concerns in similar language. Sometimes, a simple "I see" or "Now I understand" is enough.

• *Get full information and weigh any requests for changes carefully.* Sometimes you can give the customer exactly what he wants. It doesn't always happen this way. Graphics might have wanted Gina to increase the time she spent on them by 20 percent, or provide a special service that every other organization would want if they heard about it. Listening doesn't mean automatically saying "yes."

• *Be as responsive as possible both to the needs of the customer and the needs of your workers.* Here, good negotiating skills come into play. If it's not reasonable to do exactly what a customer wants, focus on the heart of what the customer wants—the real interests underlying its request. You may be able to provide some or all of that in a different way and still not overcommit your workers.

Is doing what you did ever right?

No. No matter how sure you may be that a customer's request will be "off the wall," you never simply ignore it. Yes, it may be far more pleasant to say "no" in the comfort of your office than to have to confront a customer you're sure will be unreasonable. Do it anyway. In the long run, both you and the customer will come out ahead. In the short run, listening to the customer may keep him or her from running to higher management to demand that you provide the extra service. Even if the customer does go to higher management, your having taken such a clear action to consider the request will make your reasons that much more credible.

A tip for mistake-free managing:

As organizations become more flexible, leaner, and forced to deal with a constantly changing environment, managers can count on less and less stability in their relationships with their customers. These relationships will have to be renegotiated more and more often.

You need to stay on top of the organizational changes, of course, and be responsive when customers ask your workgroup for new or different products and services. But that's not enough. You need to be ready and able to propose changes of your own. Some of them may be to enable you to keep your workers on highest-priority tasks. Others may be to improve service to your customers, or even to propose that you work together in a new way.

The point? Never let your customers have all of the initiative. If they do, *they* will control the changes in your relationships with them. You don't want that.

4-7   The Mistake: Not educating your customers

The situation: "Tab, you look really upset. What's wrong?"

                        "It's Elena Garcia, over in the Finance Department. She's insisting that we get her our report a day early."

                        "It's only been a couple of months since she and I had our talk and I told her we just couldn't do it. Apparently, she's forgotten already. Well, I'll give her a call and repeat what I said back in September. Then we'll wait and see how long it takes before she bugs us again."

Why was it a mistake?

When your customers don't understand the constraints under which your workgroup performs, they make requests that seem reasonable to them but that are beyond your ability to produce. When you say "no," they believe you're not being responsive to them. Unless you find a way out, this process of request and rejection is a vicious cycle—one that builds bad feelings into the relationship.

How can you recover from it quickly?

There is no quick way out of this. You cannot educate a customer with one phone call. Even if you could present the situation so convincingly that your reply appeared inevitable, the basis of trust isn't there. The customer would never be sure whether or not she had been sold a bill of goods.

You can take a first step. If you were the manager in the example, you should arrange to visit Elena in her office at her soonest convenience. If you make that gesture and take that time, you'll demonstrate a level of responsiveness that no phone call ever can. But it will still be far short of enough.

How can you consistently do it right from now on?

Educating customers is never a one-shot, or even a three-shot, affair. It's never so simple as walking into the customer's office, pulling out your charts, and demonstrating in half an hour where the limitations are. Nor is it a case of repeating over and over that something can't be done. It is, instead, a patient process that occurs over time—a process that depends on both parties developing a strong and trusting relationship.

Now let's roll the calendar ahead on the example above. Several months have passed and the manager has had her workers spend time getting to know their customers' needs *and* ensuring that these customers understand the workgroup's limitations. In other words, the workgroup has been educating its customers. Now Elena calls the manager directly, and we pick up the conversation after initial pleasantries:

> "Elena, why do I have the feeling that you're going to ask me if we can't have our report to you a day sooner?"

> "You're right. Corporate is all over us to get them the monthly flash report by the third work day, but you don't get us your report until the third work day. Is there even some way you could get it to us early that morning?"

> "I wish there were, but we basically need all of that day to consolidate the information for our report. [Pause] You say that Corporate really wants to squeeze that extra day out?"

> "Do they ever. You'd think that . . . well, never mind."

> "I'll tell you what. I still don't have any idea that we can do what you want. But have your representative make an appointment with Tab so he can

show him or her what's involved in producing the report. If the two of them can find any slack, we'll see if we can get it out. OK? . . ."

(By the way, just in case you think this is a lot of work for not much of a payoff, here's one of the possible outcomes. Mac, Finance's representative, looks at the report and suddenly points his finger at a page of data. "This is what we really need, and you get it together two days before you send us the report. If you can fax it to us when you assemble it, we can modify our report just slightly and get it out a day early." Don't laugh. Things do happen this way, and the better the relationship between you and your customers, the more often they happen.)

Educating customers is a reciprocal process. You don't educate customers just by giving them information, though this is an important part of the process. You educate them by building a strong mutual relationship in which you understand their needs in depth and they understand your constraints in the same depth. This doesn't happen overnight or even in a month. It happens when both sides spend time and effort developing the relationship and when each side is genuinely concerned for the welfare of the other.

Is doing what you did ever right?

If your organization is very stable, so that the relationships among work units are largely fixed and unchanging, you may be able to survive without educating your customers. But if the organization and your customers are changing, not educating them is a virtual guarantee of trouble. Your customers know what they need. They expect you to meet this need. Unless they have a good sense of what you can and cannot produce, they will be frustrated when you say you can't fulfill their requirements. You may not always be able to satisfy your customers, but you don't ever want to frustrate and anger them.

A tip for mistake-free managing:

There is yet another step beyond the reciprocal relationship between you and your customers described above: full partnership. That's very important and powerful concept. But it's not an easy one to achieve, and you ought to try for it only after you've established a strong reciprocal relationship.

How is a partnership different from this relationship? In a true partnership, both parties take responsibility for the success of both parties. For instance, when you partner with customers you may ask them to participate in your workgroup's planning sessions, so that you have the best possible information on their current and foreseeable needs. And your customers may ask you to join their planning sessions for the same reason. ("As best we can tell, we're going to have to double our capacity by February. Can you increase your support to us to that level by then?")

As you might guess, a real partnership is a very high-trust relationship. That's why it takes a long time to develop. It's also why a partnership can be destroyed in minutes.

4-8   The Mistake: Ignoring your suppliers

The situation: "Charlie, what do you mean that you can't get our new equipment installed for two more weeks?!"

"I mean exactly that, and I don't appreciate being yelled at over the phone any more than I do being yelled at in person."

"OK—I'll calm down. But, Charlie, I've just got to have that equipment in place before then."

"Sorry, ole buddy. Our headquarters has us strung out 'til you wouldn't believe. We'll give you the best we've got, but that's going to be at least two weeks. . . ."

Why was it a mistake?

Look at the unanticipated bind the manager has suddenly gotten himself in with Charlie and his workgroup. It's not that Charlie doesn't want to be responsive; we don't know whether he wants to or not. But he's coming through loud and clear that he can get the manager's equpment installed when he needs it. At the very least, if the manager had been keeping up with Charlie's workgroup and his other suppliers he would have seen this coming. As it is, he's caught flatfooted.

How can you recover from it quickly?

You can't. You might try begging, wheedling, threatening, or whatever; one of those might work. But you can't overcome months of ignoring your suppliers with one phone call or visit.

How can you consistently do it right from now on?

Remember and act on these ideas:

• *Suppliers depend on their customers—and customers depend on their suppliers.* Management books over the last decade have concentrated on the importance of taking care of your customers. That's good advice. But unless all of your supplies come from a dozen mass-marketing operations like Kmart or WalMart, your suppliers are just as important to you as you are to them. Just as they need to understand your needs, you need to understand their constraints.

• *If your suppliers don't take the initiative, you take it.* Ideally, of course, your suppliers will be customer-oriented and take the steps necessary to stay in touch with you. But not all of them will, and some of those that do stay in touch will do it only sporadically. That means the onus is on you to stay in touch with them. Ideally, most of them will have an individual worker assigned to you as a liaison. If any of them don't, ask them to.

• *Anticipate their problems and see that they anticipate yours.* You stay in touch with your suppliers, and you ensure that they stay in touch with you, to achieve this goal. If they have problems coming that will interfere with their service to you, the sooner you know about them and can plan around them the better. And when they know you have problems ahead, they may be able to help you though them.

Is doing what you did ever right?

Not unless you have so many suppliers that they have to seriously compete for your business.

A tip for mistake-free managing:

Most workgroups in most organizations are part of a process that other writers have called "a chain of customers." You depend on other units to provide you materials, services, and other support of various kinds. In turn, individual or external customers depend on what your workgroup produces to do their jobs. And when a process spans several units, the problems are going to arise at the boundaries between the units—at the customer-supplier relationships.

It's all too easy to react to your suppliers in terms of: "They don't understand that we're their customers; they don't ever make any effort to find out what we need or take care of our special requirements." If you react that way, where does it get you? Nowhere. You may feel properly and self-righteously indignant, but nothing will get better.

That's why you never ignore a workgroup that's one of your suppliers. And you never let that workgroup ignore you. Your job is to make them a good, customer-oriented supplier—in spite of themselves, if necessary.

4-9   The Mistake: Not being a good customer

The situation: "Earline, I've just got to have our supplies before the week is out. I know it's a stretch for you, but this is critical."

"I'm sorry—the middle of next week is the best we can do. It would be hard in normal times, but now we're up to our monitors getting the start-up supplies to the new office they're opening in Seattle."

"I really don't like this. I'm your customer, and your job is to satisfy my needs. You know how serious Corporate is about this. But you're telling me that you can't get me some absolutely essential supplies when I need them."

"I just can't. You're going to have to settle for the middle of next week—and I can't absolutely promise you we'll get them to you then."

"I don't like it—I don't like it worth a damn! This is really lousy customer service!"

Why was it a mistake?

Who came out of the exchange happy? Certainly not the manager who needed the supplies. And certainly not Earline. Both of them will carry negative feelings toward the other away from the exchange. And the next time a clash like this happens, it may well end up in the office of their mutual boss.

That's why it was a mistake.

How can you recover from it quickly?

A personal visit to Earline to pour oil on troubled waters, as early as possible at her convenience, will help. (Shouldn't she come apologize to you? After all, you're a customer, and she was the one who said she couldn't meet your needs.

Forget it—you want to heal the situation, not make points.) But it will be only a bare beginning.

How can you consistently do it right from now on?

• *Give your supplier the benefit of the doubt.* Was Earline's workgroup so rushed it couldn't give you that extra bit of service, or was the whole affair an excuse? You don't really know, and it's not worth your time to find out. Take Earline's word this time. If you don't, all the two of you will be able to do is fight and end up with bad feelings toward one another.

• *Understand your suppliers' constraints.* You have limits on the service you can provide. So do your suppliers. They simply cannot do certain things. They also run into temporary time binds and rush projects—just as you do. Yes, they should be concentrating on your needs as a customer and ensuring that you understand their constraints. If they don't do that, though, you need to pick up the slack. If they won't educate you to be a good customer, you need to work with them and educate yourself. The more fully you understand their constraints, the more realistically you can do your own planning.

• *Expect responsiveness on both sides.* If your supplier can't meet your need exactly, propose a reasonable alternative, one that gets your needs met with minimum inconvenience to the supplier. It's much harder for a supplier to refuse to perform when it's obvious that you're being cooperative.

The more you work with your suppliers and understand their limitations and problems, the more easily you can identify where they have the flexibility to provide extra service when you need it. It will also be easier for them, since they know you won't insist on the unreasonable.

• *Work at being a good customer.* A single contact never suffices. Use it as a springboard for getting to know all of your suppliers. Don't do it yourself, except in a very broad, manager-to-manager way. Have your people meet with their people so you can get to understand each other better. Build a strong relationship. Then, when either of you needs something special from the other, you'll each be able to assess the situation realistically and find the best possible resolution for it.

Is doing what you did ever right?

Only if you're willing to live with an angry supplier for a while, which really means "only if you have such a crushing need for the supplies that it's worth alienating a provider." If you do, common sense dictates that you use the suggestions in the section just above and set about becoming a good customer as soon as possible.

A tip for mistake-free managing:

In an ideal world, your suppliers would all value you as a customer and treat you accordingly. In the real world, though, that doesn't always happen. When it does, being a good customer means cooperating with your suppliers and making it easy for them to provide you great service. When it doesn't, being a good customer means initiating the relationship yourself and making it easy for them to provide you great service. When you act as a good customer, you make it possible for your suppliers to be good suppliers. Not only that, but the better you are as a customer, the more satisfied your customers will be in dealing with you.

CHAPTER *5*
MISTAKES IN PROVIDING INFORMATION

5-1   The Mistake: Not keeping your workgroup informed

The situation:

"Hey, boss," Derwood calls as you pass by his office. "Did you know about the pending merger between Tristron and ExecuPol? I just read about it in this month's newsletter. You didn't know this was brewing, did you?"

"As a matter of fact, I had heard they were working out a merger deal," you respond. "But it didn't seem worth mentioning at the time."

"Well, I really wish you'd said something to me," complains Derwood. "I've been negotiating with both of them for our new voucher-processing system, trying to play one off against the other, which obviously wasn't a very good strategy since they're going to be part of the same family in the next few months.

"Now I feel like a real fool. They've probably both been laughing up their sleeves at me for weeks now— talking to each other about the trick they're pulling on us and knowing full well what their bottom lines are."

Why was it a mistake?

Pretty obvious, isn't it? Because you thought a piece of information wasn't important enough to pass on to your staff, one of them has been caught in a difficult position—a position he certainly would have avoided if he'd known what you knew about the pending merger.

"But how was I to know that particular item was important?" you may ask. "If I passed on every single piece of information I learn each day, I'd be nothing more than an information conduit—and I'd never get any real work done."

129

That is exactly the problem. A major part of your "real work" as a supervisor is to be sure that your staff have the tools they need to perform effectively. In many cases, those tools include knowledge and information about areas they're involved in. Sure, you're also expected to do some filtering, extracting the truly relevant from the merely interesting and the totally extraneous. But there's still a lot of information that is truly relevant, that your staff needs to know, and that you're responsible for getting to them.

How can you recover from it quickly?

You apologize to Derwood for failing to keep him informed about the merger, then set up a time (right then or very shortly) to fill him in on all the details you're privy to that might not have been available in the short newsletter article he read.

And while you're at it, you might help Derwood strategize about how to extricate himself from the position he's in with Tristron and ExecuPol.

How can you consistently do it right from now on?

• *Keep up with your workers' assignments.* For many reasons, you need to keep up-to-date on the status of individual assignments. Knowing what's going on allows you to offer advice and assistance early enough to be of some help, lets you monitor the timely progression of project work, and ensures that you can report to your boss on important developments. It also allows you to keep track of the kinds of information that will be important to your workers and to filter out what's not likely to be relevant.

• *Make notes of important items of information that you hear.* Much of the most important information you get will not be written. Instead, it will come to you through chance conversations or overheard in meetings or at the lunch table. If you don't make a note of those items immediately, we guarantee you'll forget to pass them on to your staff until it's way too late.

One of us keeps notes on a calendar, the other uses an electronic notepad. You can use the notebook on your computer or keep a stack of cards on your desk. But whatever method you choose, be sure to record those tidbits right away, perhaps with a date and the names of the workers whom you need to inform.

The trick is in the recording—once you've noted the items, you can give out the information in staff meetings (for items of general interest) or in individual meetings or phone conversations.

• *Develop the habit of routing significant correspondence and papers to your staff.* We keep a central correspondence file that everyone in the office has access to, and we route the more important items through the entire staff each month. Other items that appear in your in-basket may also be worth routing—product announcements, memos from other parts of the company that affect your operations, notices of significant internal management decisions.

Use the copy feature on your local area computer network, but judiciously! The copy feature, sometimes known as "cc:mail" can be a convenient way to distribute significant information throughout your staff. But don't get caught in the trap of copying everything to everybody "just in case" it might be helpful. We've read horror stories of companies where workers typically have 80-100 messages a day to sort through on their computer e-mail. Those poor folks *don't* have time to do any "real work!"

• *Distribute minutes of your boss' staff meetings to everyone in your workgroup.* Although staff meetings can be incredibly boring to the people who have to sit through them, they're also valuable opportunities to share information. Well-written minutes, organized with bullets or subject headings, are easy to sift through quickly. They can also be a good source of information about what's happening elsewhere in the organization.

Is doing what you did ever right?

In this context, the question is a kind of "have you stopped beating your wife?" inquiry. Of course, it's never right to withhold information your workers need to do their jobs. Of course, you're expected to sift through the information that comes to you and decide what's relevant to your workgroup. Of course, you're going to make errors of judgment, mistakenly giving information that people don't need, or not passing on information that people do need, or forgetting information entirely. But the tips we've given here will help you sort the information and make sure it gets to the right people—most of the time.

A tip for mistake-free managing:

It's not only important to keep your workgroup informed, it's at least as important to keep your boss informed—so she doesn't get caught unawares. In the fourth case in this chapter, we describe how to keep from making that particular mistake.

As you think of information flow in your organization, think of a pipeline of information that flows in both directions: You are the valve in the middle, between your workers on one end and your boss on the other. If the valve doesn't function properly, the system can't work. Stuck open, and both ends are flooded with information. Stuck closed, and not only does the pipeline shut down, but the two ends wither from the drought.

5-2   The Mistake: Giving your workgroup incomplete information

The situation:

"Didn't you tell me that we were thinking about signing a new group to do our graphics work?" Zia asked. " I just signed up Binwell and MacCree for a big graphics project, but Lou tells me that the whole function is going back to the Hardy Harbinger. You know Binwell's had it in for the Hardy Harbinger ever since their top writer was lured away three or four years ago. I didn't even know they were in serious contention for the function—I assumed we'd be switching to Creativity Plus since the boss' daughter works there."

"I guess I knew we hadn't decided to leave the Hardy Harbinger, but it just didn't seem important," you explain. "And I really don't see what difference it makes to our customers. They don't need to know who we're subcontracting with."

"Well, they may not *need* to know, but sooner or later they're going to find out. And they won't be happy. I wish you'd told me the whole story."

Why was it a mistake?

Sometimes knowing only some of the story is worse than knowing none of the story. Zia knew that his prospective customer didn't like the graphics group currently used by the company. If he had thought that group would continue to do his company's work, he could have pitched his negotiations with Binwell and MacCree differently, perhaps by offering to split the project so they could use their own graphics firm or by trying to convince them that the overall product he was offering was worth the irritation of working with a graphics group they didn't like.

But since Zia had incomplete information, he made a wrong assumption— that there was no graphics problem because it was going to go away when the company switched subcontractors.

When you fail to give your workgroup complete information, you increase the likelihood that your workers will end up in the same box Zia did, not knowing what's really going on, even though they think they do. And if your workers find you giving them incomplete information repeatedly (and get stung for lack of the whole story), soon they won't trust much of anything you have to tell them.

How can you recover from it quickly?

In this case, you can't. That's the problem with giving incomplete information. In most cases, your workers will have the impression that they know everything of significance there is to know, and they'll act on that understanding. It's only later that they, and you, find that their lack of knowledge caused a serious problem, often when it's too late to fix.

How can you consistently do it right from now on?

This is one of those mistakes that's easy to correct. Just do it. Make sure that when you give information to your staff, it's complete information. In general, you should plan to give your workgroup as much information as you have about any specific topic.

But there are exceptions to the general guidance. The times when it's *not* appropriate to give complete information, when you *should* withhold some items, are times like these:

• *When the information concerns confidential company matters that are especially sensitive.* Negotiations with another company or with a labor union are a prime example of the kinds of issues that aren't appropriate for general dissemination, even within the company, because of the serious impact if the information gets into the wrong hands.

• *When the information concerns impending layoffs or otherwise adversely affects the organization's staff*—especially before the people affected have been told of the company's plans. Just as your group doesn't want to hear from someone in another department that two of their number are being laid off, the other department doesn't want to get its information that way either. Keeping this information on "close hold" is always appropriate, including the underlying decisions that will result in the adverse actions (like decisions to outsource or to eliminate a particular product line).

• *When your own boss, or someone higher in the chain of command, says that the information isn't to be shared.* Here you have a little more leeway. We aren't advocating that you violate a direct order, you may well have the opportunity to question the decision to withhold information if you think the lack of information will affect employee morale or productivity.

You'll probably find that many of the sensitive or adverse impact decisions that you've already decided not to share with your staff are also items you're specifically forbidden to discuss by your higher level management. Many companies have policies that limit who can release particular kinds of information, and when.

Other than in these situations, it's almost always in the best interests of the company that its workers have full and complete information about every area of the business that affects them. Especially in these days of increasing employee autonomy and empowerment, when we expect our workers to make decisions independently, it's critical that those workers have as much information available to them as possible. Bad (or incomplete) information is a sure guarantee of bad decisions.

Is doing what you did ever right?

We've discussed the kinds of situations in which it's appropriate to censor or withhold information. But remember: Those are the exception, not the rule.

A tip for mistake-free managing:

Although there are excellent reasons for carefully orchestrating the timing of announcements of layoffs or other adverse actions to employees, the longer you wait, the worse the situation becomes. Few layoffs occur in which the affected employees didn't have at least some inkling that bad news was on its way. With longer delays, workers imagine all kinds of horrible scenarios. Workers who aren't affected will believe that they are; workers who are being temporarily laid off will believe they're being put out for good. And everyone will believe that there's something sinister going on behind the closed doors of your planning sessions.

For most people, not knowing is worse than knowing—even when the news is bad. Once the news is out, everyone can deal with the situation as it really is, not as he or she imagines it to be. And the sooner that happens, the sooner all these people can get on with their lives.

5-3   *The Mistake: Not keeping your workers aware of the "big picture"*

The situation:

"I know I haven't done a lot to push our new 'Footease' with the retailers I market to," Jason admitted, "but it's just not that important a part of our line. I do much better concentrating on our established lingerie and sleepwear lines."

"How could one of our top representatives be so naive?" you fume. "The CEO announced almost six months ago that we would be entering the footwear market. Don't you know how important it is to test retailers' acceptance of our new line, which we obviously can't do if you don't push it."

Jason countered, "You may have known the 'Footease' was part of a larger line, but nobody ever said anything to me about it. Of course, if I'd known we were going full-tilt into the footwear business, I would have used a whole different approach. But you can't just say, 'Push these,' and expect me to know what that means; you've got to give me the whole picture."

Why was it a mistake?

Workers use "big picture" information for at least two important purposes:

1. It gives them information about the company's priorities. If Jason thinks "Footease" are just a sideline the company's dabbling in, he's not going to be too concerned about whether he moves any of the product or not. But if he knows that

they're an initial offering in a whole new product area that the company wants to enter, he will, as he said "use a whole different approach." He'll certainly emphasize the product more in his work with established customers; he may even pursue other customers who he thinks would be more interested in this product line than in the lingerie and sleepwear that are your mainline products. In any event, he'll give a whole lot more attention to "Footease" if he knows how important they are to the company.

2. It gives them information about where they fit into the grand scheme of company operations and how their work affects other units. This is a slightly different kind of "big picture" than the goals information we've discussed so far. Workers need to know not only what's important to the company overall, but also how they fit into those goals.

That information allows them to direct decisions toward minimizing internal friction. If, for example, Jason knows that his monthly sales projections are plugged directly into a formula that determines production quotas for different product lines, he'll be more conscientious about preparing his projections accurately and on time, particularly if he also understands the link between poor projections, resultantly lower production of items he projected wouldn't sell well, and the calls he gets later from irate customers whose items are on back order because there haven't been enough produced. But without knowing anything about those linkages and the flow of information, he's likely to slough off the projections as "just paperwork" when his real job is getting out to the customers and selling.

How can you recover from it quickly?

You can explain to Jason the CEO's announcement of a new product line—what will be included, the price range, the production schedule, and any other details you know about the company's entry into the footwear market. Although his performance over the past couple of months won't have given the company a true picture of retailers' acceptance of the product, he can easily change his approach to begin helping the company's introduction of the new line.

How can you consistently do it right from now on?

• *Give all your workers a basic orientation to the company.* If your company has an orientation program, use it. If it doesn't, get copies of the information that's sent to potential stockholders or customers about the company's overall goals and mission, activities, locations, size, and other general information. You might also have a company promotional video that includes much of the same information.

Even though some of your workers may have been on staff for five or ten years, have them at least skim the orientation material. You can't assume that this kind of information filters in through osmosis. Many workers settle into a job, knowing only their little piece of the action and not having access to (or being interested in) the big picture. It's never too late to learn.

• *Arrange briefings by other units to your staff.* Occasionally invite a manager or representative from one of the other units your workgroup interacts with to describe her operations to your unit. Use the opportunity to explore with the manager and your own staff the areas where your two operations have an impact on each other and what your group can do to make the interfaces work more smoothly. Identify potential problems areas together and suggest ways to avoid those problems.

• *Be sure your workgroup sees all the corporate level policies and announcements that apply to them.* In the first case in this chapter, we described ways to make sure you keep your workgroup informed about things going on in the company. That advice about routing correspondence and announcements, making notes and giving information during staff meetings,holding individual sessions, and copying information through e-mail all applies to big-picture information as well. In Jason's case, he may know quite a bit about the company, what it does, what its goals are, and how he fits into them, but he missed an important new development. The big picture isn't static; your employees need to see it changing.

Is doing what you did ever right?

It's always risky to neglect to explain to your workgroup the context in which they're operating. But it's also a duty that's easy to overlook. For the most part, lack of knowledge of the big picture won't hamper workers' day-to-day performance. Lack of the complete picture usually doesn't become critical until a crisis looms and workers have to make on-the-spot, crucial decisions. Then, a lack of understanding of the context of their work can make a bad situation worse. Upfront knowledge of the big picture is more often a preventive measure—a kind of insurance against the day when a decision will have to be made and you won't be there to fill in the gaps.

A tip for mistake-free managing:

We hope that you don't fall into the same category with your workgroup—knowing what happens in your own isolated piece of the organization, but having only a hazy and incomplete idea of how your unit's work contributes to the company as a whole. We've known many first-level managers, especially ones who were promoted up through the ranks of their own functions, who have never been exposed to that wider view.

If you *do* happen to fall within the group of narrowly focused managers, we urge you not only to take advantage of the same opportunities you're offering your staff, but to do even more. Talk to your peers about setting up rotation programs to allow all of you to get experience in related functions. Encourage your boss to use her staff meetings to exchange information about substantive events in each unit. Tough as it is for your staff to operate with organizational blinders on, it's even worse for you. The decisions you make should consider the welfare of the entire company or division, not just your own unit—that's part of what identifies you as a team player. And it's tough to make decisions to benefit the company as a whole if you don't know its whole agenda.

5-4   The Mistake: Not keeping your boss informed

The situation:

"I want to talk to you—right now," your boss orders as he stalks into your office.

"What's the problem?" you ask, stomach churning.

"I have just learned, from the CEO—not from you, that your people have pretty much lost the Kaiser-Prault account for us because they've been consistently late delivering on the contract. Why was I the last to hear about this? And why should I have to learn about it from *my* boss?

"Not only should I have been the *first* person you told about Kaiser-Prault wanting out, but I should have known as soon as you did that there was a problem brewing. What's the matter with you? Are you out to demolish the whole company?"

Why was it a mistake?

What's the big deal? Aren't you paid to handle these problems yourself? Sure, maybe you should have gotten back to your boss sooner about Kaiser-Prault seriously wanting out of their contract. But if you'd gone running to your boss the first time K-P started making dissatisfied noises, he would have thought you were a whiner who couldn't handle anything. Aren't you supposed to keep problems *out* of his office rather than bringing them in?

Wrong!

Your job *is* to solve problems. It is *not* to keep your boss in the dark about them. One of the fundamental commandments of organizational life is, "Thou shalt always keep thy boss informed."

No matter what else you accomplish, *always* see that your boss knows about any matter that may affect him. Good or bad, pleasant or unpleasant, your fault or not. Letting your boss be blindsided by a matter you knew about is close to the top of employee mortal sins.

How can you recover from it quickly?

Although there are some things you can do to begin recovery quickly, there's *nothing* you can do to recover completely. You've destroyed some of the trust and confidence your boss had in you, both as a manager of one of his units and as a subordinate employee to him.

So how do you start the recovery process?

As soon as you think your boss has calmed down a little (and we mean *soon*, like within the hour), go see him. Tell him you know you fouled up, that you should have spotted trouble coming and warned him. Don't make excuses; just apologize. Then promise him that it will never, ever happen again.

How can you consistently do it right from now on?

Of course, your boss expects you to handle as much as you possibly can without his intervention, and he won't appreciate being overwhelmed by details that aren't relevant to him. But there are several situations in which it's critical that you keep your boss fully informed:

• First, and most important, is when you have information that your boss needs to keep from being blindsided (by hearing the news from someone else).

This is especially important when an assignment has gone badly for you or your workgroup. Your boss *must* hear it from you first.

• When you have information that could change your company's competitive position in the market, you should also pass it on to your boss. If you hear that a viable competitor is entering one of your important markets, or is introducing a new product line, or is changing its pricing structure, you need to let your boss know (even if you think he may already have heard the news from someone else).

• Whenever you have information about *impending* problems, you should give your boss a "heads up." This doesn't mean that you should go running to your boss every time some little thing goes wrong. And many of the problems that arise are matters that you can take care of and have little, if any, repercussion beyond your immediate unit.

But whenever a problem arises that you reasonably believe your boss might hear about from someone else sooner or later, make sure you're the first one to tell him. If it's an item that you've identified and corrected, all the better, but he still has to have the information so he doesn't greet his boss with a blank stare when it comes up at their next meeting. Much better if he can respond, "Oh, yes, I knew all about that. Gribley down in Merchandising took care of it already. No problem at all."

• Finally, whenever you have information that you think would be helpful to your boss and isn't likely to be available from other sources, you should consider passing it on. Here, a little judicious filtering is in order so that you don't deluge your boss with irrelevant or redundant items. But, assuming you meet with your boss regularly, passing on a couple of tidbits of new information will be appreciated and shows that you're looking out for his, and the company's, interests.

Is doing what you did ever right?

No. Not ever.

A tip for mistake-free managing:

Different managers have different tolerance levels for detail. While it's critical that you keep your boss informed about the matters that are likely to be important to him, it's also important that you don't irritate him with detail he doesn't want to hear. Some managers want to cut immediately to the chase, bottom line issues, stark agendas, without a lot of messy details that often confuse rather than clarify. Other managers need the details to understand the bottom line and want to know many of the ins and outs of the situation in order to be sure they've got all the bases covered.

Spend some time early on getting to know your boss' personal style. In this, as in many other aspects of managing, helping your boss be successful by working to his style is an important component of your own success.

5-5   The Mistake: Getting caught up in the office rumor mill

The situation:

Jim Taylor phoned from Birmingham the other day. "Where did you hear that we were selling off our Memphis plant to PerkPac, Inc.?" he asked. "I'd been told that they were being consolidated as an off-site location under us. But Gertie from your staff was here last week, and she told me you'd announced the sale in your staff meeting the other day. Do you know something I don't?"

"I didn't exactly hear through official channels," you admit. "But I heard it from a very reliable source, and when I alluded to 'selling Memphis' with the boss, he smiled at me—that kind of knowing grin he gets, you know."

"Well maybe he was smiling at you because he couldn't believe you'd fall for a rumor like that. You should know better. Now Gertie's told half of my staff, and I'm sure Memphis will be hearing soon, too. It's bad enough that the workers pass around this gossip; I wouldn't have expected to hear it coming from you too."

Why was it a mistake?

As manager, whatever you say to your workgroup has the ring of authority. People will believe what you tell them because of the position you hold. When you give out information that you've heard only as office gossip, you run two risks:

• *The information you release may very well be wrong.* And bad information makes for bad decisions.

• *Your credibility will be seriously damaged.* Sooner or later, it will become obvious that the information you've been passing is wrong. After a few such episodes, your workers, your peers, and even your boss are likely to discount much of what you say. Then, when they can't rely on your message, the next obvious conclusion is that they can't rely on you. See where we're going here? You're on your way to a kind of corporate oblivion.

How can you recover from it quickly?

As with so many other mistakes, this one is a lot easier to prevent than to cure. You can tell your staff that your information on the Memphis sale was unreliable and that they can't draw any firm conclusions about what's going to happen to the operation. But even then, you're shutting the barn door long after the horse has bolted.

How can you consistently do it right from now on?

• *Always check your sources.* We're not going to tell you not to listen to office gossip. In fact, it's often a good source, but not always a good source of *facts*. Instead, it's a good source for finding out what your workers *think* is happening.

Workers often have a limited (and thus distorted) picture of what's going on in the company. Remember the story about the blind men who tried to describe an elephant through only their sense of touch? The one who felt his leg said the elephant must be like a tree trunk. The one who held his trunk said the elephant must be like a long snake. And each other person had an equally distorted idea of what an elephant must look like, because each had access to only part of the information about the elephant's shape.

Workers often have the same kind of distorted notions about the company information they hear. Because they know only part of the story, they interpret facts in different, and often inaccurate ways. That's one reason why it's dangerous to rely completely on what you hear through the office rumor mill.

But often those rumors do contain kernels of truth. And those are what you need to follow up on. The danger is in accepting the rumors at face value. Instead, use the information you hear as a base, then follow up with your peers or your boss or others who are in a position to know the real story.

• *Speak only about what you* know*; not about your speculations*. Maybe you heard that the company was thinking about selling off some of its operations. And that might be true. Maybe you also heard that the Memphis operation wasn't profitable anymore. And that fact might also be true.

But maybe you drew your own conclusion that the company was likely to sell off the Memphis operation as part of its downsizing because it would make sense to get rid of the least profitable parts of the company. That's speculation.

You can speculate with your peers and make your best guesses about what's likely to happen. You can ask your boss what he knows, or, as in this scenario, you can toss out an idea to see what kind of reaction you get. But you can *never* offer your speculations to the staff.

As we said before, what you say as a supervisor has the ring of truth. You're in a position of authority, so your workgroup assumes that whatever you tell them is something you know about. Offering speculation is a breach of the trust they have in you, not because you intend to mislead, but because it has the effect of misleading.

• *Be clear. Don't offer opinions in a way that makes them seem like facts.* Does this mean that you can talk to your workers only about things you're absolutely sure about? No, of course not. Oftentimes you have a pretty good guess about what's likely to happen and you want to prepare your workgroup as well as you can, but no decision has yet been made. It's usually fine to offer an opinion, as long as there's no doubt in any listener's mind that it *is* an opinion.

"Looks like we're going to be moving some of our staff to Charleston." This is a very ambiguous statement. Coming from a supervisor, it's probably going to be interpreted as a fact, not an opinion.

"I think we're going to be seeing some cutbacks in the very near future." While this is framed as an opinion rather than as a fact, the "I think" is likely to be lost very quickly as your statement is reported from one worker to another. You've been clear, but not quite clear enough.

"It's just my opinion, but I think we're likely to merge our marketing and advertising operations in the next few months."

"There's been no official decision, but I wouldn't be surprised to see some departmental changes soon."

"Understand that this is my opinion, not a firm decision: I don't think we're going to get enough early retirements to cover the number of people we'll have to downsize, so I'm expecting some layoffs to follow."

These are all unambiguously opinion. None is presented in a way that any reasonable person would interpret as fact. The introductory phrases may seem like overkill, but, depending on how starved your organization is for news, even they may not be enough to keep your statements from being quoted as if they were gospel a week or two later.

Is doing what you did ever right?

No. At the very least, you must check out any rumor you hear with a reliable and authoritative person in the company before you repeat the information to anyone. In your position, anything less is irresponsible.

A tip for mistake-free managing:

A manager must be very careful about what she says. Even the most cautiously worded statement is likely to be passed from one worker to another until, over time, it doesn't sound anything like what you originally said.

Whenever you have really significant information to give to your workers, you should consider recording it in some way so that people have access to the original version—your statement, rather than what "He said she said to someone who told his buddy in the cafeteria . . ."

That doesn't mean that you shouldn't talk to your staff to explain the information in detail or to answer questions about it. You can prepare a memo that contains the essential information your workgroup needs to have, then have a staff meeting to discuss it. Especially if your staff is large or workers tend to be out of the office on assignments (so that it's difficult to get everyone together), you can videotape your staff meetings or explanation. Information can be posted on bulletin boards (either the cork kind or the electronic kind). You can never be too careful about making sure that your workers get the real message, not some version that's passed through many other, less careful, messengers.

5-6   The Mistake: Not inviting negative information from your boss

The situation: "So you think the Rettinhaus project went pretty well?" you ask your boss.

"Oh, uh, yes. It was fine," she responds, rather distractedly, as she flips through the papers piled on her desk.

"Well, you know we put in a lot of hours on that one. Tried that new database program and then imported everything into our high-powered graphics package to make all the charts and diagrams. I had some fairly new people on that project too. Made it a lot harder for some of the more experienced folks, since they had to teach the new people at the same time they had some pretty heavy analysis to do themselves. I'm glad you're happy with the results."

"Sure, yeah, no problem," she mutters.

"Well, thanks for the feedback. Rettinhaus seemed happy too. Tough bunch to convince. You should have heard all the questions at our presentation. Asked about everything from how we gathered the data to who worked on crunching the numbers. But they seemed satisfied by the time we were finished. I'll let you know more after Wendy talks to them again next week."

"Okay. Glad it all went well. Stop in anytime." Your boss glances up as you close the door, then settles back down to her paperwork.

Why was it a mistake?

Several things went wrong in this conversation.

First, you've obviously caught your boss at a bad time. Whenever you want more than just a superficial acknowledgment of work you've done you need to schedule a specific time to talk, or at least confirm that your boss is ready to discuss your work in some depth.

Second, you did all the talking. At best, your boss confirmed your own good feelings about the Rettinhaus project. More likely, she intended to be noncommittal. If you look at the dialogue again, you'll see that she never really said, "Good job." Phrases like "it was fine" and "glad it went well" are the sort of things you say when you're not *un*happy. They convey nothing of your boss' real feelings about your work.

Finally, you never really gave your boss a chance to give you constructive feedback. Even in your opening question, you've assumed that her reactions are the same as yours.

Given the tenor of this conversation, your boss would have to interrupt whatever she's currently involved in, sit down with you, get your attention focused on the fact that her perceptions of your work on the project are not as positive as hers, and then begin to address each item with which she's displeased. Your self-congratulatory tone doesn't invite open communication at all. It invites only affirmation of your own good opinion.

How can you recover from it quickly?

As soon as you have another opening to discuss the project (maybe after Wendy talks to the Rettinhaus team next week), make an appointment to discuss the project with your boss again. This time, let *her* do the talking and you do the listening.

How can you consistently do it right from now on?

• *Set a specific time to talk to your boss.* Don't just walk in the door and start talking. Even if you have an open and casual relationship with your boss, you need to be sure she has the time to talk, free from distractions. That may well be the minute you open her door—but it may also be next week, and you need to be flexible.

• *Describe what you think went especially well on the project and what areas you have concerns about.* Begin the conversation with a short summary of the project. She probably has numerous projects and decisions occupying her days. Unless this is a super-hot project that you've both been intimately involved with, take a few minutes to set the context: "This is the study of Rettinhaus' problems with inventory inaccuracies that they asked us to help with last December. We started out by interviewing some of the supervisors to see what they thought the problems might be, then we went out to some of their stores to do some on-site research."

Summarize your conclusions, then talk about one or two things that went especially well and one or two that you have concerns about. Your concerns need not be specific criticisms; they might be just areas where you're not sure what your boss' preferences are: "We didn't talk to all the store managers because we were just trying to get a representative sample and not all the managers were available when we were coming through. I had thought about doing a follow-up written questionnaire with the ones we missed, but wasn't sure that was really necessary."

• *Invite her comments, both on your concerns and about any concerns she may have.* Ask your boss to give you her reactions to the project. These may be her own perceptions or things she's heard from others, maybe people on your staff or people in the customer's organization.

Then stop talking. Give your boss a chance to say something. Unless she has serious concerns, she's likely to let you rattle on for a while without contributing anything herself, just as in the dialogue above.

Silence becomes uncomfortable. If you don't talk, your boss will be more likely to fill the void with her own comments.

• *Listen carefully.* Your boss is likely to talk in generalities about her concerns. She didn't perform the project; she probably is a little fuzzy about the details. But she will have some important reactions nonetheless.

Your job is to try to make her impressions more concrete.

Say your boss remarks, "Rettinhaus didn't seem to know much about what was going on when I saw him a couple of weeks ago. Are you sure your people were keeping him informed?"

Is your boss suggesting that you should have talked to Mr. Rettinhaus himself rather than working solely through someone in his organization? Is she suggesting that you should have let her know that information didn't seem to be getting through so she could talk to Mr. Rettinhaus?

Ask her. But don't just ask, "What would you have liked for me to do instead?" Offer alternatives: "Would you have liked for me to talk to Mr. Rettinhaus? Or maybe let you know so you could update him?"

She now has a frame of reference to fill in the details of her concerns. She can either affirm that one of the alternatives you've offered is the appropriate approach, or she can use your ideas to explain her own.

What if she says, "I think your analysis was a little weak?"

Here, more probing is in order. But, just as before, you need to be prepared with some alternatives to offer. "Do you think we needed a larger data sample? How about the possible causes for the problem? Would we have been better off to identify some more possibilities before we started to zero in? Was the analysis itself okay, but the explanation weak? Should we have spent more time in the report explaining how we came to these conclusions?"

Don't grill. But offer enough alternatives to make concrete this fairly general concern. Your boss may not be able to pinpoint exactly what she's dissatisfied with until you identify alternatives, but once you've hit the right one, she'll jump on it.

Is doing what you did ever right?

Sure. If you've just completed a great project and there's no doubt in your mind, or anyone else's, that it was a masterful piece of work, a little self-congratulation is certainly in order.

But, even so, be sure to take a minute or two sometime down the road to check in with your boss, making sure she's as thrilled as you are.

A tip for mistake-free managing:

Not all managers are particularly forthcoming about the criticisms they have of their subordinates' work. Yours may be one of these.

Does she always make a point of saying something good about most of the work you do? Even when you're not happy with the results of an assignment, does she remain, at worst, noncommittal about your performance?

Some people just aren't comfortable giving criticism. Sometimes these are basically good-hearted people who genuinely think well of almost everyone. Sometimes they're folks who have well-formed opinions, but don't like confrontation and try to avoid situations that they believe may become confrontational.

The best way to get information about your performance, positive or negative, is to invite it. When you offer your own critical comments about the work your unit has performed, when you receive criticism in a constructive way, suggesting alternatives to improve rather than defending what you've done, you're inviting your boss to be open and honest with you. If she knows you won't respond confrontationally, if she knows that you welcome her perceptions and consider them seriously, and, most of all, if she sees that you actually change your performance in response to her suggestions, she'll gradually become more willing to share her concerns with you. And you'll both benefit.

5-7   The Mistake: Not inviting negative information from your workgroup

The situation: "I'm glad to see everyone's in agreement on how we should handle these input errors. Are there any questions?" You conclude your meeting with the staff, prepared to begin a new procedure for checking and correcting problems with data input to your payment system.

"I have a concern," Dennis offers. "What about the input that's done over in the other section? We're still going to be responsible for making correct payments, but we can't be sure their input is accurate until it shows up for payment. It seems as if we've addressed only part of the problem here."

"I agree," adds Patsy. "We could be doing everything right, and still be making payments that are wrong. We need to go farther."

"I don't agree," you respond. "We've made a decision, and we're going to go with it. If we find out later that we need to make some adjustments, we will. But we're not going to try to fix the whole world at once." And with that firm pronouncement, your staff disperses.

Why was it a mistake?

Workers often have insights that aren't available to higher levels of management. Your workers know how the work gets done, whom they interface with, what kinds of problems arise with the input they get to work with. When you ignore, or brush off, their insights, you lose valuable information that will make the organization run better. After you've established a pattern of ignoring or discouraging their ideas, your workgroup won't even offer them anymore.

How can you recover from it quickly?

Before you institute your new error correction process, call your staff together again. Begin by acknowledging Dennis' contribution: "As I was beginning to get ready to implement this new system, I realized that I made a mistake when I brushed off Dennis' ideas the other day. I think we need to look again at the problem he raised with the data input that's done in the other section. Dennis, what do you think?"

Dennis might not have a solution yet, but he does have the opportunity to voice his concern again. Then, the group can brainstorm ideas for fixing the problem.

How can you consistently do it right from now on?

• *Give your staff regular opportunities to provide feedback.* Structure your meetings and problem-solving sessions so that your workgroup knows that they're not only allowed, but encouraged, to comment and criticize.

Workers are often reluctant to disagree with the boss. Make sure that you affirm clearly and often that you welcome disagreement and that you'll take it seriously.

• *Listen, don't react.* The surest way to keep people from disagreeing with you is to become defensive when they offer their criticisms. Especially coming from the boss, defensiveness is a sure sign that you're not really interested in the feedback.

Give everyone a chance to be heard. As each opinion is presented, wait for other reactions. If you don't get any, invite others' opinions. The first few times you use this technique you almost certainly will find yourself with a whole group of people waiting to see your reaction before they reveal theirs. That's exactly what you *don't* want. And, with time and your consistent permission to disagree, your workgroup will feel more comfortable offering and enlarging on one another's ideas.

• *Consider each idea and comment seriously.* Don't dismiss ideas out of hand, no matter how silly or trivial they may sound at first blush. Matters that you consider unimportant may have a profound effect on the people who are actually performing the task under discussion. Unless you've done the work yourself, you're likely to miss important information when you dismiss ideas without discussion. Even if you have done the work, you'll find that the longer you're a supervisor, the farther you'll draw away from the technical intricacies of the day-to-day work. Systems and processes change. Problems and conditions that were once important as you performed tasks seem less important from a management perspective, but often they're still important at the workers' level.

When you do disagree or overrule the criticisms or negative comments of your workgroup, be as sensitive and as nonjudgmental as possible. Address the issue, not the person. And explain the basis for your disagreement in a way that your workers can learn how you've evaluated the issue.

• *Implement and acknowledge.* Whenever you accept a criticism and act on it, be sure to acknowledge the person who offered the idea.

You can announce the change by acknowledging the person: "I've thought over Patsy's idea and decided we ought to implement it. Thanks for your suggestion, Patsy. This is how we'll go about it. . . ."

You can designate that person as the one to be in charge of the implementation team: "Since Patsy came up with such a good way for getting around this problem, I've asked her to work out the implementation."

Or perhaps she can be a resource person as you make the change: "Patsy's the one who made this suggestion, so as we implement the new process, I've asked her to be available to answer any questions you may have about what we're trying to do and how to do it."

Is doing what you did ever right?

Sometimes *you're* the one with special insights—because you have more information about how a process fits into the company's overall goals or because you know about planned changes that haven't been announced yet or because you are more familiar with the people from other sections who're involved in the process. But even in those situations, while it may not be *bad* management not to invite disagreement, it's not *good* management.

At worst, you will have spent a little extra time getting negative information you either already knew or didn't need. At best, you will have gained insights that wouldn't otherwise be available to you.

A tip for mistake-free managing:

Workers have greater buy-in and accept decisions more enthusiastically when they believe that their concerns have been heard and considered. If workers are discouraged from using their brains, they won't use them. They'll be likely to follow an ineffective process to the letter until someone higher up notices that it's not working. Many crises can be avoided by hearing and heeding the warning signals your workers send you. But if you don't care, neither will they.

5-8   The Mistake: Not passing information to other managers

The situation: Jolynn calls to you as you pass her office. "Hey, I've got some news for you. Did you hear about the new procurement system we're supposed to be implementing in the next couple of months? Purpero is all excited about it, but it looks to me like it's going to be a lot more complicated than the one we're using now."

"Well," you admit, "I had heard something about it, but I've been so snowed under with end of the year purchase requests, I forgot to say anything to you about it."

"What do you mean, you've been snowed under? We all have. But I always make a point to let you know whenever something's going on that might be important. How come I never get any information in return? Do you think you've got some kind of an edge with the boss or something?"

Why was it a mistake?

It's always a mistake not to pass on information to your peers. As Jolynn pointed out, to get information, you're expected to give information. When you don't pass on what you know, other managers are less likely to want to help you out. On the other hand, when you share information with others, they're more inclined to share information with you. (You might call this a "tit-for-tat" theory of information flow.)

Even more ominous is the threat to other managers that you're hoarding information because you have some kind of special relationship with the boss (or are working on one). That kind of one-upmanship is more likely to backfire than to succeed. And even if your failure to communicate really was an oversight, the seed of distrust has still been planted.

How can you recover from it quickly?

You can recover in this same conversation. Admit your fault in not approaching Jolynn with the information, but then fill in all the details you know: "You're right, Jolynn. I should have at least mentioned the new system when we were in staff meeting the other day. But, if you have a few minutes now, I'll fill you in on the gory details I know something about . . ."

How can you consistently do it right from now on?

• *Keep your eyes open and your ears tuned for information that might be helpful to your peers.* Not everything that you hear is important to your unit, but it might be to someone else's. Learn about the work that your peer managers are engaged in so that when important items of information arise you can identify them and alert your peers, even though you probably won't understand all the implications of the information you've learned.

• *Make notes of information you receive.* Keep a planner; mark adhesive notes; use an electronic notepad. One way or another, be sure to capture the information you come across. Your memory is *not* always a reliable source.

• *Get in the habit of sharing what you know.* That doesn't mean that you need to become the office chatterbox. It means that you should develop a network of peers within the organization—people whom you trust and who trust you. These are people with whom you share information, bounce ideas, garner advice and counsel. These are the people whose interests you are trying to protect when you listen for useful information.

• *Respect confidences—your peers' and your boss'.* At the same time that you need to be alert to information that will be useful to other managers, you need also to be sensitive to the kinds of information that are *not* appropriate for sharing. These include items of information about personnel issues (selections, terminations, layoffs), confidential decisions, and other items that you've been specifically asked not to share.

When you know when to speak and when to keep silent and you show other managers that you respect the information they confide in you, you build a reputation for trustworthiness. As a result, others will be more willing to share information with you.

Is doing what you did ever right?

Failing to share information with other managers is one of those mistakes that won't get you into trouble immediately. Rather, the results will become apparent later—when those other managers don't share information with you or deliberately withhold information because they believe you've been holding out on them.

A tip for mistake-free managing:

Long before you became a manager you learned that success in business requires cooperation with your peers and associates. That's just as true for peers in management as it was for peers in worker-level jobs.

The level of cooperation and assistance you lend to others is directly proportional to the level of cooperation you can expect to receive in return. In other words, you'll reap what you sow. If you share information, help out when other units get overloaded, encourage and support other managers when they're having a rough time, those same managers will be more likely to give you the same support when you need it. And sooner or later you'll surely need it!

CHAPTER *6*

MISTAKES IN RELATIONSHIPS WITH OTHER WORKGROUPS

6-1   The Mistake: *Letting your workgroup hold a grudge against another workgroup*

The situation: You walked into the break room to hear Graham and Althea in the middle of a heated conversation.

"Can you believe that they want to us work with Zamora's bunch?!" Graham exclaimed.

"I know," Althea replied, just as forcefully. "After what those guys did to us last month. They're the last people on earth I'd ever want to work with!"

"I don't want to work with those turkeys either—so, what're we going to do?"

Why was it a mistake?

When a workgroup holds a grudge, it carries negative emotions from the past into the present. This fouls up the present, because it cuts the group off from potentially useful alternatives. Zamora's workgroup may have skills that your workgroup needs. Or you may just need the extra people power that the group can provide. On the other hand, there may be valid reasons for not working with Zamora's unit, but what it did some time in the past isn't one of them. In fact, whatever the situation, holding a grudge will interfere with evaluating it rationally.

How can you recover from it quickly?

It won't be easy to recover in time to salvage the current project with the other workgroup, but you need to try to do so. If it interferes with this project, it may be that much harder to resolve in the future.

How can you consistently do it right from now on?

Try following these steps:

• *Find out from your workgroup exactly what the problem is.* Do your people believe that the other workgroup promised something it didn't deliver? That it misled them about what it would or could do? Whatever happened, your people probably believe that the other workgroup exercised bad faith with them. Get as much detail on it as you can.

• *If possible, find out whether the other workgroup is also holding a grudge.* Is there bad blood on both sides now? Perhaps the other workgroup feels just as let down or even betrayed as your group does. Whether they do or not, you're going to need to get them to talk with your group, and vice versa. But how they feel about your group will heavily influence what they're willing to do.

• *Get representatives of the two groups together to discuss the matter.* This almost certainly won't be pleasant, and if your organization has individuals trained to facilitate this kind of encounter you will certainly want to use one of them. Here's a small slice of the kind of exchange that might open the joint meeting—just so you'll have an idea of what you might be getting into:

> Wallie, one of the representatives of the other workgroup, begins. "Graham, I agreed to come to this meeting because you and I go back a long way—and that's the only reason. This thing about us selling you out is a bunch of crap."

> "Yeah—and the moon is made of green cheese! You guys set us up so we'd look like we dropped the ball. And, boy, did we fall for it." Graham almost spit out the last sentence.

> Norma, another member of the other workgroup jumps in. "I can't believe you're such a bunch of crybabies. Yeah, we missed one of our deadlines, and we tried to tell you why, but all you wanted to do was feel self-righteous and blame us for your troubles."

• *Get everyone focusing on the events, not on their reactions to them.* Notice that in the discussion above the participants are describing their reactions to and evaluations of what happened. You probably can't prevent this altogether, because these reactions have strong emotions tied up with them. As soon as possible, though, you want to get them out of these reactions and dealing with the events themselves. As an example, here's how you, a member of your workgroup, or a facilitator might pick up from Norma's last comment.

"Norma, you said you missed a deadline but that we wouldn't listen when you tried to explain it. Can you tell me some more about that?"

"Well . . . I guess so. We told you we'd have everything packaged like you wanted it on . . . I think it was a Tuesday. We would have done it, too, except Charlene had that auto accident on the way to work Monday and missed the next two days. You wouldn't believe us, but she was the only one that understood just how the whole package went together. There simply wasn't anything we could do."

"You're telling me that you have only one person who could do that?!" Althea jumped in. "I think that . . . ."

"I don't care what you think," Wallie interrupts "It's true! We're still trying to train a backup for Charlene, but we just don't have the staff."

"OK, I'm sorry I got so hostile," Althea says in a much calmer tone. "I guess the same thing could happen to us if Tony were off." She looks at Graham, who nods. . . .

Don't expect a real encounter to develop this rapidly; it won't. But if you can help direct the focus to the events and keep it there, you'll make it easier for individuals to get past their emotions and talk about the facts.

• *Develop a common understanding of what happened and a joint commitment to overcome it and work together.* You may not be able to get both or even one of these, but your goal is to walk out of the room with both workgroups willing to try working with the other. You might get a complete reconciliation and warm feelings on both sides, but don't count on them. If you can get an honest agreement that they'll try working together, you'll have laid the necessary groundwork for cooperation.

• *Build on this commitment.* Don't let the matter end there. Ensure that every member of your workgroup sincerely tries to cooperate with the other group. If problems arise, don't let them fester. Bring them up with the other workgroup immediately and try to get them resolved. Act from the beginning as though the relationship is going to be a success—and it probably will be.

Is doing what you did ever right?

No. Letting grudges grow and fester is highly destructive. Whenever you believe there may have been a misunderstanding with another workgroup, get to work on it right away.

A tip for mistake-free managing:

When workgroups have to depend on each other to get a job done, the situation can all too easily create bad feelings on one or both sides. The longer one or both workgroups allow these bad feelings to continue and develop, the more destructive they become. Anger is a normal reaction, an internal sign that we need to respond to something. (It's appropriate to get angry if someone is attacking your workgroup or questioning your integrity.) But when no response is made and the anger is held in, it becomes resentment.

Here's the difference. Anger is an emotion in the present time, pushing us to do something *now*. It may or may not be sensible to act, but at least we can make a choice. Resentment is always past tense. There's no present action we can take to correct the situation that gave rise to it. Instead, it corrupts our current relationship with whomever we resent and very often leads to actions that increase rather than diminish the resentment.

When you and your workgroup are angry about something another workgroup has done, deal with it as quickly as possible. You may not always resolve it. You may decide that the other workgroup really is undependable. But that's a reasoned conclusion, one that doesn't burden you down with bad feelings. Most of the time, though, you and the other workgroup can work through the incident and regain the ability to cooperate. That's always your goal.

6-2   *The Mistake: Letting your workgroup take competition between workgroups too seriously*

The situation: "Hey, I've got a great idea!" Donnie exclaimed.

"Let's hear it."

"I'll bet that Reichauer's unit expects us to put a really big push on this month, since they beat us out last month. Suppose we held back instead and just stockpiled stuff."

"Wait a minute," Jamal said, "we've gotta get something out the door."

"Sure we do, and we will. We'll get enough out to look good, but not enough to push those guys. Then, with what we save and a good month next month, we can swamp 'em for the quarter."

"We sorta lull 'em down a little, huh?"

Why was it a mistake?

If your workgroup is consistently reacting to other groups they compete with this way, they're putting too much attention into the competition itself. Quite possibly, if they follow the strategy they're discussing, neither they nor the other group will produce as much as they could over the next two months. But if they're this wrapped up in the competition, it could get even worse. They might, for instance, begin spreading rumors about members of the other group.

Even that's not the worst. Does either group need to depend on the other at some point to get its job done? Are there any products, for instance, that your workgroup provides to the other where that group adds something of their own and sends it back for you to finish? If so, there's an obvious opportunity for either group to try to delay the other or otherwise attempt to make them look bad.

Take your pick. They all add up to competition that's becoming more important than getting the basic job done.

How can you recover from it quickly?

You probably can't. Even if you were to confront Donnie and Jamal with what you heard, they might assure you that they'd never do such a thing—and then do it. You need to examine the whole situation and if possible restructure it to make it more productive.

How can you consistently do it right from now on?

Will Carl Reishauer cooperate with you in reducing the competition? You won't really know that until you talk with him. Set up a meeting. After the small talk is done, the conversation might go this way:

> "Carl," you begin, "I don't know what you think but I'm afraid that my people are getting too wrapped up in the competition between our two groups. They're paying too much attention to the competition and not enough to getting the work out."

> "I don't know," Carl says cautiously. He pauses, then continues: "Yeah, I guess I am seeing some signs that beating your group is more important to them then just doing a good job. But what can we do—the department said we'd compete with one another. And my folks like to compete."

"I know, and that's OK. I'm afraid, though, that my people will get so wrapped up in competing that I'll have more and more trouble getting them to focus on the work. I don't need those extra headaches."

"I see what you mean. It could get out of hand. But what can we do?"

"Here's one approach, Carl. Do you think you could get a list from your folks of what they don't want my folks to do? If you could, I could get the same kind of list from my folks. Then we could see if we could work out some ground rules from the lists, and you and I could serve as referees."

"I'm willing to try that. When do you want to get back together?"

The real conversation, of course, would have lasted much longer. And it would have taken time and effort to develop the lists and the ground rules. If it succeeded, it would be because the managers realized and practiced three points.

• *They dealt with each other directly.* The manager might have been tempted to go to higher management and complain about the problem. If his attempt to work out an agreement with Reishauer and his group failed, he might still have to do that. But he began by attempting to work with the other manager face to face— a much better way to begin.

• *They found reasons for themselves and their workgroups to limit competition.* This will be a key point. The two managers need a reason to tone the competition down, or they'll never reach an agreement that they're willing to live by. And they need to find reasons that will persuade the members of their workgroups to limit themselves. In the conversation, the managers began to find reasons that they thought mattered, but they would still have to find reasons important to their workgroups. (For instance, some of the members of the workgroup might be just as upset that the competition was distracting them from doing a good job.)

• *They developed trust in one another and, as much as possible, between their two groups.* The success or failure of the attempt will hinge on this. If the two managers build up a sufficient trust level between themselves, they'll probably be able to develop and enforce ground rules successfully. If not, one of them will sooner or later sabotage anything they do. If they do learn to trust each other, helping the two workgroups develop this trust in each other will be the next step.

Is doing what you did ever right?

No. You don't want competition to distract your workgroup from focusing on their primary jobs. If the competition were friendly, it might well help production. As soon as it becomes this serious, though, it starts to get in the way.

A tip for mistake-free managing:

Not only workgroups but whole organizations can hurt themselves by focusing too much on competition, or focusing on it in the wrong way. Why? Because when you focus only on competing you give the other organization the initiative. Unless you're very careful, you end up playing a constant game of "catch-up."

How does that work in the real world? Let's take the two groups in this example. Reishauer's unit finds a way to speed up part of its process. It pulls ahead, so the other group works to find out what Reishauer is doing. Perhaps this takes a couple of months, during which productivity in the other group drops off slightly. It finds out what's different and pulls back into the race. But now Reishauer's group has worked out another improvement, so it moves ahead. . . .

What would happen if the two groups limited competition or simply decided to cooperate? When Reishauer's group finds a new process, both groups use it. This frees the other group to concentrate on different improvements of its own, which it can then share. And on it goes.

Neither competition nor cooperation is the cure for all problems. It always takes a blend of the two. An effective manager looks for the best blend in each situation.

6-3   The Mistake: *Letting your workgroup look down on other workgroups*

The situation: "Whatta ya think, Marie," Charlie asks. "The department wants us to take the lead and work with Berg and Martinelli's branches on the space redesign project. Do we want to work with either of the two on this?"

"I hate to say this because I have friends in both of the branches," Marie responds, "but neither of them is really that good."

"Yeah, but won't this stretch us something fierce for the next few weeks?"

"I'm sure it will," Paula joins the discussion, "but I agree with Marie. Those folks just aren't up to our standards. We've worked really hard to get the reputation we have, and I don't want to take a chance on having either of those branches mess it up."

Why was it a mistake?

This case and this example have been included to illustrate a major fault that really good workgroups develop: a distinct superiority complex. The group may be very good, and perhaps better than almost any other. That's all to the good. But legitimate pride in this can turn quickly into arrogance. How do you know when that's happened? When the group "knows" it's better than any other group.

Arrogance can make a group sloppy: "We know we're the best, so we don't have to worry about this." It can make the group unwilling to listen to ideas or criticism from outside: "We can't learn anything from them." And it can cut the group off from other groups that, while perhaps not quite as good, can still be valuable to it: "We just don't want to take a chance on messing up our reputation by working with them."

How can you recover from it quickly?

You can't. Arrogance takes time to develop, and it takes time to get over. But you can make a start, and the situation in the example provides you the opening you need. Get the group, or at least several of the key workers, together. Then do something like this:

"I understand you don't want to work on this new project with either of the other branches."

"That's right," Marie responds. "It'll push us, but it's better than working with either or both of them."

"Why?"

This time Charlie answers. "They're just not that good. We're afraid that if we depend on them they won't deliver on time. Then either we get egg on our faces or we have to work like the devil to get done what we thought they were doing to do."

(Other workers express similar sentiments.)

"OK—I hear all that. But I'm concerned that this is too much work in too little time for us to handle it well. If you could pick either of the two branches and give them the part of the project they could do best, who would do it and what would it be?"

(Much discussion. Then Paula speaks.) "We're more or less agreed that Berg's branch is pretty good at data consolidation. They have some software that none of the rest of us know how to use, and they're pretty good at it. We'd be willing to let them do the consolidation, if they can meet our time frames. And Marie suggested that we ask Martinelli's branch to do the illustrations. They seem to have half the clip art ever published. . . ."

"Yeah," Charlie interrupted, "we're willing to give them both a chance. But they better come through for us, or else!"

How can you consistently do it right from now on?

The discussion above, while just a beginning, illustrates several key points for preventing workgroup arrogance:

• *Remember that it grows from pride based on performance.* This is good. If your workgroup is arrogant without reason, you've really got a problem, and this case isn't designed for you. Most of the time, though, the arrogance has its beginning in real performance. Don't forget this. Your job is to minimize the arrogance, not the pride. And the sooner you begin after your workgroup develops pride, the easier it will be.

• *Keep your workgroup working with other groups as much as possible.* Pride becomes arrogance, in part, from ignorance. The workgroup knows how good it is, but doesn't know how good other workgroups are. The workgroup members tell each other how good they are, and this then makes it easy to look down on "those other guys."

The best cure for this arrogance is constant contact with other groups. If your workgroup has to cooperate with other workgroups, it will get a realistic picture of how good these groups are. On the whole, none of them may be as good as yours. But most of them will have individuals and small groups that can match yours, and perhaps have some that are better. If your workgroup deals with them constantly, they'll recognize both the strengths and weaknesses in the other groups, and that will help them get the highest payoff from cooperative efforts.

Notice that in the discussion above the workgroup turned the corner because several of them did know of specific talents the other workgroups had. Without this knowledge, the discussion might have gone nowhere. This illustrates again the important of your workgroup not isolating itself from the others.

• *Develop and maintain cooperation whenever possible between your group and others.* This simply builds on and extends the previous point. For instance, you might want to ask another workgroup to train your group in something they're particularly good at and in return you'll share some of your expertise with them. (In the example, the workgroup might want to learn about the data consolidation software used by the other branch.) This mutual training/learning builds relationships at the same time that it builds stronger workgroups.

On another, different level, you might want to explore picnics, bowling leagues, or other activities involving several workgroups. Firsthand knowledge of the people on several teams, even in a purely social setting, will reinforce cooperative relationships on the job.

Is doing what you did ever right?

There is a fine line here. You want your workgroup to perform at a very high level, and you want each member to take pride in this performance. So you don't want to do anything to discourage that. But letting it turn into arrogance is always wrong; it has no payoff for you, the group, or any other workgroup. Instead, use the ideas above to keep your workgroup involved with and cooperating with as many other groups as practical.

A tip for mistake-free managing:

The better your workgroup gets, the more you want them thinking: "We're really good, and we're going to get better by working with everyone we can and by learning from everyone we can."

You can begin building this approach in the workgroup from day one. The more the group is open to new ideas and new ways of doing things, the more effective it will be. If it practices this openness from the beginning, it will take pride in its ability to learn, and it will never have occasion to be arrogant.

In short, the best way to deal with any mistake is to prevent it from occurring.

6-4   The Mistake: Letting your workgroup blame problems on other workgroups

The situation: Gordon leaned forward over the table toward you. "You know we'd have finished the job for Marketing on time if Tony's group had done what they said when they said."

"Yes," Bernice joined in, "I'm getting tired of our taking the rap when somebody else screws up."

"It's getting to the point that we don't dare work with anyone else," Edie added. "They just keep making mistakes."

Why was it a mistake?

According to your workgroup, other workgroups are to blame for all of their problems. Now put yourself in the shoes of one of these workgroups. Do you want someone going around telling the organization that you're a bunch of screw-ups? How are you apt to feel at the thought of having to work with that group again?

In other words, when a workgroup blames other workgroups for its problems, it begins to sow the seeds of serious dissension. Unless it stops, the entire organization may begin to get resentful, and the workgroup may become an outcast. Or it may be disbanded.

How can you recover from it quickly?

You can't fix the basic mistake quickly, but you can take immediate steps to keep it from getting worse. Call your workgroup together and make a firm statement that the behavior is unacceptable, that it has serious repercussions (like no other group wanting to work with yours in the future), and that you expect immediate improvement.

How can you consistently do it right from now on?

You can help develop a workgroup that doesn't look for others to blame if you follow these points:

• *Ensure that your workgroup understands how blaming others will hurt it.* It doesn't matter how good your workgroup is, if it gets a reputation for blaming the workgroups that work with it, then no one is going to work with you. Why should they put out energy in what they know will be a losing effort?

But the problem goes deeper and further than that. Other workgroups will have a strong motive to show that yours isn't really that good. Your workgroup may find that supplies it needs come late, key people it needs to contact aren't in (again and again), or that basic support it needs to get a job done isn't available.

As much fun as it may be to put the blame on others, it's long-run results are somewhere between painful and disastrous. Your workgroup needs to understand that.

• *When a problem arises, ensure that your workgroup looks first at how it may have caused it or at least contributed to it.* A good workgroup always looks first at how it can improve. One of the most powerful ways it can do this is by looking at its own contribution to any problems that come up. In the example, another workgroup let yours down by not doing what they said when they said. This provides a great place to start looking at what your contribution might have been. For instance, did your workgroup

1. give the other workgroup such a fuzzy request that it wasn't sure just what you wanted or when;

2. fail to follow up appropriately with that group to see that it was on target in what it was doing;

3. fail to provide the information that the other workgroup needed to complete its job successfully; and/or

4. fail to work with the other group when it needed your cooperation to succeed?

You will almost always find that some variation of these or similar problems played a part in the other workgroup's failure, perhaps a major part. And this brings us to the last point.

• *Ensure that when your workgroup collaborates with another group, your group takes responsibility for making the project successful.* This point has two important aspects. First, if you really believe you can't work successfully with another workgroup, *don't work with them.* If they really are mediocre performers you can't depend on, do your best to avoid them, or at least to work with them on projects that are within the scope of what they can do.

Second, if you work with another group—whether by choice or by direction—do what needs to be done to make the project successful. Give them clear guidance, follow up, provide the information they need, work with them however and whenever you need to. "That's their job—if they can't do it right that's their problem" has no place in the collaboration. Concentrate on their strong points and avoid their weaknesses whenever possible.

At the end, you may conclude that the other group was more trouble than it was worth. That's OK—but you didn't give either them or yourself a black eye in the process.

Is doing what you did ever right?

No.

A tip for mistake-free managing:

What's the best reputation your workgroup can have? For being very good at what it does? That's part of it. But what about the reputation for being a great group to work with—one that makes everyone who deals with it successful? If you want to live long and prosper in the organization, the latter is the best possible way to be known.

You can't necessarily build this reputation quickly and easily. First, your workgroup has to learn to be very good at its primary job. As it gets better and better, though, you want to use the ideas in this case to help it turn into a "success factory." What's a success factory? It's a group that other groups want to work with because they know the outcome of the collaboration will be successful and that they will share in the success.

Remember, the more groups that want to work with yours, the more picky you can be in the ones you select and what you ask from them. As they say, this ain't chopped liver.

6-5   The Mistake: Letting other managers steal workers from you

The situation:	"I've enjoyed working for you and with the rest of the group here," Laetitia said, "but a week from Monday I'm going to transfer over to Martin Sengal's group. It doesn't have anything to do with you or working conditions here. I just think I have a better chance to get ahead with his workgroup."

You wish Laetitia well and tell her that you'll be glad to consider her for her old job back. But your smile doesn't really reflect how you feel. This is the third worker you've lost to other workgroups like yours in the past four months.

Why was it a mistake?

As you'll see below, there are times when it isn't a mistake. But if other workgroups are picking up your better workers without a promise of a raise or promotion, it may well be a mistake. It means they believe they'll get something from other workgroups they can't get from yours. If that something isn't money or a higher-level job, what is it?

By the way, don't put too much stock in the reason a worker gives you for leaving. Laetitia says her decision had nothing to do with you or with working conditions. That may be true. It may also be the case that she's leaving specifically because of you and/or the working conditions, but doesn't want to burn her bridges behind her.

How can you recover from it quickly?

Since you don't really know what you're recovering from, you can't.

How can you consistently do it right from now on?

Let's assume that Laetitia really does believe she will get a better break by working for another workgroup (just as the last two workers who left you believed). Your number one task is to find out why she and other workers believe this. Here are some possible reasons:

• *Your workgroup has a poor reputation.* Workers believe that as long as they're part of the group they have little chance to get ahead.

• *They don't believe you appreciate their efforts.* If they can't get any more money, at least they can work for someone who appreciates them.

• *Your workers really don't like you as a supervisor.* They believe the other workgroup managers are better to work for.

• *You try too hard to hang onto workers.* They believe that as long as they work for you you'll try to prevent their leaving. So, when they get a chance they go.

There are many more reasons, of course. Whatever the reasons, other workgroup managers believe they can hire good people away from you easier than they can from other workgroups—or from outside the organization. You want to stop that.

How do you stop it? Begin by looking through this book at the different mistakes and see if you can identify ones that you're making. This won't be a pleasant process, but if you want to stop losing workers it's a necessary one. Each case not only describes the mistake but provides suggestions on how to overcome it. Follow these suggestions.

You can augment this with another approach. Are any of these managers friends of yours? Will they level with you? Ask them why your workers are so easy for other groups to hire away from you. If you get even a part of the answer, you'll be ahead. But why limit this to other workgroup managers? Does your boss know how you and several of the others operate? Ask him or her to tell you what the advantage is that the others have. Then pay attention to anything you've been told and start to make changes. (If other managers or your boss do identify shortcomings in the way you manage, see if they aren't described in this book. They probably are—and the cases that describe them will also have suggestions on how you can overcome them.)

Is doing what you did ever right?

In at least one circumstance, yes. Could it really be the case that you have such a good reputation for selecting and training workers that other managers want your workers in preference to anyone else? It does happen.

This is the proverbial good news/bad news situation. The good news is that you're not doing anything wrong. In fact, you're doing something very right. The bad news is that because you are doing well your turnover stays high. How do you deal with this. *Don't* try to hang onto workers. Instead, use the fact that everyone wants to hire them away as a recruiting tool. If individuals believe their chances of getting ahead are best if they work for you, you'll have the cream of the crop. And they'll be motivated. So make sure you train them well and quickly and develop them into the best workers you can. You'll get more than enough return from them to be worth the whole effort.

A tip for mistake-free managing:

One of the best reputations you can have as a manager is that of someone whose people get promoted or assigned into really good positions. One of the worst reputations you can get is that of someone who hangs onto his or her workers. Don't combine the two reputations.

Instead, be known as a manager who hires nothing but good people, trains them well, and then works to help them achieve their ambitions. This has several important advantages.

1. Many of your people will stay with you for a long time, simply because they like the way you manage and believe that you're looking out for their best interests.

2. Regardless of how long they stay, you'll get their best effort. They won't have to be rocket scientists to realize that slacking off won't work for them.

3. And you won't have people working for you who would rather be somewhere else. Don't underrate this. If your workgroup has a mediocre reputation or you try to hold onto your workers, you'll have people working for you who genuinely want to be somewhere else. You won't get their best efforts, and they may complain about you to other workers. You don't need that. Keep the ones who want to stay and let the others go—with your blessing.

6-6   ***The Mistake: Letting other workgroups take over parts of your workgroup's mission***

The situation: "Have a seat," your boss says.

You sit.

"Let me get right to the point, because I know you're not going to be happy with what I say. After a good deal of thought, we've decided to give responsibility for software evaluation to Tom Broadman's workgroup."

"Wha . . . . what?" you sputter. "But we've always done the software evaluation."

"I know you have, and you've done acceptably well at it, especially when you were evaluating mainframe software. But now that we're all dealing with personal computers and networks, I don't think your group can keep up with all its responsibilities. Tom wants the responsibility, and I think he'll do it well. That'll give you and your people more time for your other responsibilities, and you've been telling me how overloaded you are."

You protest a bit longer, but it's obvious—your boss's mind is made up.

Why was it a mistake?

When the organization takes any significant responsibility from you and your workgroup, it's seldom meant as a compliment. Your boss may believe you haven't been performing the duties that well, and another workgroup manager has made it clear that he or she would like to pick them up. You may have been complaining about your workload, while the other manager has reorganized his or her workload to accommodate more work. Most harmful of all, the organization may be downsizing and instead of trying to plan for extra work you've been trying to avoid it.

Whether it was one of these causes or a similar one, it led to your losing a key responsibility. It's not far from that to the reputation that your workgroup just can't cut it and/or doesn't want to shoulder its share of the organization's increasing workload.

How can you recover from it quickly?

You can't. What you can do is lay the groundwork for a longer-term recovery. You can begin by calling your workgroup together, telling them about the duties that are being taken away, and then saying: "You may be happy that our workload has dropped, at least for now, but don't be. We didn't lose something simple, like keeping track of the software or finding out which units wanted upgrades. We lost a key responsibility, one we've performed for a long time. Don't kid yourselves—we lost it because somebody wasn't happy with how we're doing it. And don't kid yourselves another way—Tom's group got it because Tom made it clear that they wanted it and that they would do a good job. We've come out of this one with a real black eye."

How can you consistently do it right from now on?

• *Focus on your customers and keep them satisfied.* Nothing else will make you and the workgroup look better than this. Why did your boss take software evaluation away from your group? Almost certainly, he had heard directly or indirectly from your customers that you weren't doing a good job. (Can you picture Tom saying to your mutual boss: "Look, I've had three of their customers in the last week tell me that they thought I'd do a lot better job of evaluation. You've just got to do something about this situation!")

The cure is simple: Stay in touch with your customers, find out what they want, and see that you do the best possible job of giving it to them. Don't give the Toms of this world a chance to make a pitch for part of your mission. (And, of course, make sure your boss knows you're focusing on your customers.)

   • *Be responsive to the needs of the organization.* Just as you want to respond to customers, you want to respond to the needs of the larger organization. You may have lost the software evaluation mission because higher management thought you were trying to get more workers than you needed. Or the organization may be downsizing, abolishing some units and giving their work to other groups—and you fought taking on any extra work.

Either way, you convinced your boss and other managers that you were interested only in your own job and workgroup, and not in the organization as a whole. You shot yourself in the foot, badly. What do you do? You make it clear that you understand the larger situation and that you want to support the organization.

Keep these two points in the forefront of your mind. See that your workgroup understands them and commits itself to them. Practice them.

Is doing what you did ever right?

Only in a very narrow circumstance. You may have duties that your workgroup finds boring and repetitive. Keeping track of who has what software may be one of those duties. If another workgroup wants that duty *and you can substitute a new, more interesting and demanding duty for it*, it's fine to let that workgroup take it.

It's almost always a good practice to be willing to give up less challenging duties for more challenging ones. Do that, and then do the new duties well—and your reputation in the organization will get better.

A tip for mistake-free managing:

People like duties that challenge them. What kind of duties do this? All kinds—and what kind challenges a specific individual depends on that individual. Patricia may like quantitative work with spreadsheets, and the more complicated the spreadsheet the better. Vince may like dealing with other workgroups, negotiating and resolving problems. And Fred may like most of his work to be repetitive, because he challenges himself to see how efficient he can get at it.

One of the smartest goals you can have as a manager is seeing that as many people in your workgroup as possible have challenging jobs. You may want to switch workers at times, or cross-train them, to make their jobs more interesting. As they get better and better, you want to have more demanding work for them to do. You may want to go looking for this challenging work, which may be exactly what Tom was doing when he got the software evaluation mission for his workgroup.

6-7   The Mistake: Accepting boring or no-win duties for your workgroup from other workgroups

The situation: "Have a seat," your boss says.

You sit.

"Let me get right to the point, because I think you're going to like what I'm going to say. I've been talking with all of the workgroups in the branch, and we've decided to take all of the under-$30,000 contracting responsibilities and put them in your workgroup. And Alicia Gutierrez has even volunteered to give you a slot to help absorb the workload."

"We're always willing to take on extra work when we need to," you respond, "but why give us all of the small contracts? They're pretty repetitive, and the people who send them in always want them awarded as soon as possible."

"All of the other workgroup managers agreed that you have the right balance of people and skills for this job, and I think they're right. But don't worry—we'll be finding some more jobs for them in the next few weeks. Everybody is taking on extra work this time around."

Why was it a mistake?

If we put aside your boss's good words, the truth of the matter is this: Several other workgroups have just dumped work they didn't want on you. Why didn't they want it? It's low-level, repetitive work, and its customers expect unrealistically fast service.

Why did you get it? Evidently your boss thinks your workgroup can handle routine work better than it can handle more challenging work. And she expects that the other workgroups can handle the more demanding work better than yours can. A double whammy: You end up with work you don't really want, because your boss doesn't feel as confident as she should about the capabilities of your group.

How can you recover from it quickly?

You can't. This deed is done. But you can set about preventing anything like it from happening again.

How can you consistently do it right from now on?

• *Get the new work organized as efficiently as possible.* When life hands out lemons, make lemonade. When you get stuck with routine tasks, organize and perform them as efficiently as possible. You may have a worker who excels at running routine operations, but you don't necessarily want to start with that worker alone. Is there another worker who excels at setting up operations so they require the simplest processes possible? Get the two of them together and have them get the duties organized. Then give the responsibility to the person who runs routine operations well, along with the people it takes to run it. Provide them any incentives you can for doing an effective, low-cost job.

Don't forget, by the way, that part of this job is dealing effectively with your customers' expectations. Start working with your customers right away, so they know you intend to serve them well *and* that there are certain realistic limitations on how quickly you can do it.

• *Demonstrate that the workgroup is handling the new work well.* Once you get the new work organized, make sure your boss knows how well it's organized. Here's a sample of how you might bring this up to her: "Mrs. Esterbrook, I hope you've noticed that we have the under-$30,000 contracting really well organized. Actually, it turned out to be a much easier job than you and the others led us to believe. It looks like it was a good idea to give it all to us, so we can do it efficiently. I'm not exactly sure, but I think we're doing it with just under half the work months the other groups were taking."

Isn't this dangerous? Won't you get stuck with more of the same kind of duties? Not necessarily, which is why you need to follow the next point, too. But before you take that route, stop and ask yourself (and your workgroup) how you really feel about these "boring" duties now. Are they still boring—or has organizing and executing them well made them a lot more interesting, or at least a lot less time consuming? You might want to collect some more duties like them. After all, there is merit in showing that you can do routine work more efficiently than anyone else.

• *Find more challenging work and get it assigned to your workgroup.* More likely, though, you and your workgroup are going to prefer adding more interesting and less routine work. Don't just stand around and wait for it to come to you. Go find it. Is another workgroup overloaded, and do they have interesting duties you'd be glad to perform? Is there a workgroup whose reputation isn't that good, so that its customers might be happy to have someone else serving them? Or is the organization downsizing, so that duties performed by a workgroup due to be disbanded will have to be performed by someone else? The possibilities are endless.

Is doing what you did ever right?

Well, maybe sometimes. If you believe your workgroup can take the duties, boring as they might be, and organize them much more efficiently—well, perhaps you should just let others "unload" on you. It doesn't hurt to get the reputation as the workgroup that can consistently produce at the lowest cost (or quickest time, or whatever).

Be very careful, though. Other workgroups won't reliably give you duties that will make you look good and, by comparison, make them look not quite so good. In short, be extra careful you're not being sold a bill of goods.

A tip for mistake-free managing:

Many ways exist to build a solid reputation for your workgroup. You can take duties dumped on you because no one else wanted them and turn them into a success story. You can find ever more challenging duties and do them well.

A strong word of caution, though: Do this in ways that help other workgroups, not in ways that make them look bad. Look at the two sections above. Unless your workgroup sells itself and what it can do to other workgroups, they'll look on it as self-serving and a potential danger to them. Earlier cases in this chapter stressed how important it is to operate in ways that help other workgroups be successful. The same applies in situations such as the one in this case. Don't fight others. Do your homework and develop win-win solutions.

Remember, the more people you can help look better, the more supporters you'll have for what you want to accomplish.

CHAPTER 7

MISTAKES IN USING TECHNOLOGY

7-1   The Mistake: Rejecting new technology

The situation: "But we're willing to give you the software, install it, train your people in it, and then support it for you until you're completely comfortable with it."

"That sounds good, Jack, but doesn't the software require the new computers and networking?"

"You don't have those yet?"

"Frankly, Jack, we haven't seen much advantage from them. A lot of what we do is still manual, and it works pretty well. I think you can just count us out again. We'll stick to what we know works for us."

Why was it a mistake?

New technology is generally disruptive, and it doesn't always produce the benefits you expect (as other cases in this chapter will point out). But you don't solve that problem by turning down anything new. Not only do you miss out on changes that could materially help your workgroup, but you get the reputation for being "anti-technology." In today's world, you don't want that reputation.

How can you recover from it quickly?

You simply change your mind. Let's suppose you do this in a hurry, and you catch Jack as he's about to leave. This is how the conversation might begin:

"Jack, hold up a minute if you don't mind. I was a little hasty and I'd really like to discuss the new hardware and software with you a little further."

"Sure. You think you want it?"

177

"Not so fast. Let's talk about the hardware. I've heard horror story after horror story about how some of the other groups have lost their data and had to reenter it all by hand. We don't have time for that."

"Unfortunately, it was a real mess. One of our contractors hadn't had the experience it claimed, and we had to bring in someone else to correct their mistakes. But we haven't had a problem now for several months."

"All right, we'd consider it, then. But let's talk about the software. What will it really do for us that we're not getting done now? . . ."

Notice that the manager doesn't simply shift from "no" to "yes." She shifts from "no" to asking the right questions.

How can you consistently do it right from now on?

The key, as the section above suggests, is a balanced approach. If you're the kind of manager who sees the problems in technology more easily than its benefits, you might want to concentrate on these points:

• *Look at where and how lack of technology is keeping you back.* You can do this in three effective ways:

1. Read the magazines and journals in your field that deal with new technology.

2. Talk with other managers who try new technology. How do they look at it? What results do they get? If you can join an association with these people in it, do so. If you can afford to go to a conference or two where they discuss new technology, do that.

3. Above all and as the basis for both of the suggestions above, look continuously for the problems and bottlenecks in your group's work. Does recording and then retrieving information manually slow things down? Does recopying information lead to errors? Develop a list and keep it up to date. Then when you read or talk with others about new technology, you'll know where the payoff areas are for your workgroup.

• *If you're not comfortable evaluating new technology, find someone you trust to evaluate it and discuss it with you.* This can be someone in your workgroup, or it can be someone in an organization that services you where new technology is concerned. Look around as long as necessary to find a person whose judgment you trust. Then if the individual comes up with an evaluation very different from your own, you'll at least be willing to listen.

Note that you're not asking the person to evaluate it *instead* of you. Even though the individual's evaluation may be much deeper and more technical than yours, you don't want to delegate the basis for a decision to anyone. Besides, if the person knows that you're interested and want to discuss it, he or she will do a better job.

• *If a new technology looks promising but you're not sure, see if you can test it for a while without committing to it.* This may be difficult, but if there's no other way for you to make a decision on new technology, try to arrange it. You might get an individual or small group within the workgroup to try the technology for a few weeks and get their feedback. Some companies will let customers try software for as long as 60 days before making a commitment to buy, which makes a reasonable test easy. The flexibility is out there; do your best to find it and use it.

Is doing what you did ever right?

Turning down technology without understanding what it can do for you seldom pays off. There is perhaps one exception. If your workgroup is trying to assimilate one or more new technologies but hasn't mastered them yet, you might want to turn down any other new technology that's offered. If you do, though, make it clear that at some point in the future, when your workgroup has learned to use what it has now, you'll consider the technology.

A tip for mistake-free managing:

Technology, especially technology based on computers and communication, changes and develops rapidly. By the time you can get it installed and running, it's usually been superseded by a "new and improved" model. And it's often difficult to decide which of several developing technologies will be most useful in another year, or in five years.

What do you do in this environment? The single most useful step you can take is to build a network of people who understand both your business and the ways that technology is developing. If you can do this through a group of managers in the organization or the community, it will help immensely. Visit them and see how they use technology. Ask them to visit you and suggest ways that technology can help your workgroup. Then pay attention to their suggestions.

If we had been writing this book ten years ago, we would scarcely have mentioned technology. If we had been writing it five years ago, we would have suggested that you stay generally aware of new technology. In today's world, though, technology is becoming more and more important to effective performance. However you do it, keep up with it.

7-2   The Mistake: Getting technology for technology's sake

The situation: "But we're not completely convinced that the new software will perform the way you think it will. We can install it, train your people in it, and then support it until you get going, but we can't really assure you that it'll do what you think it'll do."

"I understand, Jack, but this version of this package is the hottest thing out there in our field. You know how strongly I feel about staying on the cutting edge—and this is the cutting edge."

"You don't want to wait until you're sure the new machines and the networking software are working as they should?"

"We're still having a few problems with the setup, Jack, but I think we'll have them licked by the time you get the new software in. Like I said, we don't want to miss out on what's happening in the field."

Why was it a mistake?

New technology is generally disruptive, even when it produces the benefits you expect. And the fact that it's new doesn't necessarily mean that it will produce benefits worth its cost and its problems. While it's often useful to have a reputation for being strongly "pro-technology" it can also lead you to (1) adopt technology that doesn't help that much and/or (2) keep your workgroup in turmoil and reduce its production by implementing new technology before everyone has assimilated what you already have.

How can you recover from it quickly?

You simply change your mind. Let's suppose you do this in a hurry, and you catch Jack as he's about to leave. This is how the conversation might begin:

"Jack, hold up a minute if you don't mind. I was a little hasty and I think I'd better discuss the new software with you a little further."

"Sure. You want to wait before you get it?"

"Not necessarily. It really does look like an improvement, and we really do need to keep up. Is there any way I could let one or two of my people play with it and see what they think?"

"The company puts out a demo, but it's not a very reliable guide to what you really have to do to make the product work. I think Micro Tools has a real copy up and running. Suppose we make an appointment with them and your people and mine take a look at it?"

"Jack, that's an excellent idea. Just let us know when."

Notice that the manager doesn't simply change his mind and decide not to get the software. Instead, he decides to get more information, good information, before he makes up his mind.

How can you consistently do it right from now on?

The key, as the section above suggests, is a balanced approach based on solid information. If you're the kind of manager who sees the promise in technology more easily than its problems, you might want to concentrate on these points:

• *Look objectively at how new technology has affected your group's performance in the past.* This may be painful, but it's where you need to start. If you've implemented significant amounts of new technology in your workgroup over the past few years, look at each implementation and ask yourself what the payoff has been from it. "It would have worked, but the workers wouldn't use it right" is a cop-out. That still counts as a failed implementation. As several later cases in this chapter will point out, technology and people have to work together effectively, or else.

Don't be afraid to ask your workers, both those who love technology and those who dread it. How do they like the implementations? More important—how have the implementations helped them improve their work, and particularly, their productivity?

The future doesn't always follow the past. If the technology implemented in the group in the past hasn't been successful, though, that's the best predictor of what future implementations will accomplish. The reverse is also true: If past implementations have been successful, future ones are more likely to be successful also.

• *Find someone you trust who's more cautious about new technology and let him or her be a "devil's advocate."* Pick someone in your workgroup, in another workgroup, or in an organization that provides you technology support. If necessary, find someone in another organization. You need someone whose judgment you trust and who can ask all of the hard questions about the new technology. You also need to make a firm decision that no matter how thoroughly he or she disagrees with you, you will pay close attention to the individual's judgment.

One great benefit of this is that when you do it right some of the other's critical judgment begins to rub off on you. Then you can become your own "devil's advocate."

• *If possible, let the workgroup or several key members make the decision on the technology with you.* This requires a mature workgroup and a great deal of maturity in yourself as a manager. But it can be done. The more sophisticated workgroup members become about technology, the more they will be able to help you decide what new technology offers the greatest payoff. They're the ones who'll have to use it, so they have a real stake in how well it works. Once they realize this, they'll begin to be highly motivated to make the best decision.

Is doing what you did ever right?

Sometimes, particularly if your judgment on new technology has been good in the past or if the workgroup understands and uses technology well. These two "ifs" are big ones, though. Unless one or both are clearly true, and perhaps even if they are, you're better off spending time evaluating new technology carefully before making a decision.

A tip for mistake-free managing:

Most of us accept that technology is becoming more and more important to organizations and the jobs of the individuals in them. Even when this is the case, though, we have hard, hard decisions to make. How does an organization balance mainframe, client-server, and stand-alone personal computers? How does your workgroup decide which of a dozen competing software packages will work best for it? And on and on as the pace of change, particularly in electronics, does nothing but increase.

In this environment, it's particularly important to keep focused on where the problems and opportunities are in your workgroup. Technology that helps you do better or less expensively what you're already doing is very helpful. Technology that enables you to serve customers in a new and valuable way is much more helpful. And technology that takes your attention away from your mission is positively harmful. (What kind of technology could that be? Do you use software to create charts and drawings? How much time do your people spend getting something to look really spectacular when looking accurate and authoritative is quite good enough?)

7-3   The Mistake: Letting someone else be responsible for picking new technology for your workgroup

The situation: "Hey, aren't you coming with us to watch the demonstration for the new telephone system we're probably going to get?"

"No, Selina—I'll let you guys do that. If it works for you, I can figure it'll work for me."

"You know, we really would like your opinion. Each one of us has a slightly different organization, and you might not reach the same conclusion I would."

"Thanks. I really appreciate your stopping by, Selina, and I very much want to know what you think of the new system. But your evaluation's going to be good enough for me."

Why was it a mistake?

To begin with, it was a mistake for the exact reason Selina said: Each workgroup operates slightly differently. The system may have had a feature that was great for your group, even though it was useless for the others. Or vice versa. A second reason is just as important: You would not only have learned from but would have added to the discussion. By letting someone else decide what technology you should have, you end up with a system you're not familiar with and can't "sell" to your workgroup. Or you end up without the technology, when perhaps your workgroup needed it worse than anyone else.

How can you recover from it quickly?

Grab your coat and catch up with Selina. Tell her you changed your mind and thank her again for thinking to say something to you.

How can you consistently do it right from now on?

Let's tune in on the two managers as they walk back from the meeting:

"Well," Selina says, "what did you think?"

"Frankly, I'm confused. Did I understand right that this system has a much more convenient Speed Dial than our current system?"

"I'm not really sure. Is Speed Dialing important to you?"

"About three of my people live and die by it. I need to get some more information on it. I'm also not sure whether their system has a better data transfer rate than ours. Is that something you care about?"

"You better believe! I got everything they have on data transfer. You want to go over it together? . . ."

What conclusions might we draw from this brief conversation?

• *Get at least the basic information for yourself.* After a second thought, the manager decided to go to the demonstration himself. He made a wise decision. This gives him the opportunity to see what the system looks like, to hear the pitch for it, and to get material on it. Just as important, he now knows enough about it to intelligently discuss it with other managers.

Notice, by the way, that even if he decided this wasn't the system for his workgroup he would have a clear idea of why not. Then, if someone tried to push it on his workgroup he would be able to oppose it effectively: "Look, no matter how good the rest of it might be, there's no point in spending money on a system that doesn't have far higher data transfer rates."

• *Take advantage of knowledgeable people's ideas; discuss the proposed technology with them as much as you can.* The manager got the point on this one and started picking Selina's brain as soon as they left the session. She may or may not have understood what his needs were, but if she understood her own and could explain them the other manager couldn't help but learn from her. His logical next step would be conversations with other managers, particularly with ones whose workgroups were much like his own. All this would have helped him get a clearer idea of how the new system would or wouldn't have met his workgroup's needs.

• *Concentrate on the features important to you and your workgroup.* Most of us at one time or another fall into the trap of buying something just because we've gotten a general recommendation. This is a kind of "If it's good enough for them, it's good enough for me" approach to purchasing. If you act on that kind of general recommendation, you're back where you started—letting someone else make your decision for you. Don't do that. Identify the features that matter to you and your workgroup and focus on them.

• *If necessary, build coalitions with other managers to get just the technology you want.* Much of the time, individual workgroups don't get a choice for or against a new technology or even much voice in exactly what features it will have. In these cases, it's extremely important for workgroup managers to talk with one another until they reach agreement on whether they want the technology and what features it should have. Then they can present a united front to whomever will make the decision. This doesn't guarantee that you and other managers will get what you want, but it certainly increases the likelihood that you will.

Is doing what you did ever right?

Virtually never. Look at the disadvantages to the approach under "Why was it a mistake?" above. It's hard to think of a situation in which letting someone else decide on your technology has advantages that outweigh these disadvantages.

A tip for mistake-free managing:

Many managers are uncomfortable around new technology. Perhaps you're one. You don't want to turn the new technology down, but you're not comfortable simply saying "yes" either. So it seems simplest to find someone (or someones) you feel you can trust and make a decision based on their judgment.

Don't do that. Technology is becoming more important every day. Selina was concerned about the data transfer rate of the new system. That rate could affect everything from her access to videoconferencing to her ability to use the organization's networks effectively, to the simple task of sending a long report to the Los Angeles office. Make a hasty or uninformed decision and you can be stuck for a very long time with a technology that doesn't work for you. As you probably know by now, getting rid of an inadequate technology is much harder than getting it in the first place.

Learn all you can from others, but make the technology decisions for your group yourself.

7-4   The Mistake: Not letting workers use technology fully

The situation:

"Hey, boss, I think we've found a way to modify our database so we can capture some of the costs we've been trying to get a handle on."

"Suellen, that's a noble goal, but you're going to alter the format we've been using?"

"Not a whole lot. And I'm not going to do it. Matt's spelled out the changes that need to be made, and Arsenio Washburn has agreed to implement them for us."

"Slow down! Why hasn't anyone mentioned this to me before?"

Suellen was visibly taken aback. "Gosh, we didn't know you'd have any problem with it. We're just trying to make the system more useful to us."

"Like I said, Suellen, that's a noble goal, but I don't think I like your way of getting there. Why don't you get Matt so he can explain to me what he thinks needs to be done. If it sounds workable, we'll write up a request and let the folks who installed it decide whether it should be modified or not."

Why was it a mistake?

This short example actually treats three different questions about workers and technology:

1. Should workers use technology in ways it wasn't designed to be used?

2. Should workers be allowed to "play around" with technology to see what they can accomplish with it?

3. Should workers attempt to adapt the technology they use to their work?

The first two questions are obviously valid ones. Why, then, is what the manager did a mistake? The manager essentially answered "no" to the first two questions. By doing so, however, he answered "no" to the last question—and that's a different kind of question. True, he said he would send in a request if the change sounded feasible, but that almost certainly meant delaying the change for weeks or months. And it meant that anyone in his workgroup would have problems learning more about how the system might be modified to be more effective for the group.

You have to be careful about letting your workgroup experiment with using its technology in ways that weren't planned. But if they don't experiment, the technology will never do you or your workers any more good than it did on the day it was delivered.

How can you recover from it quickly?

Simple—catch Suellen before she gets out the door, or call her back, and amend the last paragraph of what you said to something like this: "Like I said, Suellen, that's a noble goal—but we need to be careful we don't cause problems getting to it. Why don't you get Matt so you and he can explain to me exactly what you think needs to be done. If it sounds workable, go ahead and have Arsenio make the changes. Then we'll see what happens and go from there."

Notice that the manager didn't simply tell his workers to go ahead with the project. He sensibly asked them to explain it to him in some detail. Then he can make an intelligent decision about whether the potential benefits of what they want to do outweigh the risks. And if this change sounds too risky, perhaps they can decide on another experiment that has more promise.

How can you consistently do it right from now on?

Most of us who've been around organizations for long learned about computers, and most other technology, in an environment where this technology was highly centralized. It was something that someone else brought in, installed, trained us to use, and then told us to use exactly as they said. Experimenting with the technology, though often done on the sly, was strictly forbidden.

Times have changed. You may have one or two workgroup members who actually understand the technology better than the people who installed it. Every member of your workgroup should understand how it should help him or her—and even have some ideas on how to improve its usefulness. Here are some suggestions on how to help turn their ideas into practical steps. All of the suggestions assume that your technology is computer based, but the general ideas can be used even if it isn't.

• *Ensure that everyone understands the importance of backing up his or her work.* Of course, the technology may be more than just computers. To the extent that computers are involved, though, make sure that the group has backup copies of all of its programs and that every worker backs up his or her work regularly. How often is "regularly"? For most of us, at least twice as frequently as we think is required.

• *Ensure that one or more workgroup members understand how each program works and how it can be changed with minimum risk.* This begins as a training problem. Whenever your workgroup gets new or upgraded programs, they get the training that goes with them. Most of them will take this, learn the little bit additional they need to do their work on the new software, and stop learning there. Don't encourage this. Encourage they to browse the program's help system to look for features they haven't yet used. Encourage them to experiment with program features: Both spreadsheets and word processors normally have extensive macro facilities. Just this much knowledge may help individuals and the workgroup as a whole make the programs significantly more useful to them.

• *Let everyone play with the software, but if you attempt any real changes ensure that one worker is responsible for them.* Encourage everyone to experiment with small changes that can be easily undone. But if you try more significant changes—and you should—put one individual in charge of each change. You can have a group work on the change, but one person needs to make the decisions. The people who make suggestions can have any level of expertise and creativity; the person who decides which suggestions to implement needs to have a solid understanding of the software and the impact of the changes. It doesn't have to be the same person for all the projects. You'll be better off if several people develop this expertise. But you need to ensure that only one person is responsible for the success or failure of any project.

• *No matter how much or how little experimentation takes place, ensure that all your workers understand that the technology is there to support them, not vice versa.* Encourage workers to let you know of changes that need to be made or, if you have technically competent workers, you might allow them to make their own changes. Remember that the technology is a tool. It shouldn't drive the work.

Is doing what you did ever right?

Only if your workgroup is unused to computers. Then they need time to learn about their strengths and weaknesses and how to back up work regularly. During this time, you may want to be very cautious about letting them make any changes. As they become more proficient, though, you need to communicate clearly that they need to make the system just as useful to themselves as humanly possible.

A tip for mistake-free managing:

You don't want your people becoming enamored of your technology—becoming "techies." On the other hand, you and your workers all need to understand how it works and what its strengths and weaknesses are. And you need to understand how to modify it to increase its usefulness without causing new problems. How do you combine all these concerns?

Not easily. You'll probably have some workers who would love to become techies and spend most of their time playing with the technology. Others want to know just enough to get their jobs done, but no more. Somehow, you create a work environment that keeps the would-be techies focused on their jobs and not the technology, while you encourage the determined non-techies to learn more about the technology.

Here's a basic tip for accomplishing that. Encourage your technically oriented folks to spend time with those who aren't. Don't encourage them to spend the time on technology as such, though. Instead, let them discuss problems that the nontechies are having using the technology for their work. In many cases, they can show the nontechies simple ways to solve their own problems. And in some cases, the techies will get ideas for more significant changes that they can make to help everyone.

7-5   *The Mistake: Trying to solve performance problems with technology*

The situation:

"Beverley, I called you because I need some help."

"Sure—what's up?"

"One of my people—you probably know who it is—just isn't cutting the mustard. I thought if I could find him a more up-to-date spreadsheet I could help him cut down on his errors."

"That won't necessarily work, but I'll see what I can do. Suppose I send Carolyn over tomorrow around 2:00 to talk with you about the options we have?"

> "Sounds fine. Thanks a million, Bev—I knew I could count on you."

Why was it a mistake?

The manager has no reason, other than a fond hope, to believe that new technology will help overcome his worker's performance problem. Most of the time, it just adds expense and complexity, and you end up with the same problem with which you began.

How can you recover from it quickly?

You can call Bev and tell her to hold off until she hears from you again. Then you can deal with the performance problem.

How can you consistently do it right from now on?

Where might the manager have gotten the idea that new technology would help? Let's listen to a little of the conversation between her and her nonperformer, Phil:

> "Phil, there's been at least one major error on each of the last three reports you've given me."

> "I didn't think it was quite that bad. Besides, the spreadsheet I have to use doesn't help me catch the mistakes. If I had one of the newer spreadsheets, there wouldn't be as many errors."

> "OK, Phil, we'll give that a try. I'll get you an up-to-date one as soon as I can."

Note that Phil shifted the problem from his performance to that of the software. If nothing else, he bought himself some time. The manager bought nothing, and learned nothing.

Let's look at how the conversation might have gone:

> "Phil, there's been at least one major error on each of the last three reports you've given me."

> "I didn't think it was quite that bad. Besides, the spreadsheet I have to use doesn't help me catch the mistakes. If I had one of the newer spreadsheets, there wouldn't be as many errors."

"Maybe a newer spreadsheet would help, Phil, and we can consider that. But what do you mean when you say that the spreadsheet doesn't help you catch your errors?"

"Well, if I make a mistake in a new formula or put the decimal point in the wrong place, it never warns me or tells me I'm making an error. I'm sure there must be newer spreadsheets that catch things like that and tell you."

"Again, maybe they do. But why do you put the wrong formulas in or put the decimal point in the wrong place to start with?"

"We're all under such pressure to get the reports done that I can't help it. . . ."

Just a few sentences more, and suddenly the problem looks quite different. Phil is responding poorly to pressure, or perhaps just using the pressure as an excuse for mistakes he would make anyway. It's hard to see how technology helps cause the problem or how it could help cure it.

You might find the following suggestions useful when you're trying to decide whether technology is causing a performance problem and/or might help cure it:

• *Get as much detail as possible about the problem.* One clear difference between the first and second conversations above is the amount of detail that the manager got in the second conversation. But that was just a beginning. If a worker has a problem, spend all the time necessary to understand the problem in depth. The better you understand it, the more effective your response will be.

• *Explore to find out whether there is a deeper problem.* Perhaps Phil is making so many mistakes because he and everyone else are under pressure, but he doesn't tolerate it well. Or perhaps he's a slower worker and doesn't have time to review his spreadsheets for error. Or perhaps the spreadsheet itself was poorly set up, so that he has to keep interrupting his input to fumble through paper reports. Take long enough to see if another problem is underlying the problem you began with. If so, it's far more important to solve that problem.

• *Ask the worker what he or she has done to try to solve the problem.* You don't want workers who want someone else to solve their problems, or who hope that if they ignore the problems they'll go away. Instead, you want them to face and deal with the problem, then bring it to you only if they couldn't solve it. Has Phil attempted to deal with the input errors? How? How determinedly? Did he use the program's help system? Did he ask other workers how they handled the same problem? He should have made a serious attempt to solve the problem himself, instead of letting you catch it.

• *If technology is contributing to the problem or might help solve it, find out specifically how.* If technology is part of either the problem or solution, it will be in specific ways. Phil said that the spreadsheet wouldn't help him catch errors. Is that a cop-out? Perhaps not, but you won't know unless you ask. For instance, it may really be that in this or another spreadsheet he could write a macro that would warn him whenever a decimal point was outside a set range. Whatever the situation, new technology will help only if (1) you can tell exactly what's going wrong and (2) a new program will cure that specific problem.

Is doing what you did ever right?

No. It never works to jump to quick conclusions about the cause of a performance problem.

A tip for mistake-free managing:

As many organizations have found to their pain, no technology—not even the latest and slickest technology—will cure most human performance problems. Sometimes people perform poorly because they lack really effective tools. In these cases, the right technology can help them perform better. Far more often, they perform poorly because they don't understand the objectives of their job, don't understand what's really expected of them, don't get useful feedback on how they're doing, aren't allowed to do what's required to perform really well, or simply don't care whether they perform well or not. Technology not only doesn't help in most of these situations but diverts effort and attention away from the real causes of the problem.

Effective performance is always a balance. Where technology is concerned, effective performance occurs when it supports the skills and motivation of the workers who use it. The more effectively your workers perform, the more use the right technology will be to them. If they perform poorly, though, new technology seldom helps. Whenever there's a performance problem, look first at the human elements in the problem. Deal with them—then call on technology to help them improve already effective performance.

7-6   The Mistake: Automating an existing process without improving it first

The situation: "Hello, Rosina—what brings you over this way?"

"Believe it or not, we want to give you some help. How'd you like to have your document receipt process put on the computer?"

"Wow—I've been waiting years for someone to say that. When can you start?"

"Stewart is the best I have a using programmable databases, but he's awfully busy. Do you think you could arrange for a couple of your most knowledgeable people to spend as much time as possible with him on Monday and Tuesday? Then he can bring the information back and try to put the process into a database over the next three weeks."

"That would be wonderful, Rosina. My people will be delighted to give you as much time as you want. I just can't wait until this gets on the computer."

Why was it a mistake?

You can be almost certain that any manual process that has been operating for a while without change—such as the document receipt process in the example—will have two characteristics. First, it will not be as efficient as it could be; it may, in fact, be very inefficient. Second, if it's put on a computer without change it will make inefficient use of the computer. In other words, if you start with an inefficient manual process and automate it without changing it, you'll get an inefficient automated process. And, strange as it sounds, the automated process may turn out to be even less efficient than the manual process.

How can you recover from it quickly?

How are your workers at analyzing process flow? If several of them are proficient at it, and if there's time, put them to work diagraming the flow of the document receipt process. They won't have time to diagram it in great detail at this point, but they should be able to get the basic flows in place. Then look at what you've got. How inefficient does it appear to be? How many times does each document have to be handled? How many times does the same individual or subgroup have to handle it? How much time does it spend waiting for someone to do something with it? You may find you have only fuzzy answers to these questions.

Now it's time to call Rosina back and change the game plan. If Stewart or another of her workers is very good at diagraming processes, ask if that individual can meet with your team. Let all of them look at the process. If you've very lucky, Stewart will end up with enough to do a reasonable first pass at the computer-based system. It's more likely that you'll have to do a great deal more work before Stewart or anyone else can automate the process.

How can you consistently do it right from now on?

Reengineering is a formal method for analyzing and improving processes so they can be automated effectively. You probably don't have the time or the resources for a real reengineering effort. But you do have the time and effort, perhaps aided by one or more of Rosina's people, to take these steps:

• *Step 1.* Define the purpose of the process as clearly and specifically as possible.

• *Step 2.* Diagram the current process in detail. There is software to help you do this, but it doesn't require software. It does require time and a willingness to deal with detail.

• *Step 3.* Using the definition of the purpose of the process, revise the process to be more efficient and, perhaps, more effective. Start by asking: Why do we have to do this? Then omit all steps you can. Then, and only then, ask: What's the fewest steps we can do this in? Then simplify these steps. Omit every step that doesn't help meet the objective of the process. Simplify those that do.

• *Step 4.* Give the revised process to someone familiar with computers. Ask him or her if it will materially help to automate the process. You may find that you get enough benefit just from revising the process that automating it won't help that much more.

• *Step 5.* Now, either implement the revised process or give it to the appropriate office to develop an automated version of it.

Most of the time, analyzing and improving the process will yield a greater benefit than automating it. So, no matter what the situation, start by looking at the process in depth. Many organizations have formal process analysis training course. If your doesn't, perhaps a local community college offers this kind of course. Seriously consider putting every one of your workgroup through the course—yourself included.

Is doing what you did ever right?

No. Don't ever automate a process without analyzing and improving it first. Various experts estimate that from 30 percent to 70 percent of the improvement from automating is actually the improvement made *before* it's automated.

A tip for mistake-free managing:

You don't read about this a lot, but here's an iron law of automating: Once a process is changed from a manual one to an automated one it becomes *less flexible and harder to change* than it was when it was done manually. Think long and hard about this and make your decisions about automating accordingly. If you want to put a process on the computer, you must ensure that it is as efficient and effective as possible *before it's automated.*

7-7　*The Mistake: Letting technology make work more boring for the workgroup*

The situation:　　　　"I've heard about expert systems, Andrea, but I'm not completely sure I understand them."

"They do exactly what it sounds like. You get workers' expertise and code it in the form of rules, and then the expert system can make the decisions that the workers used to make."

"But, Andrea, what about the workers?"

"Oh, it makes their job a lot easier. Really all they have to do is put the data in and then do what the system tells them—except for the most complex situations, of course."

"And you want us to implement one?"

"Yes, I think it would be great. I could have one or two of my people get the basic expertise from your folks and create an expert system from it."

"Well, if you think it will work we'll certainly try it."

Why was it a mistake?

Because it reduces the skills of your people.

Because it makes their jobs more boring.

Because they will fight it (because it reduces their skills and makes their jobs more boring.)

Because whenever a change needs to be made in the system, you're dependent on someone else to make the change.

Because expertise is changing so fast in many jobs that the system will have to be updated constantly, and you won't be able to get it updated fast enough.

How can you recover from it quickly?

By not having the conversation in the first place.

By turning down Andrea's offer.

By asking Andrea to build your workgroup expert systems to perform the "extrinsic" tasks that it has to do.

How can you consistently do it right from now on?

What are "extrinsic" tasks? They're the work that all workers have to do that isn't really part of their core job. Say, your unit's basic work is doing financial analyses on small businesses your company works with. That's what your staff was hired for, and that's what they enjoy. You don't want to interfere with that. But they have other jobs, maybe ordering supplies or preparing reports, that are part of the job, but not an essential part. That's what you should automate.

• *Be sure you understand what the core work of your workgroup is.* This may sound silly, and we hope it's unnecessary. But workgroups do accumulate duties that aren't related to their basic work, and these duties can be very time consuming. For instance, most workgroups are established to produce a product or service, but they must spend time and effort generating reports, summaries, and other documents that don't actually help produce their primary product or service. It's not that long a jump for people to be valued for their ability to do the paperwork and only secondarily for their ability to accomplish the real mission.

If your workgroup is in this situation, ensure that both you and they understand the difference between what they're hired to accomplish and the secondary, extrinsic duties they also must perform.

• *Don't let technology reduce the skill required to do this core work.* Once you and your workers have a clear focus of the core work of the group, don't permit technology to take over the skills required to produce this work.

There's a fine line here. Sometimes using technology to take over the basic skills can free a workgroup to take on even higher-level skills and perform more complex and useful duties. In the example at the start of this case, new technology might have been able to take over the simplest aspects of financial analysis. This could give the workers more time to spend on the more difficult, and more important, parts of the analysis. That creates a definite "win-win" situation.

• *Use every bit of technology you can to reduce the skill and time required to do the extrinsic, noncore work.* This is where the heavy-duty payoff comes from technology. Let the computer fill out your requisitions for nonstocked supplies and capital equipment. Let it do the basic paperwork that supports a worker's analysis. Why are spreadsheets so popular? Because they take over so much of the day-in-day-out calculations and leave the performers who use them free to concentrate on the end results they're after. Some with word processors—they take care of many of the routine processes and let writers like us concentrate on what we want to say. (On the other hand, neither a spreadsheet nor a word processor will protect its user from dumb ideas.)

Is doing what you did ever right?

Unless you and your workgroup are getting a very specific payoff from it, you should never let technology make the workgroup's job more boring. In the long run, the only people who benefit from that are the people who write the software.

A tip for mistake-free managing:

Technology can be used in three different ways in a workgroup:

1. It can perform the basic work of the group, with the remaining human beings inputting data and handling the most unusual situations. This happened to most payroll offices and inventory branches—their computers do the work they used to do.

2. It can support the basic work of the group, making it easier for workers to do their basic jobs. Most software that supports "knowledge workers"—engineers,

architects, writers, and so forth—works this way. So does any software that takes care of the extrinsic work and lets workers focus more sharply on the core mission.

3. It can do the part of the work that it does best, while supporting humans in doing the part they do best. Computer-aided drafting (CAD) software does this to a large extent; the human handles the creative side and the "what ifs?" while the computer handles the precise details. However, very few people really understand how to design technology to perform effectively as a partner to people.

Do you want to use technology so it helps your workgroup? Avoid the first use of technology like the plague. Implement the second use whenever you can. And keep looking to see if someone in your organization is beginning to understand the third use and might help you implement it in your workgroup.

CHAPTER *8*

MISTAKES IN MANAGING TEAMS

8-1   The Mistake: Trying to manage a team as a traditional supervisor

The situation: "We've just about got the assignments worked out for this job," Li said. "I think we've distributed the work pretty well."

"Wait a minute—you've done all the assignments?"

"Yeah, isn't that what we're supposed to do?" Li frowned.

"While I want you to try your hand at this kind of thing, Li, I certainly never intended for the team just to go ahead and make decisions like this without talking with me. Now why don't you bring me the assignment sheet and I'll look at it and see whether it needs to be changed."

Why was it a mistake?

If organizations establish teams, it's to take advantage of workers' ability to manage themselves and produce without having to be told what to do. If you continue to perform as a traditional supervisor, this can't happen. In the short run, there will be conflict between you and the team. In the long term, if you don't change, team members will stop taking the initiative, and all of you will be back where you started. The organization will not be happy about that.

How can you recover from it quickly?

Before Li comes back with the assignment sheet, shift gears. This is how the beginning of the conversation might go:

"Here's the assignment sheet," Li says flatly.

199

"Good—but I don't think I made myself clear before. This really is up to you and the team to do."

Li brightens noticeably. "You're not going to overrule us?"

"No, not at all. If I can help you any with it, that's fine. What I really want to do is get an idea of who's doing what, so if I need to ask questions later on I know whom to talk to."

Note the significant shift in the manager's intent. Now his purpose is to keep himself informed, not to make decisions for the team.

How can you consistently do it right from now on?

You need to make the basic shift from being a supervisor to being a coach. What does a coach do? He or she ensures that the team develops the skills it needs, is properly motivated, has the equipment it needs, and otherwise is prepared to play its game effectively. He does not run the ball or play the hand in the actual game.

How do you make this shift? Let's look at how the conversation at the opening of this case might have sounded if the manager acted like a coach instead of as a supervisor:

"We've just about got the assignments worked out for this job," Li said. "I think we've distributed the work pretty well."

"Did all of the team members participate?"

"Yes, all except Delena, who isn't going to work on it, and Vic, who said he was OK with any assignment we wanted to give him. He's still trying to get his last project closed down."

"Is everyone happy with the results, though, Li?"

"Pretty much. Wally really wanted a different assignment, but we convinced him that the one he got would work best for the team as a whole. Everybody else got pretty much what they wanted."

Note how different this discussion is. It's based on a set of guidelines that a manager who wants to be a coach rather than a supervisor would follow.

1. He would make sure that the team followed all the steps it should to produce an effective decision. As the team becomes more proficient, he would do this less and less frequently. The manager in the discussion just above did it by asking a series of helpful questions.

2. He would use questions, rather than statements, to help team members think problems through. Suppose Li had said that, no, Wally wasn't satisfied with his assignment. The manager might have asked how the team made the decision and how fully it allowed Wally to express and defend his preferences. Then he might have followed this by other questions designed to help Li and the team think more effectively about the situation and how to handle it next time.

3. He would never tell the team or any member what to do unless he were sure that he had knowledge, information, or expertise that the team did not yet have. Then he would find a way to help the team or individual develop, so that in the future the manager wouldn't need to make that kind of decision.

4. He would get a real kick from watching the team develop and take over more and more of its own management.

Is doing what you did ever right?

It might be a way to begin a discussion if the team were new and not used to taking responsibility for decisions such as making assignments. Teams, like individuals, don't always know what they don't know how to do. Even then, it's not enough for the manager to make the decisions. He needs to use the coaching techniques described just above and to explain to the team all the factors involved in particular decisions. Since learning takes time, he might begin by being somewhat directive, then backing off as the team gained expertise.

None of this would work, though, unless you had already begun to think of yourself as a coach rather than as a supervisor.

A tip for mistake-free management:

How self-managing should a team be? That really depends on the answers to three questions. How self-managing does it want to be? How self-managing do you want it to be? And how self-managing does the organization want it to be? These aren't questions with simple, quick answers. The fact that a group of people are called a team doesn't make them one. They may still want to be told what to do. You may still want to tell them what to do. And the organization may want you to tell them what to do. And nothing changes magically if, starting one Monday morning, the organization calls them *self-managing* teams.

Here's the place to begin: Decide that you want the team to be as self-managing as possible. Don't worry about whether they're called "self-managing" or not. Just do it! Help the individuals learn to work together and depend on one another. Help them accept conflicting opinions and learn to resolve them. Help them pick up the skills they need to make their own assignments, control their own workflow, perhaps even evaluate one another.

The individuals on the team will probably like working this way. You will probably like working this way. And if you've done it right, their productivity will probably go up, which means the organization will probably like them working this way.

8-2   *The Mistake: Not developing commitment to the team's mission*

The situation: "Bonnie, how come your team seems to get so much more done than mine?"

"I don't know. Is your team really committed to its mission?"

"They know what they have to do, Bonnie, and they do it—just like they did before they became a team instead of a workgroup."

"That's not enough. Is each member committed to getting the team's overall mission done and done right? And is each member committed to the team's success and not just his or her personal success to?"

"No. I just ask each of them to do their individual job and do it well."

Why was it a mistake?

If a team is to function any more effectively than a traditional workgroup, each member of the team must commit himself or herself both to the team and to its mission. Team members must believe in the mission and work together to achieve it. They must also be committed to the team and its success, not just to the small part of its overall mission they may be responsible for at any given time. If members don't commit themselves to the mission and to the team as a whole, the team will never really become a team. It will remain a collection of individuals working more or less closely together.

How can you recover from it quickly?

You can't. Commitment to the team's mission and to the team as a whole takes time. But you can certainly begin taking the steps outlined in the next section.

How can you consistently do it right from now on?

Follow these suggestions:

• *Ensure that everyone on the team knows what the overall mission is.* In a traditional workgroup, individual workers know only their own jobs. They may not even understand how it fits into the overall mission of the group. A team can't function that way. Every team member needs to know the overall mission. Suppose your team is responsible for producing newsletters for the organization. Some of these are published regularly, others are one-time ones to meet specific management needs. You have editors, writers, graphics specialists, and production specialists. You might describe the fundamental mission as "getting high-quality newsletters into customers, hands, when promised, and without running over budget." Even in a traditional workgroup, this focus on the overall mission helps tremendously. For a team, it's an essential.

• *Ensure that everyone focuses on achieving the overall mission, not just on their job at the moment.* Once everyone knows what the mission is, everyone needs to focus on it. In practice, that means that sometimes workers have to sacrifice their own specific jobs for the good of the entire unit. Someone who's working on a production report, for instance, might have to drop that to fold and staple when the team gets behind in production.

• *Encourage all your workers to work together and to think of themselves as one team.* Workers often find it hard to make this transition. Those who've worked for traditional organizations are used to being rewarded or penalized on the basis of their individual work. (See the next case.) It takes time for them to make the shift to valuing helping one another more than getting their individual jobs done. As workers demonstrate team cooperation, be sure to praise their efforts *and* use them as a model for the rest of the group.

Is doing what you did ever right?

If you want an effective team, it never works to let its members concentrate only about their individual jobs. You need to help them keep primary focus on the team's mission, always.

A tip for mistake-free managing:

For a team to commit itself to its mission, the mission must have three characteristics:

1. The mission must be *clear.* All the team members must understand it and understand it in basically the same way. ("Satisfy customers" is relatively clear; "produce a quality product" is not quite so clear.)

2. The mission must be *worthwhile.* For team members to commit to it, they must believe that it is worth their time and effort. "Provide high-quality newsletters to our customers" is relatively worthwhile; "meet the deadlines that higher management assigns us" is not quite so compelling.

3. The mission must be *pressing.* Team members need to see that it needs to be done now, not that it could wait while something else more important gets done. "Design newsletters in time to meet our customers' needs" is relatively pressing; "prepare a report on the number of newsletters produced" (that no one may ever read) is not.

If you want an effective team, make sure its mission has all three of these characteristics.

8-3   *The Mistake: Dealing with team members solely as individuals*

The situation: "Drew, I need to talk with you about the job analyses you're doing in Manufacturing."

"Sure," Drew said, still standing, "but the whole team is doing them. Shouldn't I get the rest of the team in here with me so we can all take part in the discussion?"

"That's not necessary. I know that you work together more closely than you used to, and teams are just fine, but we still depend on the performance of each individual to get our job done. I want to see how you think the analyses are going and maybe make a few suggestions to you on some changes you might make in your approach."

Drew shifted his weight noticeably. "You know, I'm really uncomfortable talking about this without all of my team taking part in it."

"Don't be. I'm planning on having the same conversation with two other of your team members later today. . . ."

Why was it a mistake?

Most workers are accustomed to being supervised and evaluated on the basis on their individual efforts. Even when they're told they're part of a team, they tend to keep thinking in individual performance terms. A manager's basic job at this point is to help these workers shift their focus from individual performance to team performance. (See the case just before this one.) When the manager doesn't help them shift focus, when she keeps them focusing on individual performance, she prevents them from becoming an effective team.

How can you recover from it quickly?

It's simple. The manager can shift the focus for this discussion to where it should be just by changing her last statement in the dialogue above. This is how it should sound: "I'm planning on having about the same conversation with two of your team members later today. . . . Well, wait a minute. It isn't just you, it's your whole team that's concerned in this, isn't it? Can you round them up so that all of us can meet right after lunch and go over this?"

This one change won't be enough, of course, but it's a significant move in the right direction.

How can you consistently do it right from now on?

• *Focus on team performance first, not on individual performance.* Individual performance still counts, of course. But team performance counts more because if the team isn't successful no amount of individual performance will make up for it. So keep your attention on how the team as a whole is performing and how individual members are contributing to its overall performance. Once you're focused there, you can help team members do the same.

• *Let the team correct individual performance.* In the past, part of a manager's job has always been correcting individual performance. Once a team becomes a true team, though, that changes significantly. Effective teams are far more effective at correcting and improving the performance of their members than most managers could be. Of course, you have to help the team understand that this is part of its responsibility and that you expect it to take it seriously. You may even have to intervene once or twice until the members learn how to correct and help one another effectively, but then the team should handle most of its own performance problems.

• *Don't reward individual performance that doesn't contribute to team success.* Teams have stars, but they're not the individual stars traditional workgroups are accustomed to. Team stars are the individuals who help the team achieve its overall goals. Over time, almost anyone on the team can be a star—making a particularly important contribution to the team's effort at a particular point. So don't single out an individual for his or her contribution. If the team believes the person made that great a contribution, they'll recognize the fact. Let them.

Suppose Drew did an unusually effective job of the job analysis in Manufacturing. If this were still a traditional workgroup, you might call the group together and recognize him in some way. But not if this is a team. You might still call everyone together, but your contribution might be no more than an introduction of the *team member* who would describe Drew's accomplishments.

• *If you use individual performance appraisals, make team performance a major item on each individual's appraisal.* Individual performance appraisals aren't really compatible with effective team performance, but most teams have to deal with individual appraisals, at least in the beginning. You may be required to have individual achievement factors on the appraisal; if so, use them. But ensure that at least one of the most important items is the individual's performance as a team member—the person's willingness to cooperate and to put the team's goals ahead of his or her own.

This changes the content of the appraisal and of the evaluation you give. Before, you might have called Drew in for his annual appraisal and spent all of the time on how effectively he accomplished his work. But not in a team environment. In that environment, the evaluation might well begin with his contributions to team performance.

Is doing what you did ever right?

No. You need to spend your time and effort helping individuals integrate into the team, not forcing them to focus on their individual performance.

A tip for mistake-free managing:

There is a conflict between performing effectively as an individual and performing as part of an effective team. When teams begin to develop strong cohesion, they often err on the side of pushing everyone to be compatible and "one of the group." This isn't all bad, but it needs to be dealt with. (And it is, later in this chapter.)

While the team is making the switch from a workgroup to a true team, though, too much "group think" isn't normally the problem. Instead, the team needs to discover how to become a team and how to offer each individual a valuable role on the team but keep everyone focused on the team's goals.

You play a key role in this. The better you understand the kind of closeness and cooperation that an effective team needs, the better you can pass this understanding on to team members. Particularly in the early stages of becoming a team, your help here is critical.

8-4   The Mistake: Not developing and living by team norms

The situation: "Why do you always have to put other people down?!" Kyle demanded.

"You're the one who gets personal about problems!" Sylvia responded.

"Hey, wait a minute," Vi broke in "I don't think we ought to talk to one another this way."

"Well, I wouldn't if Kyle didn't attack me instead of my ideas."

"Yeah—I think we ought to have rules about this kind of thing," Vi said emphatically."

"Who needs rules?" Kyle responded. "All we need to do is treat each other with a little respect."

Why was it a mistake?

The discussion disintegrated into personal attacks, then into comments about the attacks and what the team needed—with no resolution to any of the problems. It's not enough that team members should want to treat one another with respect. The team needs to develop ground rules that everyone commits to abide by. Until then, the scene above will be repeated again and again.

How can you recover from it quickly?

It's probably better not to try. You could interrupt at this point and suggest that the team develop team norms (ground rules). And it might work. But you'll have greater success if you wait until everyone calms down, the next day perhaps, and then call a team meeting to begin developing the team norms. The memory of the painful scene above will be fresh in everyone's minds, but they'll have calmed down enough to discuss it without as much emotion.

How can you consistently do it right from now on?

Get the team together. Explain that every team needs two kinds of norms: administrative norms and interpersonal norms. Administrative norms guide the conduct of meetings. For instance, "No meeting will last longer than one and one-half hours unless the team votes to extend it" is an administrative norm. Relationship norms describe how team members treat one another. "If an individual has not expressed an opinion, we will not assume that he either agrees or disagrees" is a relationship norm.

Don't assume that because a norm sounds good it is one that will work for the team. Here's an example:

> "I think this is an easy norm," Vi began. "We'll begin meetings on time and everyone will agree to be here when they start. That way, we won't have to waste time summarizing what's happened for someone who comes late."
>
> "Sounds good to me," Sylvia added.
>
> Kyle shook his head. "Hang on a minute. I have to make three or four customer visits a week, and there's just no way I can predict how long they'll last. I think it's a good idea for meetings to start on time, but we've got to find some way to cut me a little slack."
>
> "Would this work?" Sylvia asked. "Could we do our meetings first thing in the morning and you not schedule customer visits until afterward?"
>
> "It's worth a try, but it means that we need to agree on how long the meetings are going to be . . . ."

Why worry so much about administrative norms? Because if some team members have expectations even on minor matters that other members don't share, they can be a source of irritation and resentment to everyone. (Suppose Vi assumes that everyone should be at meetings on time and Kyle assumes that spending time with customers takes priority. If they don't find a norm they can both agree on, they may be a constant source of irritation to one another.)

A team must have relationship norms, though, to be effective. And each team member must commit to the norms and be willing to be called on them. How does that work? Let's suppose that the team has agreed that members will never label each other's ideas, but always respond to the content of the ideas. Here's how a situation might develop:

> "You know, we could simply agree not to accept calls on Wednesday afternoon and Friday afternoon. That way our customers would know what to expect but we wouldn't have to interrupt ourselves to handle calls at least for those two times."

> "What a harebrained idea, Sylvia! That's about as customer hostile as I've heard for . . ."

> "Hold it," Vi broke in. "That sure sounded like Kyle is labeling Sylvia's idea. Sylvia, did it feel that way to you?"

> "It sure did. I really felt put down.

> "Ok, you got me!" Kyle responded with a grimace. "I did label her idea. Let me put it another way. Sylvia, do you really think the idea would give us the kind of reputation with our customers we want?"

> "Thanks, that's much better," Sylvia responded. "Now, let me tell you why it occurred to me. . . ."

The team shouldn't waste time developing norms unless *everyone* on the team commits to living by them and enforcing them. As the example above illustrates, everyone has to be free to call everyone on a perceived violation, and has the right to expect the other individual to deal with the issue then and there.

When the team first begins to use norms, members may be hesitant to call one another on violations. You may have to intervene until everyone is comfortable insisting that the norms be respected. But get yourself out of the picture as quickly as possible and let team members take responsibility for enforcing the norms. That's part of being a team member.

Is doing what you did ever right?

No. If you have a team made up of individuals with a lot of experience on teams, they may unconsciously bring effective norms with them. But unless these norms are made explicit and committed to by everyone, they will sooner or later prove inadequate.

A tip for mistake-free managing:

One norm is critical for most teams: Always criticize ideas, never people. It's critical because it's so important, but also because so many individuals have never learned to practice it. For instance, how many times have you heard someone respond to an idea with "Oh, you're always trying to push that off on us" or "If you cared anything about costs, you'd never suggest that."

Why is it so critical? First, because when you attack a person rather than an idea you're inviting an emotion-laden response. For instance, the last comment in the paragraph above could easily draw a response like "What do you mean—you're the one who's always trying to get us to spend more money." The main point, whatever it was, is already lost, in a budding argument about who does best at controlling costs.

But there's at least one other reason. It's terribly difficult to judge an idea when it's first presented. What sounds like a fantastic idea may end up useless, while a really "dumb" idea may have the seed of a truly useful idea within it. A team that reacts to ideas emotionally in terms of individuals is unlikely to put in the time discussing and developing the ideas they need. See that the team recognizes every idea as a contribution and responds to it on its merits.

8-5   *The Mistake: Pushing the team to make decisions too quickly*

The situation:

"All right, I've given you all kinds of time to decide how to approach the special project for Engineering. I need you to make a decision."

"We will, boss," Shad replied. "We just have a lot of different ideas on how to approach it, and it's taking us time to decide which one is the best."

"Now teams are an excellent idea—you know I believe that. But we can't let the fact we're working as a team bog us down. We still have to make decisions quickly, you know."

"We know," Eileen chimed in, "but it takes time for us to give everyone a chance to be heard. And we think that's important."

"I'm sure it is, but getting a decision made is important, too. I need you to decide what approach you're going to use, and I need you to decide it quickly. . . ."

Why was it a mistake?

Particularly in the beginning stages, a team can take a long time to make a decision. It has to find a proper balance between reaching a conclusion and letting everyone be heard, between the requirements for a decision and the requirements for team participation. Pushing the team to make a quick decision interferes with their finding this balance. For instance, if pushed too hard a team may turn into one or two people offering ideas with the rest of the team rubber-stamping them. When a team does this, the members who aren't expressing their opinions and fully participating begin to lose commitment and motivation. Then the value of the team begins to decline sharply.

How can you recover from it quickly?

You can't cure the situation in general quickly, but you can deal effectively with this specific situation. All the manager has to do is add a few sentences to his last statement: "I need you to decide what approach you're going to use, and I need you to decide it as quickly as you can. But I also want you to take the time you need to see that everyone's ideas get considered. What do you think is a reasonable time for us to meet together again to see how close you're getting to a decision? . . ."

Note that this puts both factors back into the situation—making a decision without undue delay and not short-circuiting the team process.

How can you consistently do it right from now on?

Making a decision has three basic steps:

- *Step 1:* Identify a variety of alternatives.
- *Step 2:* Evaluate the alternatives.
- *Step 3:* Select the alternative to implement.

An individual can go through the steps relatively quickly. For a team to make effective decisions, however, it must involve all of its members at every step. This means that a team will often take longer to arrive at a decision, particularly while it's learning to function as a team. If it's given the time and guidance it needs to learn these decision-making skills, it will get more and more effective at making decisions.

How do you help the process along? You can explain the decision-making process itself just as we have here. You can also offer the following three tips:

1. First of all, encourage the team members to listen carefully to one another. Often each one's first impulse will be to wait impatiently for the other person to stop speaking so he or she can make his or her own contribution. The team needs everyone's contribution, but it also needs to listen carefully to that contribution and not rush past it to something else.

2. Second, encourage team members to ask questions that will help them understand what other people are getting at. An idea that turns out to be useful may sound awkward and even silly when it's first presented. The better each team member is at asking questions that draw out the heart of an idea, the better the team will function.

3. Third, caution the team not to rush. As they get more experienced at making decisions as a team, the process will go more quickly. But, in the beginning, team decisions will take a while. Until they become proficient, the team needs to take extra time to see that everyone gets listened to.

Is doing what you did ever right?

There are times when you need a quick decision, or when the team gets stuck in the process and can't seem to get to a decision. For instance, higher management may require the team to start acting immediately, but (as in this case) the team needs to spend time deciding how to begin. Or the team may have factions that normally work together but can't seem to agree on this particular decision.

What do you do? Telling the team to hurry up isn't normally the best answer. Instead, you might want to explain the time crunch to the team, acknowledge their normal decision style, and then offer an alternative: Either they can shortcut the normal process and make a decision more quickly, or you'll make the decision.

A tip for mistake-free managing:

Just as there are different levels of delegation to individual workers, there are different levels of delegation to teams. A fully self-managing team makes nearly all of its own decisions, but teams don't get to be self-managing overnight. While a good manager doesn't push the team to make a decision more rapidly than it should, he or she doesn't just tell the team to make decisions and then leave them alone to muddle through.

Your organization may have good training in team decision making, or you may be able to get the training from a community college or private contractor. By all means get it. But also be clear with the team how much authority it has. For instance, you may begin by asking the team to look at a problem or project and bring you their recommendations. Then you'll make the decision. When they get proficient at that level, you'll probably want to ask them to go a step further and make a tentative decision. You discuss the decision with the team, and it becomes the final decision unless you have specific objections.

The final level of delegation, the one that makes a team fully self-managing, is the authority to make and implement the decision. You expect the team to let you know what the decisions was; you may even ask them to give you a formal briefing. But none of this happens until *after* they've made the decision and begun to implement. That makes it clear that the decision is truly theirs.

8-6   The Mistake: Not supporting the team

The situation: Pali lost no time getting to his point: "Boss, you let us down!"

"You mean on the proposal for Finance?"

"Yes. We spent a lot of time on that, and then when they didn't like it you told them you'd have us come up with something different."

"After all, Pali, I do have the final responsibility for what we do. If our customer doesn't like what the team gives him, I have to take action."

"Yes—but you could have come to talk to the team first. It's awfully embarrassing to have a customer call and tell you your own boss has overruled you. . . ."

Why was it a mistake?

Either a team has the authority to make a decision or it doesn't. If it doesn't, you make the decision and everyone goes on from there. If it does, and then you later overrule its decision, you create an entirely different situation. The team will be disappointed and that much less willing to make any hard decisions in the future. Your customer will see that all he or she needs to do to get a team decision redone is, come directly to you. Have this happen just two or three times to and you'll be back to making most of the decisions, and the team will be a team in name only.

How can you recover from it quickly?

In this case, you can't. You've already overruled the team, and the customer knows it. All you can do now is start building so that the situation doesn't occur again.

How can you consistently do it right from now on?

Let's say that a year has passed. You've worked with the team, you trust their decisions, and you support them. Once again, the team prepares a proposal for Finance. Once again, Finance is unhappy with it, and Bert French, chief of the branch, calls you. You go through the pleasantries, and then this happens:

> "The reason I called you is the proposal your folks gave us yesterday. It really doesn't meet our needs, and I need you to do something about it."

> "I understand your concern, Bert, and we want to be responsive to you. Do you really want to handle it at our level, or do you want to let my folks work it out with your folks?"

> "I wouldn't have called if I didn't want you to get involved." Bert sounds a bit irritated.

> "That's fine. If your calendar's free day after tomorrow, I'd like you to put me and Heidi Schloss, the project leader for your area, down for a time that's convenient with you. I'll talk with Heidi tomorrow and have her explain the team's rationale to me. That way, I'll come prepared. Then we can meet, and after she goes over it with you we can discuss any changes you might want to make."

"Hey, I was thinking that just you and I could do this." Now Bert sounds puzzled.

"Maybe in the old days, but not today. My folks are really effective at working together, and I never even think of overruling them on anything without discussing it with them. Wait until you talk with Heidi; you'll see what I mean. . . ."

That takes care of the customer. What about the discussion with Heidi, the project manager? Let's listen:

"Heidi, you told me a couple of days ago that Finance wouldn't be happy with you, and you were right. Bert French called me yesterday afternoon and wanted me to come to talk with him."

Heidi looks a little edgy. "Are you going to?"

"Yes. Well, actually, both of us are going to talk with him. I want you to brief me sometime today on the items you think he's upset with and explain to me why the team came to the decision it did. That way, I can support you intelligently when we discuss it with him tomorrow."

"Good—but does that mean you're not going to change anything?"

"I'm not going to, no—but the team might. We both need to listen carefully to Bert's objections and take them seriously. I expect you to keep an open mind, particularly since you know I'm not going to just overrule you. If there are any items either you or I think should be reconsidered, we'll note them, give him a time when we'll give him an answer, and then the team can look at them. I might still overrule a specific item, but I wouldn't do it until I'd heard you and the team out—and Finance would never know I was the one who made the decision."

Is doing what you did ever right?

No. You never want to give the slightest impression that a customer can get around your team just by coming to you. We already noted what this does to the team.

A tip for mistake-free managing:

It's really tempting to play the "good guy." If higher management or a customer isn't happy with a decision made by your team, it feels good to step in and "correct" the problem. That is, it feels good to you and perhaps to the higher manager or customer, but it doesn't feel very good to the team.

This is the rule: Always let the team be the good guys. Never overrule them directly (except in the midst of an out-and-out crisis). See that the team continues to deal with the customer and, if possible, with the higher manager. If you must get involved, publicly support the team. If anything needs to be changed, do it in private with the team and let the team take credit for it.

If customers find that they never get a better deal from you than from the team, they'll stop coming to you before talking with the team. And even higher management might learn to deal directly with the team at times. That makes your job easier and the team more effective—a real "win-win" situation.

8-7   *The Mistake: Trying to prevent the team from surfacing and resolving conflict*

The situation: "I've called you all together because I was deeply disappointed in what I heard yesterday afternoon. You know that I stopped by to see how you were doing on the receipt processing redesign. What I heard was appalling—you grown people were arguing like a bunch of kids! I've never seen people go after one another the way you did. I started to interrupt then and there, but I thought I'd wait and give you a chance to cool down. Anyway, I don't want to see anything like that ever again."

Why was it a mistake?

Team members must be able to work together effectively. Working effectively, however, means recognizing conflict within the team, confronting it, and working through it to resolve it. None of this can happen, though, unless team members are free to express their opinions and defend them—even when this creates heated discussion. Trying to keep the conflict from occurring is precisely the wrong strategy. If the team gets the idea that it has to downplay or ignore conflict, it will fall into "group think" and be much less effective than a traditional work-group.

How can you recover from it quickly?

The way to recover from this one is not to have made the speech in the first place. Once it's made, the damage is done. Your best course of action is to start following the suggestions in the next section as quickly as possible.

How can you consistently do it right from now on?

Most workers in most traditional workgroups are taught not to create conflict. Those who do are often labeled "troublemakers." It's quite a change when these workers become part of closely knit teams, particularly teams that are expected to be self-managing. You need to help them understand that conflict is part of team performance and that their goal is to identify the conflict and then resolve it.

• *Conflict in itself isn't bad.* Conflict becomes harmful when it becomes personal, but it never has to be personal. Instead, fruitful conflict is conflict of ideas, without regard for *whose* ideas they are. Managers need to make clear to teams that conflict itself is never the problem. But teams do need to learn and use the most effective ways to express and resolve the conflict.

• *Teams need basic training in how to resolve conflict.* There are definite principles for identifying and resolving conflict. One such rule is "Keep personalities out of disagreements." But the team doesn't need to reinvent the wheel; competent training on how to resolve conflict is available in virtually every city of any size. Teams should always have the opportunity to get this training instead of having to muddle through on their own. And whenever possible, the team should take the training as a team, all at one time. That gives the members a chance to practice together in the class what they'll need to do when they return to the job.

• *Teams need the support of their managers.* What else does the team need? It needs a supportive manager—one who's willing to take the time to understand what the team needs to perform effectively and to see that the team gets it. You might volunteer to meet with the team and help it learn good listening techniques. Or you might offer to find an experienced facilitator to help the team learn to handle conflict. Exactly what you do doesn't matter as much as the fact that you take specific actions to be supportive.

It's rewarding to operate as a closely knit, self-managing team, but it's stressful to learn how to be one. When you clearly support the team and its learning process, you reduce the stress, both for the team and for yourself.

Is doing what you did ever right?

Not if you want the team to grow and succeed. The team needs to learn how to resolve conflict, not to repress it.

A tip for mistake-free managing:

As a manager, you need to steer the team between two extremes. At the one extreme is the avoidance of conflict, the temptation to "make nice" with everyone so that nothing disruptive happens. At the other extreme is continuing conflict, in which nothing ever seems to get settled. The closer a team moves to either extreme, the less effective it will become.

How do you help keep it away from the extremes? First, you need to be able to tolerate conflict yourself. That sounds easy, but you may not have had much training or experience at this. If you've worked in a typical organization, you learned to handle conflict by not letting it emerge. What happened if you had a serious disagreement with your boss? Did he or she invite you to express the disagreement openly, and then deal with the merits of what you said? Perhaps one or two of your best managers did, but they were definitely in the minority. Instead, if you disagreed you either swallowed the disagreement or found some roundabout way to express it. And the odds are good that your workers had to do the same with you.

Where conflict is concerned, you need to learn a set of new tricks. This manager did. Would you be tempted to squash conflict, or are you able to invite and entertain it as a way of getting the best possible team performance? The answer matters—it matters very much.

9-1 The Mistake: Not recognizing your boss' important issues

The situation:

"Do you have any idea what's up with the boss?" you ask your friend Gary one evening as the two of you head for the front door. "He's been acting like he's not happy about something I did, but he's never said anything to me about it. I'd think he'd be pleased, not upset. We did a really good job on the Vernon project, even corrected some of their misconceptions and gave them a better product than what they'd originally asked for. I can't imagine what he's got to be upset about."

"Actually, I think that's exactly the problem," Gary replies. "You know the boss has this thing about making the customer happy, even if what he wants isn't what's best for him. I overheard him say something about Vernon's just the other day—something about thinking we knew better than the customer what was good for him. And I could tell he was teed off about it too. What did you guys do over there?"

"All we did was point out that the two million dollars they were planning to spend on new equipment was money down the drain and show them that they could get along a lot better by overhauling the equipment they already had. Who could argue with that?"

"Well, I don't know any details. From what I heard they must have felt like they were sold up the river. You know how sticky the boss gets about that. He's made enough speeches and put stuff in the newsletter almost every other issue about customer preference, customer first, customer this and that. All that stuff about how it's

219

not enough to be right if the customer doesn't agree. Haven't you been listening?"

Why was it a mistake?

You can probably see pretty easily why it was important to be sensitive to your boss' important issues. You think you've done a great job on a project. He doesn't. Apparently you didn't even recognize that there was a conflict between the way you handled the project and one of your boss' "hot buttons." As a result, you violated the approach your boss wants you to follow, and he's not happy. Since by all objective criteria you've done good work for the customer (saved them money, improved their process), chances are that you'll never hear this criticism directly from your boss. But he'll remember—for a long, long time.

What kinds of things are important to managers? We can't generalize. One manager's hot button may be just the kind of customer approach we've described here. Sometimes the hot buttons seem like relatively trivial matters, but ones that really light up the boss. One manager we know was passionate about the terms used to refer to the people who worked for him. You could call them "associates" or "staff," but you could never call them "employees." That might seem like a truly petty issue, but for that particular manager the language used embodied all sorts of concepts about equality and empowerment in the workplace. And his staff learned to comply.

How can you recover from it quickly?

You can't. You've already made the faux pas, and the damage is already done. You need to concentrate on long-term solutions.

How can you consistently do it right from now on?

• *Listen carefully to what your boss emphasizes.* Sometimes the most critical messages are hidden—perhaps because they're so obvious to your boss that he assumes they're obvious to you too. Sometimes they're ideas that are so ingrained in your boss that he *can't* easily articulate them. But he lives them.

• *Notice which kinds of behavior tend to be rewarded and which aren't.* Two projects may appear to be of equal value, or two workers may appear to be equally competent and equally productive, but your boss rewards one and not the other. If you can figure out the difference, you may have a powerful clue about what's most important to your boss. Chances are that your boss consistently draws similar distinctions, but may not voice them. In that case, it's up to you to identify and observe them. Voiced or not, these are the criteria that count most.

• *Ask your boss about the issues you've identified that seem to be important to him.* When you think you've identified an important issue, but you're not sure what is expected of you or how to put your boss' wishes into practice, talk to him about how he sees that issue in terms of everyday work. These discussions can be great opportunities to get to know your boss and his approach to business much better.

You might begin by asking: "You've talked a lot about putting customers first and about how it's not good enough to be right if the customer doesn't agree, but sometimes it's difficult to know how hard to push when you know that what the customer is asking for isn't good for him and may even harm him. How would you handle something like that?"

Or you could begin on a more philosophical level: "Sometimes there seems to be a tension between what customers want and what's best for them. What do you see as our role as consultants? What are our professional responsibilities as experts in the field?"

Remember, these are issues that are near and dear to your boss' heart. Set aside some time for an in-depth discussion and make sure your boss has time available too.

• *Request feedback.* Once in a while, when an issue arises that's in one of the areas that you know is particularly important to your boss and you've handled it as well as you could in accord with what you think your boss is looking for, check back to see if you've interpreted his concerns correctly. After the smoke has cleared, check in with your boss. Describe the situation and how you handled it, then ask, "Is that what you were looking for? Would you have handled things differently? What could I have done better?"

This also is a discussion that you want to leave some time for. A thoughtful response won't necessarily be immediate or short.

Is doing what you did ever right?

It is never a good idea to ignore your boss' concerns. Even though you may believe that he's getting caught up in irrelevancies at the expense of the "real work," remember that he has a vantage point you don't have. There are probably good and sufficient reasons for his concerns, and they're undoubtedly shaped by a lot of previous experiences. And the bottom line is that, even if they *are* irrelevant and trivial issues, they're still *his* issues—and he's still the boss.

A tip for mistake-free managing:

How well do you explain to *your* workers the issues that are important to you and why they're important? At a number of points in this chapter, we'll ask you to measure your behavior against your boss'. Oftentimes the things that are most vexing about your relationship with him are just the kinds of issues about which your workers become most irritated with you.

And so in this case: If your workers know what's important to you and why, they'll be much more likely to comply, both because they'll know exactly what's expected of them and because they'll understand the rationale for its importance. Especially if your perceptions have been shaped by some critical experience or incident, it helps if you can relate that story to your staff and explain the conclusions you drew or the changes you made in your own behavior as a result. The more concrete you can make the issue and your expectations, the easier it will be for your workers to adopt the behavior you're seeking.

9-2   *The Mistake: Not working to make your boss successful*

The situation: "Yeah, so what if I forgot to send a copy of that BoldFil letter of appreciation up to the front office. I don't know why Evelyn's so worked up about that," you complain to one of the other managers. "It's not like she can't take care of herself. She certainly knows how to blow her own horn when it suits her. And why should she get the credit for that account anyway? I'm the one who did all the work."

"Get real," your cohort replies. "The big boss probably doesn't even know we exist. BoldFil was a hot project. It makes sense to me that Evelyn wants to get as much mileage out of it as she can."

"That may be so, and I can't blame her for wanting to look good with her boss. But being her public relations flunky isn't what they're paying me for."

Why was it a mistake?

Obviously, you have a misperception about your role in the organization. Sure, you're responsible for making sure that your part of the organization runs smoothly. And you're responsible for performing particular projects and assignments. And you're responsible for keeping customers happy and coming back. But you're also responsible for being a good subordinate to your boss. And the first law of effective subordinateship is this: *You have no responsibility greater than that of helping your boss be successful. None. Nada. Zip. Period.*

Does this sound harsh and manipulative and scheming and otherwise unsavory? Stop and think a moment about what you expect from your workers. Don't you want them to help make you successful? And when you're successful, doesn't that give your team greater stature in the organization? Doesn't it make the whole workgroup more successful?

Just as you expect your subordinates to support you, your boss expects you to support her. It's that simple.

How can you recover from it quickly?

Apologize to Evelyn for the misunderstanding: "Evelyn, I'm sorry that I forgot to send a copy of BoldFil's letter to the front office. I know we're trying to get support on some of our initiatives, and having that letter from such an important customer would help our credibility. You can count on me to be more vigilant next time. I'll be sure to pass on all the kudos we receive. You've got my support."

How can you consistently do it right from now on?

• *Look for opportunities to share credit.* The only person who really needs to know how wonderful you are is your own boss. Of course it's nice to be recognized by other managers, and even by higher level managers in your organization. But if your boss is happy with you, she'll reflect that in her interactions with other managers and people above her in the chain of command. You'll get the recognition you deserve, along with the recommendations for awards and promotions, but through your own boss.

Once you recognize that basic rule of progression, it becomes much easier to let go of the credit and help your boss look good. When work is well done, there's plenty of glory to share. Whenever the "higher ups" recognize your unit for outstanding performance, be sure to acknowledge the contributions of your boss to the effort—her support and encouragement, her suggestions, her willingness to run interference on difficult projects, perhaps her ideas and specific participation. She'll appreciate your loyalty, and your reward will follow.

• *Make sure your boss sees the good work that you do.* As a subordinate manager, you probably don't have a lot of opportunities to interface directly with your boss' superiors. She's more likely to be the one who reports successes to the front office. Make sure she's well-armed. If your unit gets a letter of appreciation or a note from a satisfied customer, if one of your workers gets an award or is recognized by another organization for helping out, if you achieve especially challenging performance goals or beat your goals—make sure your boss knows about your achievements, so she can pass on the information to her superiors and share in the credit.

• *Help your boss prepare for criticisms that arise.* One of the worst mistakes you can make is to let your boss get blindsided by criticism she wasn't prepared for. Whenever problems arise that are likely to come to your boss' attention, make sure she hears about them from you first. That advice doesn't just apply when you've made an error, it applies even if you know you may be *accused* of making an error: "Evelyn, I've heard from one of our reps that we're likely to get some complaints about the BoldFil project. Thought you ought to hear about them before anything comes up officially."

Then make sure she knows the real story, so she's prepared to respond to the complaint.

• *Foster a sense of participation and supportiveness in your own workgroup.* The corporate world works best when everyone on the team supports everyone else. Your support of your boss should be part of a larger effort to support the company as a whole so that everyone can be successful. Do you share credit with your subordinates? Do you recognize their contributions? When you talk to your boss, do you mention contributions your workers have made that are especially worthwhile?

When you support your group and they support you, that mutual respect and team spirit will naturally carry over to other relationships within the company, including those with your peers and your boss.

Is doing what you did ever right?

Failing to take pains to make sure your boss gets credit for a project (or has the means to claim credit) is not a fatal mistake unless it becomes a pattern of behavior. If you consistently fail to act to make your boss successful, she'll notice that you're not acting as a team player. When you don't support your boss, she'll be less likely to support you.

A tip for mistake-free managing:

The single most important contribution you can make to your boss' success is your own successful performance. Even though it's tempting to get caught up in office politics and the trappings of success, competence still counts—a lot. The manager who is all glitz and glitter but without depth is soon pegged as all show and no substance. Effective managers have both political skills and leadership skills—the skill to lead a group to produce outstanding work consistently, as well as skill in identifying and sharing the credit to be gained.

9-3   The Mistake: Knuckling under to your boss

The situation: "I see just what you mean, Doris. I'll go right back and see that we change those accounts to stop the automatic billing notices."

You walk away from your conversation with Doris, fuming and fussing to yourself. You know that collections have improved markedly since you began the automatic reminders for delinquent customer accounts. And there haven't been any complaints at all. The notices are respectfully phrased; they're not threatening, and some customers actually seem to appreciate being reminded that they've forgotten to make a payment. It saves them interest charges too. If only you'd been able to say all that to Doris, but then she'd probably overrule you anyway. So what's the use?

Why was it a mistake?

Supervisors don't have all the answers. You don't, do you? So why should you think that Doris knows as much as you do about your billing procedures?

But she can't make good decisions unless she's well informed. And she'll never be well informed if you fold every time she criticizes, or even questions, one of your processes. You need to be prepared to explain and justify those processes that are working well, as well as admit when some aren't working well.

When you knuckle under at the first hint of disagreement from your boss, you reduce your value to the organization—big time. Part of your value as a first-line manager is your more in-depth knowledge of the work and how it relates to other parts of the organization. Failing to share that with your supervisor, even when it means disagreeing with her, does you, her, and the company a disservice.

How can you recover from it quickly?

Return to Doris and ask to revisit the decision she just made: "Doris, on my way back to the office, I had some second thoughts about the change in billing procedures we just discussed. I understand your concern about not wanting to alienate customers, but this has been my experience with the new process we've instituted . . ."

This is a respectful, but clear, way to reopen the discussion. It's not threatening to Doris, nor does it challenge her authority to make the decision she did, but it ensures that she has all the information she needs to make a better decision.

How can you consistently do it right from now on?

• *Be prepared.* If you don't know any more about your processes than Doris does, it's hard to convince her that your methods are more effective. Get to know the flow of every major segment of work that your unit is responsible for. You needn't learn it in the depth that your workers do, but you should understand how work moves from one step to the next and what happens at each stop along the way.

Learn the goals of each process: Who is the work produced for? What does that customer do with it? Is it the input for another process? Or information used to make a decision? Or maybe the decision itself? Who is affected if the work is done poorly? How important is the work? How visible to others?

What are the management concerns connected to the process? In this example, are higher-level managers more concerned with recovering accounts due to the company? Or are they more concerned about not doing anything to alienate good customers? Are there ways to reconcile conflicting goals?

And what are your boss' high priority issues? What kinds of concerns do you need to keep in mind when you discuss work methods and processes with her?

• *Develop a confident, but respectful style of discussion.* Are you concerned that you'll be seen as argumentative if you disagree with the boss? That's not necessarily so. There are two ways you can present your point of view: You can be *aggressive*, or you can be *assertive*. Assertiveness works. Aggression doesn't.

Aggression sounds like this: "That's all wrong, Doris. If you keep us from sending these automatic reminder notices, we'll never get anyone to pay their bills. You may have lots of customers, but you'll never earn any income from any of them. Are you trying to ruin the company—on my back?"

See the accusatory style? Notice that the attack becomes personal: "Are you trying to ruin the company?" The focus is not on the issue of reminder notices, it's shifted to Doris herself. The attack is made up of very pointed remarks, and the emotional level of the speaker is high. If not actually shouting, the speaker has probably at least raised his voice and might be pointing his finger or shaking his head at Doris as he speaks—emphasizing his message with negative body language.

In contrast, assertiveness sounds like this: "Doris, I understand your concern about not wanting to get customers teed off at us for badgering them with reminder notices. But we've also developed a real problem in getting people to pay their bills. I think we can work out a solution that will meet both those concerns, and here's why . . ."

This is an entirely different approach. It lets Doris know that you disagree with her direction, but it's not offensive. It focuses on the issue entirely. Notice that the speaker never explicitly says, "Doris, you're wrong." Instead, he acknowledges Doris' legitimate concern and then points out the difficulties with her approach. Doris knows that he's listened and *thought about* the things she's concerned about. So she'll be more willing to listen to his equally valid concerns. The approach is sensitive, almost deferential. And the discussion is reasonable and calm—no wagging fingers or shaking heads here. You can almost see yourself smiling and nodding as you explain to Doris the other piece of the puzzle. And together, you will solve it in an open give-and-take exchange.

• *Offer alternatives.* Suppose that, after your very reasonable explanation, Doris says, "I'm still not comfortable with the reminder process we've set up. I understand your position, but I still think our customers will feel as if we're badgering them." What then? *Now* do you knuckle under?

No. Not yet. Now you present one or two alternatives that move progressively closer to Doris' position without capitulating completely.

What if you sent out reminder notices only for bills sixty days past due instead of thirty days? What if you re-worded the reminder notices? What if they looked more like personal letters than computer-generated dunning notices?

There may still be a compromise you can reach with Doris that will effectively meet both of your interests. Pursue that until you have reached a satisfactory solution, or until it becomes apparent that Doris has moved (if at all) as far as she's going to. She may call off discussion herself: "I hear your position, but this is what I want. I don't see any point in more discussion."

Or it may be apparent from the tone of her voice or her expression that she's heard enough and isn't going to change her mind.

At that point, accede gracefully and be prepared for the next issue that comes up.

Is doing what you did ever right?

If the issue is one that's not of particular importance to the achievement of your workgroup's overall goals or if it's one that you don't have a very strong opinion about, one way or the other, there's no problem with knuckling under right away. But if the issue is important or if you have strong, reasoned arguments for doing things a different way, it's your responsibility to voice your objections. Not to bring out the difference of opinion isn't fair to your workgroup or to your boss.

A tip for mistake-free managing:

A valuable management skill is knowing when to fight and when to walk away. Some battles just aren't worth the effort. When your boss is especially sensitive about a topic or issue, when the weight of the whole organization is poised in the other direction, when the issue is a relatively minor part of a much larger concern, these are all times when you need to stop and think about whether this is a battle that's worth waging.

On the other hand, those may be just the times when your disagreement is *most* valuable to the organization. You've probably heard the fable about the "trip to Abilene" that illustrates the dangers of being too agreeable and ending up somewhere no one wanted to be. Sometimes your lone dissent is just what's needed to encourage the rest of the group to reconsider a position they've taken or a step they're about to take.

As a manager, you need both courage to speak up and restraint to keep from speaking up at the wrong time—and the wisdom to know the difference.

9-4   *The Mistake: Not acting like a team player*

The situation:

"What's with you and Herb?" Loretta, one of the other unit managers, asks you. "He treats you like a pariah—not exactly hostile, but as if he doesn't want to be around you anymore."

"Yeah, I've noticed the change," you reply thoughtfully. "I don't know of anything I've done to make him unhappy. In fact, I thought he'd be happy about the last quarter's statistics. Instead, he seems to hold it against me that my team's been successful."

"I think you've hit the nail on the head," adds Grady, another manager. "He thinks you're just out to make yourself look good, even at the expense of the rest of us. I don't see you that way, but there are times when I can see why he does. What about staff meeting last week when you started arguing with him about his work-at-home policies? You got really agitated about that one, and some of the other folks there looked as if they weren't too comfortable being part of it."

"Well, I'd think he'd be glad somebody is willing to stand up to him. I'm not out to undermine him or anything. I'm just trying to be helpful. I guess he must not see it that way."

"I don't think it's that you're doing anything bad," explains Grady. "I think it's just the impression you give, as if you know what you're doing and he doesn't, or as if your unit does well just because of you, not because of anything anyone else does. It's all just a matter of style."

Why was it a mistake?

It's *not* just a matter of style. Although self-aggrandizement is condoned in a very limited number of occupations, in most companies people are valued for their contributions to a team, not for their ability to make themselves look good. That's more than a "style" of interacting. It's a whole attitude toward work and working within a company.

Your boss, and his superiors, won't value the real contributions you make to the organization if he also thinks that you're out for his job, that you're out to make yourself look good (especially at others' expense), that you always have to be right, or that you won't work with the team to make everyone successful.

When you don't work actively to support others (and make it clear that you *are* being supportive), they won't support you either. And we all need support from someone else, sooner or later.

How can you recover from it quickly?

The perception that you're not acting like a team player isn't one that's built overnight, nor will it be cured overnight. You *can* begin immediately to change the perception, though, by following the tips below.

How can you consistently do it right from now on?

For most of the mistakes we've discussed in this book, we've offered you positive steps to take to avoid making the same mistake in the future. We've told you how to do it right the next time.

Here, it is as important to know what *not* to do as it is to know what you should do. So here's a list of actions guaranteed to convince your boss that you're *not* on his team.

• *Grabbing the glory.* When a project is completed successfully, when your unit's production statistics look great, when a new cost-saving idea has been effectively implemented—how do you react? Do you congratulate yourself for your great achievement? Or do you downplay your own contribution, and share the credit with your workgroup and with your boss?

When you take all the credit for yourself, no one else will give you any, even when it's due.

• *Fighting in public.* When you disagree with your boss or with another manager, how do you react? Do you jump right in and take the first swing (figuratively, of course) by attacking the idea, the person, the unit? Do you always have to be right? Do you embarrass your boss or your peers by correcting their errors in front of others?

When you're so convinced of your own "rightness," everyone else will be irresistibly drawn to disagree—just to prove you wrong for once.

• *Telling tales out of school.* When you think your boss has made a poor decision, when one of the other unit managers messes up a project, when things seem disorganized or stalemated—to whom do you talk? Do you spread the bad news through the hallways? Do you "confide" in the other managers on the putting green? Do you discuss the problem with your friends at corporate headquarters?

When you can't keep bad news at home, other people will look for bad news to spread about you too.

• *Being a "naysayer."* How do you respond to others' ideas and suggestions? Do you always have a critical word to offer? Are you the official "devil's advocate" for any proposal that's offered? Can you always do the suggester "one better" or do you freely acknowledge good ideas that come from others?

When you never support others' ideas, you'll have a hard time finding support for your own.

How do you convince your boss that you *are* a team player?

• *Give credit where credit is due.* When your workgroup completes a project successfully, be sure their contributions are recognized. When your boss is a part of that success, be sure to thank him for his help. You don't need to toady or give credit that's not deserved, but you *do* need to emphasize others' contributions rather than your own achievements. Demonstrate by the way you credit others that the team's success is more important to you than any individual accomplishment.

• *Handle disagreements and errors sensitively.* Just as you don't want to be embarrassed by your mistakes and errors in judgment, neither do your boss or your peers. Disagree calmly and respectfully, emphasizing the issues and the areas of agreement. Start with your common ground, then extend to areas where you don't share the same views.

• *Keep inside matters inside.* Don't air your organization's dirty linen in public. Instead, work from within to make things better so that the image you can present to the rest of the world will be positive and confidently successful. During tough times, act as a pillar of strength to bolster others' confidence.

• *Encourage others' ideas; don't discourage innovation by criticizing every new idea.* If you're not making mistakes, you must not be doing anything new. And any change involves some trial and error. Be supportive during that process by offering encouragement and suggestions for improvement, rather than negatives and critical comments.

Is doing what you did ever right?

Once you've established yourself as a dedicated team player within the organization, you can brag once in a while about something your group has done particularly well. You can almost *always* voice your concerns about a decision or direction the organization is taking, but a confrontational approach usually backfires.

So, although individual actions we've discussed here may sometimes be acceptable, it's *never* good management practice to act as if you're not part of the team. Your contribution to the team's success is the main reason why you're in this position.

A tip for mistake-free managing:

Many managers are chosen from among the ranks of the best, most technically competent workers in the organization. But the skills needed for technical success and the skills needed for managerial success aren't always the same. One big difference is in the approach to assignments. While there are still a significant number of jobs in which an individual worker needs to be concerned about only his own individual accomplishment, management requires that your focus be on the team as a whole. The shift in emphasis is critical to your success as a manager.

9-5   The Mistake: Not taking on high-payoff but risky assignments

The situation:	"I don't know about this, Zephnie," you grumble to your boss. "We've never tried to do focus groups before. We're good at questionnaires and personal interviews for gathering information, but this is something we just don't know much about. I don't want to jump into something brand new and have us fall flat on our collective faces."

"Look here," Zephnie argues, "we've done all kinds of analysis projects before, and we've got a good reputation in the field. But if we don't stick our necks out this once and try something new, our customers are going to go somewhere else, and not just for focus groups but for all kinds of other research projects as well. We just have to get up to speed on this fast and make this bid. We can do some learning on the job, since we'll be doing other data collection work at the same time. And we certainly know what to do once we get the data. I just don't see that we have any real choice but to give it a try. And if you're among the first groups to actually get this process working, you'll be a real hero."

"I'm sorry, Zephnie. I know Frank's group is anxious to try this out, but I'm just not ready to sign up. This isn't just like a personal interview. There are certain kinds of questions to ask and different techniques to get people talking and get the information we need. We should have some time to learn and practice before we take on an assignment like this. I'm afraid that unless you order me, I'm going to have to pass on this project."

Why was it a mistake?

Running a business is a series of risks. Will the public like this product? Will sales be high enough to cover expenses? Will technology save us money or will it drive up our costs just to stay competitive? Do we have the skills to take on this work? As a manager, one of the things you manage is risk. The company that's not moving ahead is really running behind, so change and its accompanying risks are inevitable. Your job is to manage the changes in such a way that the likelihood of success is increased and the costs of failure are minimized.

How can you recover from it quickly?

Tell Zephnie that you've reconsidered. Ask her to set up an initial session with you, her, Frank, and any other units that are going to be involved in the project to see how it can best be managed. Then get to work to convince your unit that this is a risk worth taking.

How can you consistently do it right from now on?

We're not suggesting that you find the nearest lion and stick you head in its mouth. What we're suggesting is that you support your boss in taking reasonable risks that are necessary to further the organization's goals.

In assuming an assignment that has significant risks (even though there may be high payoffs in the end), there are some things you can do to increase the chances of success and to minimize the chances of failure. How can you do that?

• *Assess the risks realistically.* What stands in the way of your success? Here, you're concerned that your team doesn't have the skills it needs (and can't get them in time) to perform competently. In another case, you might not have the equipment you need. Or you might not have the management support you need. Or the factors may be entirely outside the company's control. The public might not like a new product you're bringing to market, despite all the preliminary research results. You might invest in new technology and find that it complicates the job without any payback. There are myriad things that *might* go wrong in any project. One of your first steps is to identify what is *most likely* to.

• *Do damage control* before *the damage occurs.* What happens if your people can't learn the new skills in time to perform competently on this project? Does the whole project come to a grinding halt? Are there other methods you could use to gather the data that might compensate for the inadequacies in the new methodology?

Develop a fallback strategy, something you can do to save the project or minimize the damage if your risks do materialize.

Sometimes that's not possible. What you're taking on is all or nothing. Even then you can be prepared to backtrack if everything falls apart. A number of years ago a major soft drink manufacturer decided to change the formula for one of the world's best-selling cola drinks. *That* was an all-or-nothing venture. The change was announced with great hoopla and fanfare—and fell absolutely flat. To this day, we're hard pressed to find anyone who liked the "new" cola. But the company recovered almost overnight by reintroducing its original cola drink as the "classic" version. Within a few weeks, while folks were still laughing over the company's marketing blunder, its cola drinks were as popular as ever.

You may not be able to devise a recovery that spectacular, but you probably also won't ever have a failure that horrendous (or visible). The point is that, with careful planning, you can prepare in advance for almost any problem that may occur.

• *Enlist the support of your superiors.* While your boss clearly wants you to accept this risk, what about *her* superiors? Especially if this high risk assignment is also a high-visibility assignment, you'll want to be sure that everyone up the chain of command knows what you're trying to accomplish, its potential payoff, and the risks incurred. Your boss' assistance is important to getting the support you need from higher management. But she can't do it alone. You need to arm her with the information at your disposal so she can sell your project.

Having the support of higher levels in the company doesn't give you permission to fail, but it does guarantee that, if the project *does* fail, you won't be left hanging.

• *Enlist the support of your staff.* The people on whose shoulders the success of this assignment rests are the staff members who will actually carry it out. They also need to get pumped up to go out and conquer this project. Like your superiors, your staff needs to know why you're taking on the assignment, what it involves, and what its risks and payoffs are. They also need to participate in assessing the risks and in figuring out how to control any damage before it occurs. This is a team effort, and the team should be involved in the planning as well as the execution. That's the only way to get the buy-in you need to complete the assignment successfully.

Is doing what you did ever right?

It depends. Sometimes turning down a risky project is *exactly* the right response. The next case describes a way to identify those projects that have high enough potential for payoff to be worthwhile and those that should be set aside. But remember that one of the benefits you accrue when you accept a risky assignment at your superiors' behest is the appreciation of those superiors. Many managers—at all levels—have the same fear of failure you do, even though they recognize the necessity of trying new ideas and accepting challenges. Your willingness to be a guinea pig for an occasional experiment marks you as a loyal, contributing member of the management team. And reinforcing that perception is a benefit that can't be ignored.

A tip for mistake-free managing:

The inevitable outcomes of risky assignments are that sometimes you win and sometimes you lose. Good managers recognize that people do make mistakes and that mistakes are an inevitable part of change and improvement. No one gets every-thing right the first time. NO ONE. When you accept mistakes from your staff that are made in the course of well-reasoned, sincere efforts at innovation, you encourage more innovation. But when your people are afraid to make mistakes, they'll also be afraid to try anything new. Remember what we said before? If you're not mov-ing ahead, you're falling behind. And the only way to move ahead is to try new ideas. Some will work and some won't. But you'll never have the chance to find out if your workers are so focused on perfection that they're not willing to experiment.

9-6   The Mistake: Taking on risky projects with little payoff

The situation: "Sure, I'd be happy to work on that change management program with Brice," you volunteer enthusiastically. "You know I like a challenge."

"Looks more like a suicide mission than a challenge to me," Vikki remarks wryly. "Nobody except you and Brice care anything about this project, but you could both fall flat on your faces if it comes out badly. Why would anyone in his right mind volunteer for something like that? Not only are you and Brice going to look like fools, but Jan is going to have to bail you out. How happy do you think she's going to be about that?"

Well, you have to admit you hadn't looked at it from that angle before. This scheme of Brice's just seemed like something that would be interesting to try out—a kind of self-affirmation system to encourage people to enthusias-tically embrace change. But if your boss gets caught up in it because it flopped, she probably *won't* be very happy, will she?

Why was it a mistake?

There are projects that are worth falling on your sword for and projects that aren't. Whatever Brice has cooked up here looks like a sure miss, a corporate lose-lose situation. If you don't succeed, your boss will have to bail you out. And if you do succeed, all you'll get is a big yawn from everyone else. That's the prob-lem with this particular project.

The bigger problem is that by using poor judgment in deciding when it's the right time to put yourself and your unit at risk, you undermine Jan's confidence in your supervisory abilities. She'll wonder whether you're a kind of will-o'-the-wisp, chasing after every fantastic proposal that comes along. That lowers your credibility among the management team and makes your boss less likely to trust you with the really sensitive and important issues.

How can you recover from it quickly?

Easy. Unless you're already so far along on the project that backing out would mean certain failure for Brice and leaving him hanging out to dry alone, you tell him that you've reconsidered the payoffs and the risks and decided that the project isn't worth the potential losses. If you can, you might offer some alternative sources of help to Brice, but, even better, encourage him to reconsider his involvement in the project too. The reasons for your backing out early are equally applicable to him.

How can you consistently do it right from now on?

• *Weigh the risks and benefits of any new project that seems to have significant risks.* Have you ever heard of cost-benefit analysis? It's a rather technical-sounding term for a process of evaluating the risks and the payoffs of any endeavor to decide whether it's worthwhile. In its most elaborate form, it entails mathematical modeling of probabilities and application of sophisticated statistical formulas. But you can do essentially the same kind of analysis much more simply.

1. Draw a line down the middle of a sheet of paper (or columns on your computer, if you'd rather). Label one side "risks" and the other "payoffs."

2. Now list, under the appropriate heading, all the factors you can think of that should affect your decision whether to volunteer for the project. Risks could include long start-up times, equipment investments that may not be recouped, harm to your reputation if you fail, lack of support from your superiors or from your own staff, lack of available staff to work on the project, or the need to divert staff from other projects to take on this one. Payoffs might include enhanced reputation in the organization if you succeed, increased sales or profits, enhanced skills among your staff, the opportunity to justify investments in equipment or technology that you couldn't justify otherwise, or a chance to develop contacts in your industry or discipline that wouldn't be available without this project.

At this point, list *every* potential benefit and cost you can think of. Don't worry about whether the likelihood of the cost or benefit is high or low or whether the magnitude of the cost or benefit is great or small. This is like a brainstorming exercise. First you list all the factors you can, then you evaluate them.

3. This is the first step in evaluating the potential costs and benefits you've identified. At this step, you classify each cost and each benefit by assigning it to a category—A, B, or C.

    An "A" is a cost or benefit that's almost certain to occur and is very important or of large magnitude. If the risk to your reputation is high and is very likely to occur because the project is likely to fail, then the cost you've identified as "harm to reputation" should be an "A."

    A "C" is a cost or benefit that's not very likely or isn't very important. If the project might develop skills in your staff that they don't have already, but those skills aren't very important and aren't likely to be helpful in other projects in the future, then the benefit "enhanced skills of staff" should be a "C." If you have to buy a new computer to work on the project, but you'd likely have bought one anyway, then "equipment costs" might be a "C."

    A "B" is anything in between. You may have a tendency to make everything a "B" ("just to be safe"), but that will defeat the purpose of classifying. Some risks and payoffs will clearly be more important than any of the others. Those are "As." And some aren't likely to occur or really don't matter much, even if they do. Those are "Cs." "Cs" are still worth listing, regardless of their individual importance. Sometimes there's no one big reason for taking or turning down a project, but there are lots of little things that, cumulatively, do make a difference—if you take the time to identify them.

4. Next, you do a little math. Score each "A" item a 5, each "B" item a 3, and each "C" item a 1. (Why score 5, 3, 1 instead of 3, 2, 1? The wider spread gives you a better picture of the real importance of items.) Add up the scores for each column. Then compare the two column totals.

5. That's not quite the end of the analysis. There's one more step that's a kind of a "pit of the stomach" test. It goes like this: When you look at the numbers at the bottom of each list, how do they *feel?* Even though we've assigned numerical values to these factors, making management decisions isn't an exact science. All we've tried to do is to express externally what's already been swimming around in your brain and your heart internally.

If the numbers and your "pit of the stomach" feeling are in sync, you've made your decision.

If they're not, go back and look at your factors again. Have you identified everything that's really important? Remember, this is *your* list; factors that are important to you that you might not want to share with your boss are still fair game. Have you weighed everything the way you really believe it should be weighed? If so, and the numbers still don't match, find somebody to help talk you through the decision. It could be your boss, or a peer manager, or even someone on your staff who has good management instincts. The numbers we've derived here are not a formula; they're only a guide.

• *Once you've made your decision, stick with it.* You now have a good, solid basis for talking with Brice about his proposed project. You also have well-defined reasons to present to your boss to justify your decision. Even if she wasn't aware that Brice had approached you with this idea, you might want to let her know about the offer and your reasons for declining. Knowing that you have thought through the decision carefully and logically, she'll be more comfortable with other decisions you make in the future.

Is doing what you did ever right?

Only if the payoffs are very high. In that instance, look at the preceding case to find out why you *should* accept the project.

A tip for mistake-free managing:

Deciding whether to accept or reject a new project isn't the only application for the cost-benefit technique we've discussed here. You can apply it any time you have a decision to make that involves some risk to you or your workgroup. Decisions like whether to hire a particular applicant, whether to make an equipment investment, whether implementing a new policy is likely to cause grievances, whether you can sustain a disciplinary action against an employee—these are all occasions when you need to weigh the risks and the payoffs before making a decision. Getting comfortable with the process through repeated applications will help make it almost automatic and will give you a better basis for making those difficult decisions.

9-7 The Mistake: Telling your boss "that's not my job"

The situation: "I'd like you to handle the inspection reports for the next couple of months while Griff is recovering from his surgery," your boss tells you.

"You know I don't mind filling in," you reply. "But Pam's section can handle that a lot better than we can, and I'm pretty backed up right now. Maybe you could let her slide on some of the initiatives tracking she's been doing so she'd have the resources to do the inspection reports. I don't think she'd mind."

"I suppose I could ask Pam," muses your boss. "It seems to me, though, as if you've got a couple of people who aren't too busy right now. I'd rather your section covered for Griff."

"There are one or two people who have a little slack," you admit, "but they're not people who could handle the reports, and I really don't have time to handle them myself. I think this is a lot closer to Pam's area of responsibility, so it would be much easier for her to take on the reports."

"Well, I'll talk to her and see what she says. I can usually count on Pam to help out. But I may still have to ask you to handle them if she's too overloaded."

Why was it a mistake?

We assume that no one who's made it to the managerial ranks would be so crass as to actually say, "That's not my job." But there are lots of subtle, albeit equally clear, ways to convey the same message.

Telling your boss you're unwilling to handle an assignment is a violation of one of the fundamental commandments of corporate life: *You must participate enthusiastically in any reasonable endeavor for which your superiors ask your assistance.*

Why? For several reasons:

1. First, because your boss is counting on you to help. Your dependability and cooperation are important assets that helped you *get* a managerial job and will be essential in your keeping it.

2. A related reason is that your avoidance of the assignment will be an indication that you're not a team player. Even though you may think that the assignment is beneath you or that you shouldn't be asked to cover for someone else, remember that what goes around comes around. Your unwillingness to support the team when one of its members is down will translate into the team's unwillingness to support you when you need it some time in the future.

3. Finally, your refusal to help out will make more work both for your boss (who now has to find someone else to cover the assignment) and for the other manager who gets the work. Neither will be pleased at your refusal to carry a fair share of the load. This is more than simply not playing as part of the team; it's a shifting of workload that you could have covered. That's worse than not helping— it's hurting the others.

How can you recover from it quickly?

Catch your boss before he approaches Pam with his request. Tell him that you've reviewed your workload and decided that you could cover Griff's inspection reports while he's recovering. Apologize for any negative impression you may have given, perhaps by implying that you weren't trying to avoid work, but wanted only to make sure the work was covered as effectively as possible. (That's not true at all here, and your boss probably knows it, but offering the explanation will help you to save face, and your boss will likely be gracious in accepting your explanation.)

How can you consistently do it right from now on?

You want to maintain a balance. You want to be cooperative, but you don't want to be taken advantage of.

• *Cooperation*: Whenever your boss needs someone to cover an assignment or take on additional workload, keep in mind your own ongoing workload. Make a good-faith effort to evaluate whether you could take on the additional assignment without substantial degradation of the work you're already performing. If you can, then you're in a position to accept the new assignment enthusiastically (without, of course, implying that your unit normally doesn't have enough to keep itself productively occupied): "Yes, we'd be glad to help out for a few weeks. We've got a new project starting in about a month that's going to take up most of our resources, but in the meantime we could fill in with no problem."

• *Not being taken advantage of*: When your workload is truly overwhelming, so that any additional assignments will seriously hurt your ability to perform the work you're already assigned, you must let your boss know that you're not in a position to accept anything new. That's not being uncooperative; it's being realistic. You know the limitations of your own staff better than anyone else. Make sure your boss also understands what they are.

If he insists that you take on the workload (probably because he doesn't have anyone else he can give it to), examine your current assignments to see if there's anything you're doing now that really doesn't need to be done, or doesn't need to be done to the same level of exactness. Once you've identified that work, stop doing it, or change the way it's being done. That may require the concurrence of your superiors, but often there are steps in your processes that could be shortened or reports that could be eliminated without anyone noticing at all. Anything you're doing that no one else notices is a good candidate for elimination. And unless you can identify an extraordinarily good reason for continuing the task, stop doing it.

There's one other time when it's not only acceptable to decline an assignment, it's necessary that you decline. That's when you're asked to take on a project in an area in which you neither have the skills on the staff nor the means to acquire the skills in the near term. If your boss wants you to take on review of engineering drawings, but your staff members are all administrative workers who have little or no familiarity with drawings and specifications, you have no choice but to decline. Your boss may sincerely believe that people with jobs such as your staff perform could do the assignment. But if you know that you couldn't do the work competently, even with a reasonable period to get up to speed, you have an obligation to refuse.

Taking on work you're not qualified to perform hurts the company; it doesn't help. The result will be either significant rework further down the production chain or poor products sent to customers. Neither is acceptable.

Is doing what you did ever right?

Not unless "uncooperative" is an adjective you'd like to see on your next performance review.

A tip for mistake-free managing:

What happens to your work when your unit gets overloaded or you're short on staff? Does your boss have to scurry around the office trying to find someone to cover for you? It's much more efficient (for both you and your boss) if you already have a "buddy system" in place. Among your peer managers there's probably someone whose work is relatively like yours, someone whom you'd trust to handle your work and whose work you'd be willing to cover. Talk to her about making an informal agreement to cover for each other. The work will be handled more effectively, because your units will have repeated opportunities to get familiar with each others' assignments. And your superiors will be pleased that when they ask questions such as, "How are you going to stay caught up on all of Griff's assignments when he's out for his surgery?" you can respond, "No sweat, boss, I've already got it covered."

9-8   The Mistake: Not representing your workers to your boss

The situation:

"I was really disappointed in what I heard about Will's performance in the presentation to Murgatroyd Industries," your boss, Arlene, comments. "I was told that he stumbled through questions and got defensive when people raised concerns about some of his suggestions. We can't have somebody like that representing us. Maybe we should just keep him here at home base from now on."

"That wasn't the impression I got about this presentation," you respond. "But I've known Will to get defensive once or twice in the office. I guess I could give him assignments that limit his customer interaction. I'll see what I can come up with."

You walk away from the conversation, disturbed about Arlene's perception of Will. You always have considered him a pretty reasonable person. Sure, everybody gets a little defensive once in a while, and you'd heard that the people in the Murgatroyd presentation attacked pretty hard. But that's not a reason to tell him he can't work with customers any more. Why is Arlene being so harsh?

Why was it a mistake?

One reason Arlene is being so harsh might be that she's acting on the only information that was available to her—and that information made Will's performance sound pretty bad. Your failure to represent Will to her in a more balanced light means that she has no other information to counter what she's already heard. So she acts on what she knows.

We've said it before: Bad information makes bad decisions. And Arlene's information is bad—or at least lopsided. By your failure to give Arlene complete information, you've contributed to the bad decision she's just made. And, in addition, you've undermined your own staff.

How can you recover from it quickly?

You can revisit your discussion with Arlene: "Arlene, I've been thinking about what you said this morning about Will's presentation to Murgatroyd, and it sounds to me as if you haven't heard the whole story. Will did an excellent job of explaining our proposal and justifying our recommendations. The reports I heard back from at least two other people said that the Murgatroyd group attacked him pretty hard—even got a little personal, like 'couldn't analyze his way out of a paper bag.' My folks tell me that Will kept his cool a lot longer than most people would have, and even when he did react didn't get ugly about it.

"I think I need to talk to Will about what happened, but I don't think we need to keep him away from customers (even though we might want him to lay low with Murgatroyd for a while). He's always been one of my better people in customer interactions, and I don't think we ought to react too strongly to a single instance of what might have been poor judgment."

Now you've given Arlene a more complete picture of Will's overall performance and the conflicting reports about his presentation. Arlene may still insist on limiting Will's interactions with customers (although she probably won't), but at least she'll have the information she needs to make a *good* decision.

How can you consistently do it right from now on?

• *Act as a conduit.* Part of your role as a manager is to ensure both that your superiors have accurate information about your workers' capabilities and performance and that your workers understand the bases for the decisions made by your superiors. The way you present information has a substantial influence on how it will be received. Acceptance on both sides can be facilitated by your objective assessment of the facts and circumstances and a fair account to each group. When Arlene hears bad information about one of your workers, she needs to know that he's generally a fine worker who had a particularly stressful experience. Likewise, if Arlene presses to keep Will from working with customers for a while until she's sure that he can handle such stressful situations appropriately, Will needs to understand why Arlene is so focused on customer relations and how she perceives that his defensiveness damaged the company. You're the conduit in both cases.

• *Don't knuckle under.* Don't be afraid to tell Arlene that some of the information she's working from is inaccurate or misleading. Similarly, don't be afraid to tell her that you disagree with her characterization of Will as a worker who's unable to deal productively in customer relationships. She may disagree with you, but she's deprived of the benefit of your observations and judgment when you fold too quickly. The third case in this chapter discusses the problems that arise when you knuckle under to your boss.

• *Support your workers' valuable ideas and suggestions.* Your workers need you to represent them fairly to your boss not only when one of them is being criticized, but also when they have positive suggestions for improvements or innovations in the work environment. Your role is to act as a filter for those ideas and suggestions, screening out those that have merit and are workable to advance up the management chain for approval.

This is an important function, since many of the best ideas for process and work place improvement come from the people on the front line. Your advancement of their suggestions can result in significant gains in productivity or effectiveness—both in your unit and in the company as a whole. At the same time, your advocacy of your workgroup's ideas helps build their loyalty to you as a manager and reinforces team goals.

Is doing what you did ever right?

No. That doesn't mean that you must exhibit unqualified acceptance of whatever behavior your workgroup engages in. But it does mean that you must *always* assess any criticisms yourself, objectively and fairly, before you acquiesce—even when the person who's criticizing your workers is your own boss.

A tip for mistake-free managing:

Your workers are subject to criticism from many sides: Your boss may have gotten some uncomplimentary feedback about their work (or might be looking for a scapegoat for a larger problem). Customers often want someone to blame. Other units will want to deflect criticism they've received. You may be tempted to jump on that bandwagon—to distance yourself from any blemishes on their image in order to keep your own image relatively untarnished.

Don't.

If your unit is subject to unwarranted criticism, you should be its first line of defense and its strongest defense. When a unit can't count on its own manager to stand up for its competence and reputation, there's probably no one who will. And you might as well disestablish the unit immediately, rather than watch it slowly disintegrate into oblivion.

If you're managing a unit that does have performance problems, the first person who should be identifying and correcting those problems is *you*. Once you've begun to address those problems, you don't have to apologize to anyone. You may still need to acknowledge a persistent problem now and again, but, with competent supervision, the unit will indeed improve. During that improvement period, and beyond, what the unit needs is your encouragement and support, not continued criticism. In either circumstance, part of your role as the unit's manager is to act as its spokesperson and cheerleader, to urge your workers to higher achievements, and to make sure the rest of your corporate world acknowledges them.

9-9   *The Mistake: Not representing your boss to your workers*

The situation:

"I was really disappointed in what I heard about Will's performance in the presentation to Murgatroyd Industries," your boss, Arlene, comments. "I was told that he stumbled through questions and got defensive when people raised concerns about some of his suggestions. We can't have somebody like that representing us. Maybe we should just keep him here at home base from now on."

"That wasn't the impression I got about this presentation," you respond. "The reports I heard back from at least two other people said that the Murgatroyd group attacked him pretty hard—even got a little personal, like 'couldn't analyze his way out of a paper bag.' My folks tell me that Will kept his cool a lot longer than most people would have, and even when he did react, he didn't get ugly about it. I think I need to talk to Will about what happened, but I don't think we need to keep him away from customers (even though we might want him to lay low with Murgatroyd for a while). He's always been one of my better people in customer interactions, and I don't think we ought to react too strongly to a single instance of what might have been poor judgment."

"I know Will's one of your best people," admits Arlene. "I can't handle this as an isolated incident, though. We've gotten some bad reports about a number of our folks lately, and I need to send a message to the staff that customer relations are a number-one priority here. I'm not asking you to do anything that will really harm Will or affect his career. But I do need to take an action that will make a statement to the entire workforce. And I need your support on this."

Try as you might, you just can't agree with Arlene. And you think it's important for Will to know that you stood up for him.. So when you talk to Will about Arlene's decision, you make your position very clear: "I want you to understand, Will, that I think Arlene's really off base on this one. She's got some bug in her ear about generally poor customer relations, and she's out to make an example of you. I don't blame you one bit for being upset about this. You have every right to be angry."

Why was it a mistake?

Every supervisor has a right to expect her subordinates' loyalty. Your supervisor deserves no less. When you fail to represent her position adequately to your staff, you are being disloyal to your supervisor in her position as a higher-level decision maker in the organization. There are two reasons why that's a mistake:

1. Your failure to represent your boss adequately undermines her confidence in you as a subordinate supervisor. She might never find out about the specific discussion you've had with Will, but she's likely to discover over time that you've shaded your conversations with your employees to put her in a bad light with them. If she learns that you've characterized her decisions as "off base" and "out to make an example" of Will, she'll be disturbed by your lack of support and so

much more cautious about how she interacts with you in the future. Proving yourself disloyal to your superiors is a dangerous step to take.

2. The reaction you receive from Will and your other employees isn't likely to be what you expected either. Rather than showing them that you've taken their side in a disagreement with your boss, your remarks are a clear indication of your disloyalty to Arlene. Your workers may well perceive that if you're not supportive of your superiors you won't be supportive of your subordinates either. So instead of reassuring your unit of your allegiance to them, you may well have disheartened them even further.

How can you recover from it quickly?

You can't. Words once spoken can never be erased completely, and here the damage is already done. But you can be very careful not to repeat the mistake.

How can you consistently do it right from now on?

• *Act as a conduit.* Part of your role as a manager is to ensure both that your workers understand the bases for the decisions made by your superiors and that your superiors have accurate information about your workers' capabilities and performance. The way you present information has a substantial influence on how it will be received. Acceptance on both sides can be facilitated by your objective assessment of the facts and circumstances and a fair account to each group. When Arlene insists that Will not work with customers for a while until she's sure that he can handle stressful interactions appropriately, Will needs to understand why Arlene is so focused on customer relations and how she thinks his defensiveness damaged the company. Likewise, when Arlene hears bad things about Will, she needs to know that he's generally a fine worker who had a very difficult experience. You're the conduit in both cases.

• *Be sure you understand completely the reasons for the decisions your boss makes about your workgroup.* You can't accurately transmit information from your boss to your subordinates unless you understand it yourself.

What if Arlene hadn't been so forthcoming about having received other customer relations complaints and the fact that Will's defensiveness is part of a larger problem? You'd have no idea why she'd decided to be so harsh with Will and would probably conclude that she was being exceptionally arbitrary in her decision. So your explanation of Arlene's decision to Will would necessarily be incomplete or reflect your feeling that she was being arbitrary.

In contrast, because you know that Arlene is having a problem with customer relationships among a significant proportion of the staff, her decision to take action is reasonable—whether you agree with it or not. Your explanation to Will should reflect that reasonable basis for Arlene's decision, without expressions of your personal opinion.

• *Look for ways to make your boss' unpopular decisions more palatable to your workgroup.* When you can gain acceptance of your boss' decisions, you not only demonstrate your loyalty to her, but you also make life easier for yourself. A grumbling and disheartened staff isn't much fun to work with. Put your superiors' decisions in the most positive light possible. Look for ways to minimize the impact on the staff. In this case, you might be able to give Will another assignment for a few weeks that will be even more challenging and rewarding than the Murgatroyd account he's been working on. He will feel less like he's being punished, even though he'll certainly understand why his assignment has been changed.

Is doing what you did ever right?

Never is a long, long time. We wouldn't go so far as to say that failing to support your boss' position to your staff is *never* acceptable, but, for the reasons we've discussed above, it's never a good pattern to fall into.

There is one situation in which it's important that your staff understand that you're in disagreement with your boss. That's the very rare occasion when you disagree with her decision so vehemently that you're taking a public stand against her. These might be occasions when *she*'s proposing an action that will alienate a good customer, when she's asking you to do something unethical, when she's proposing to disregard a directive from *her* boss and you don't want to get caught in the crossfire. In such circumstances, your staff needs to know where you as an individual stand—apart from the corporate stance. It's still important to represent your boss' position fairly, but to explain why you have such a strong disagreement with her. Then your workers can make their own decisions about where to stand during the conflict.

A tip for mistake-free managing:

Remember the Golden Rule? "Do unto others as you would have them do unto you." Whenever you're tempted to voice your criticisms of your boss' decisions to your workgroup, think about how you would react if one of your subordinates did the same in a similar situation. Is this an issue that's worth generating internal contention and discord? If one of your workers reacted as you're planning to, would you consider that he was grandstanding to further his own agenda or even undermining your authority?

Put yourself in your boss' shoes and it will be much easier to accord her the loyalty and support you want to see from your own group.

9-10   The Mistake: Going along with your boss' unethical behavior

The situation:

Your boss, Tony, begins tentatively: "Now, I'm sure that we'll just keep this between us. I think that we could recast some of these production figures to make it clear that we're doing just as much work as ever—it's just not turning out as well as we'd hoped. We could add in figures to show production, even if it required rework, instead of leaving those totals out. And there are a couple of columns here we could strike altogether.

"You know what will happen if our unit costs keep going up. The front office is going to start cutting positions, maybe yours or mine. We're not really lying here. We're just moving some numbers around to put them in a better light. Right?"

"Well . . . I guess so," you reluctantly agree. "It doesn't feel right to me, but you're the boss, so I'll go along with whatever you say."

"Don't worry so much," Tony tries to reassure you. "Nobody pays any attention to where these numbers come from; all they're looking at is the bottom line. You *do* want to keep your job, don't you? It's not as if we were doing anything illegal."

Why was it a mistake?

Just because an action isn't illegal doesn't mean it's not wrong. You already know that, but it's hard to refuse your boss when his request seems so reasonable—at least on the surface. Whether this is an ethical dilemma or not depends on the situation. If Tony is changing the report because it really doesn't reflect what's going on in the unit, his motives may be pure and the action acceptable. That's not what this looks like. This looks more as if Tony doesn't want to look bad in front of *his* boss.

Whether your going along with Tony's request is a mistake or not is really for you to decide. That's not a decision we can help you with. It's based on your own internal code—about what your responsibilities are to your employer, about your responsibilities to maintain truth and honesty, about how far you can compromise without violating an essential part of yourself. You know what you're comfortable with and what you're not. You know when you have a "gut feeling" that you're about to cross the line. Pay attention to those feelings. They're usually right on target!

How can you recover from it quickly?

If you decide that changing the production figures is beyond the pale for you, then you must simply refuse to do it. No speeches, no long explanations, no philosophical or moralistic pronouncements, just tell Tony: "I'm sorry, Tony, not to be able to support you on this. But I've thought it over and decided I'm just not willing to make the changes."

If you can identify a different, ethically acceptable way to help Tony to minimize the damage the poor production report will do him, offer it. But get as far away as you can from Tony's original request to change the production figures.

How can you consistently do it right from now on?

• *Build a wall of honesty.* Do you know the saying, "The best defense is a good offense?" The best defense to temptations to engage in unethical behavior is to develop a reputation so sterling that no one would even think of approaching you with a questionable proposal. If your boss, your peers, and your workers all know you as a fair, compassionate, and scrupulously honest person, they won't be tempted to try to entice you into something you're not comfortable with. It's only when your standards are not well known or when you've approached the margins before that you're likely to be approached again.

Ensure not only that your decisions rest on firm foundations, but also that you articulate those foundations. When you tell a production worker that his work isn't acceptable to send to a customer, when you explain to a customer support person not to make promises he knows he can't keep, when you send reports and charts back for rework because they're misleading, take these opportunities to explain why the actions aren't acceptable. Don't wear it on your sleeve, but make sure people know you subscribe to a code of ethical conduct and that you live by it.

• *Develop a network of like-minded managers.* Even the most corrupt organization will have at least a few other managers whose standards match yours. It may take you a while to find them, but those managers can form a kind of support group with you. It's much easier to say, "no" when you know you're not alone.

• *Insist upon high ethical standards of conduct among your own staff.* Your wall of honesty will begin to crumble quickly if your expectations for ethical conduct apply only to you yourself. Looking the other way when your staff engages in questionable behavior undermines the reputation you're trying to build. In fact, you may instead develop a reputation for being the person who's afraid to take risks himself but perfectly willing to put his staff on the line.

Explain to your staff what you expect of them and what standards they should use to make decisions. Offer to help them work through difficult problems. And, most of all, support their ethical conduct—even when it's not popular.

• *Find a safety valve.* We won't insult your intelligence by reminding you that virtue isn't always rewarded. We will remind you that when virtue is punished, it's a good idea to have a backup plan. You may have connections with a higher level manager who will support you. You might document any questionable directives you're given and deposit a copy in a safe place away from the office. You might want to start looking for other employment options if it looks as if your day is coming. Whatever safety valve you choose, make sure it's in place and working dependably if you're caught in an environment where unethical behavior is condoned.

Is doing what you did ever right?

As we explained earlier, ethical decision making is highly personal. Only you can decide whether you can look yourself in the mirror tomorrow morning. Only you can decide how much your soul can bear.

A tip for mistake-free managing:

These are just a few of the actions you can take to protect yourself and preserve your integrity in a difficult situation. But sometimes there's not much you *can* do to protect yourself. It's useful to remember, though, that unethical actions seldom occur in isolation. Environments foster ethical or unethical behavior, and you can usually tell fairly easily what kind of environment you're in. If you're stuck in an environment in which questionable behavior is condoned, or, especially, where unacceptable actions are part of the way of doing business, the only good long-term solution is to get out. We know that's not easy advice to take in these days of cutbacks and downsizing and outsourcing, but you *do* have to be able to live with yourself. The stress and anxiety of operating on the edge are a higher price than you should have to pay.

CHAPTER 10

MISTAKES IN YOUR REACTIONS AS PART OF THE ORGANIZATION

10-1   The Mistake: Not seeing the "big picture"

The situation: "Where are all of these cordless mice coming from lately? asked your boss, Mark, as he played with one lying on your desk. "Did we get a good deal on them?"

"We got a great deal. We found a place that's selling the mice along with some management software for an unbeatable price—CompQuik over on First Avenue."

"CompQuik!" your boss is nearly apoplectic. "How could you possibly deal with those lying, cheating schemers? Didn't you read the memo I had Legal send out a couple of weeks ago? We're in a big fight with them over a whole batch of notebook computers they sent us nearly a year ago. Legal wanted everybody to know specifically *not* to buy anything else from them until we get our claim settled. They're a small outfit, and we've given them enough business that our little boycott ought to hurt. So why weren't you on board with the rest of us?"

Why was it a mistake?

Companies employ both strategy and tactics to reach their goals. These are terms borrowed from military operations that have come into common use in the business world, but their real meanings are often misunderstood. A strategy is an overall plan for accomplishing an objective, and it encompasses many different kinds of resources and many different types of contributions. Tactics are smaller-scale actions that serve a larger purpose. Typically, tactics are employed to support the overall strategy. To put those terms into more common language: Strategy is the big picture. Tactics are the day-to-day operating decisions that advance toward or detract from the big picture.

255

In order for a strategy to work, each individual tactical decision must be made with the overall strategy in mind. If the organization is going to meet its goals, then each step you take in the wrong direction has to be compensated for—by you or by someone else. But before you can work to advance the company's goals, you have to know what they are. That's what we mean when we say that it's a mistake not to see the "big picture."

Here, you weren't aware that your company was making a concerted effort to push CompQuik into a favorable settlement of its claim to recover for defective products CompQuik supplied. By giving CompQuik more business, you've undermined an important goal of the company. (It may not rise to the level of a "strategic goal" but it's definitely a level above your goal and decision to buy a few cordless mice.) When you undermined your company's attempt to push CompQuik to a favorable settlement, that meant that the company took at least one step back in its progress toward that goal. For every step back, it takes at least two steps forward to compensate. See how much your ignorance of the company's big picture hurt?

How can you recover from it quickly?

As with many other mistakes, once you've made the mistake, there's no quick way to recover. If the mice are still in their original packaging, you could return them for a refund. But once you've bought them and put them into service, the damage is already done.

How can you consistently do it right from now on?

• *Read the mail.* Many companies have vision and goals statements that they publish periodically to all employees. Newsletters and internal publications often include statements by top level managers about where the company is headed. In the situation we described here, the company had issued a policy statement that clearly explained its expectations. Organizations are often very open about their goals, both long term and near term, and publish them in a variety of media. New rules and regulations are often designed to advance specific company goals. (Sometimes they last longer than the goals do, but that's a different problem.) Part of your job is to stay on top of the written materials prepared by your company so that you can be sure to stay focused in the right direction.

• *Develop your own self-education plan.* Getting the "big picture" requires that you know not only specific strategic goals, but also the overall orientation and mission of the company. Oftentimes managers are expected to come into the job with that kind of knowledge, or they're expected to know how to acquire it without much assistance from their own bosses. You may find yourself in that situation, but there are things you can do to make sure you know what the company's basic purposes are and where it's headed. Find an orientation video or get a copy of the orientation materials provided to new hires for very basic information. Talk to your peers about setting up rotation programs to allow all of you to get experience in related functions. Encourage your boss to use staff meetings to exchange information about substantive events in each unit. Above all, stay aware to the fact that there are often strategic, big-picture concerns underlying many day-to-day operating decisions. And become savvy in picking up clues about where those strategies lie.

• *Listen carefully to what your boss and the CEO say.* Many upper-level managers have read and heeded the message that their job is to transmit the values and vision of the company to its workers. As a result, many of the talks your boss, and especially the CEO, make to the staff will include valuable hints about where the company is headed. One of the problems you'll likely encounter in trying to translate those stated goals into practice is that they're often not explained fully. Managers frequently assume that the people who work for them in the company already understand what the company's goals and strategies are. So the things they talk about in briefings and speeches are more often tactics, implementing actions, while the underlying strategies remain unspoken. Or they'll talk about the strategies, but in vague terms because they assume that all the workers already know what they're talking about.

Your CEO might refer in a speech to "needing to ensure that our suppliers give us value for our dollars." Now, if you didn't already know about CompQuik, would you be able to guess from a vague and general statement that there was a problem with a particular supplier? Probably not.

What if your boss talks about needing "to be really careful before we award a purchase contract to some fly-by-night company that's likely to rip us off?" Sounds a little more impassioned, doesn't it? As if he might be speaking from personal experience? But you still can't exactly identify the focus of his concerns.

What you *can* glean from both of those comments, though, is that the company has some special interest in getting quality performance from its suppliers. You can figure out that there's a big picture item there somewhere; now you need to ferret it out.

• *Ask questions.* When you hear or read something that looks as if it might be a part of a larger picture, follow up.

Ask your boss, "Was there something behind your comment about 'fly-by-night' suppliers? You seemed pretty heated up about it."

Ask other managers, "Do you know what was behind the boss' speech about 'fly-by-night' suppliers? He doesn't usually get quite so heated up about things. I figure there must be more to this than I know about."

And even if you can't get the full story immediately, you've at least been alerted to the fact that you need to be especially sensitive about the purchases you make for a while. If you're not in a position to *see* the big picture, it's at least as important to know where there *is* one.

• *See where you've been.* A final suggestion: When your company has a history of dealing with particular issues in a specific, perhaps unusual, way, it often means that the issue is the focus of a larger goal. As we mentioned before, sometimes the goal that prompted the specific process has been achieved or has fallen by the wayside, while the process remains into perpetuity. But this is another occasion when it's better to ask questions than to get caught short. What if you have to jump through hoops whenever you need to get letterhead or business cards printed, going through all kinds of apparently unnecessary contortions for a simple print job?

Ask your boss or someone who's been around for a while: "Do you know why we have to get special approvals for printing services when we can make other purchases without telling anyone? I can spend thousands of dollars on software and nobody blinks an eye, but I have to fill out bunches of forms and get special approvals to do a couple of hundred dollars' worth of printing. Am I completely out of step, or is there something going on here that I don't know about?"

Maybe those special approvals have long since achieved their intended goal, or maybe the goal doesn't matter anymore. But it's equally likely that the company has an important and necessary objective it's trying to meet, and your little printing job is an important tactical operation in that overall strategy.

Is doing what you did ever right?

It's never right to miss or ignore your company's big picture. There's too much danger that you'll end up working at cross-purposes to the rest of your company.

A tip for mistake-free managing:

Just as you got caught short by making a decision without knowing how it fit into the company's big picture, your workers can get caught the same way.

You can't expect to be able to police all the decisions made by the people who work for you (and you shouldn't want to). Instead, they need the same kind of big-picture information you have, albeit in less detail, so they can make helpful, informed decisions on their own. The third case in Chapter 5 can give you some ideas of ways to get big-picture information to your workgroup.

10-2   The Mistake: Not working with other managers

The situation:

"I'm really ticked off that I'm going to have to put up with Brian's whining and snarling just to get this project done," you complain to your husband one lazy Sunday afternoon. "I could get this whole thing done in about two-thirds of the time, half the cost, and with none of the headaches if my group and I could just do it ourselves. But, no, Teresa has decided that we need to do some cross-functional teambuilding, and she thinks this project is just the place to start.

"Brian's people do know more about inventory accounting than mine do, but that's such a minor part of the whole project that I'm sure we could get the information from them and still do the project basically on our own. I just don't get it."

"Sounds to me as if you're the one doing the whining now," is your husband's less-than-supportive response. "You know, maybe Teresa's on to something here. Brian's group and yours do have to work together from time to time, and it seems as if this is a good chance to get a relationship going without a lot of pressure and heavy deadlines. I think you should give it a chance."

"Well, I don't. Anytime I've had projects with Brian before, I've just gotten the input I needed from him and did the rest of the work myself. I can do that this time too, and still get a good product out. I think all of this teambuilding stuff is for the birds. My job is to produce, not to make friends with the other managers."

Why was it a mistake?

The world's not as simple as it used to be. There are very few jobs that don't require regular and ongoing interactions between units. The work of your unit is almost certainly dependent on information, input, or products you receive from someone else in the company. And other units are almost certainly dependent on you. In that kind of situation, good peer relations are critical to your own success as a manager. Failing to foster those relationships or, even worse, refusing to work with other managers are sure ways to ensure your own quick demise.

How can you recover from it quickly?

No damage has been done yet, and you can still change your mind about not working with Brian. Monday morning, first thing, go to see Brian to begin to work out the details of your collaboration. Then be sure to let Teresa know that this mutual project has your full support.

How can you consistently do it right from now on?

• *Establish clear mutual goals and expectations.* Whenever you have an assignment to perform that requires substantial interaction with another manager, the single best guarantee of success is to establish up front exactly what you want to accomplish together and who's going to do what to get there.

Sit down with Brian and outline, preferably in writing, the goal of the assignment and each of your roles in accomplishing it. List the various tasks that will need to be performed and assign responsibility for each one.

Talk about what "success" for this project will look like. How will you know that you've done a good job together? That may be easy to define for some projects. You may know, for example, that you've succeeded in a project to identify all the workers' compensation cases each manager in the organization is responsible for when all the names on your compensation list have been linked with an organization or a manager's name. But what if you're working together on a project to develop a new incentive system for office workers? Success in that project isn't nearly so easy to define. But if you haven't developed some idea of where you want to go, one of you may decide you've gotten there while the other thinks you have miles yet to complete.

• *Set milestones.* This suggestion is a kind of subset of the first one. As you decide on roles and responsibilities and assign specific tasks to each group, it's particularly important that you work out a timeline for completion of each of the major tasks. One person's delay can back up actions in the other groups and throw off the planning for the entire project. One person's delay can also irritate the other players so much that the cooperative relationship you're trying to build is severely damaged.

It's necessary to decide both the sequence of task completion and the times when those tasks must be accomplished. Particularly in a complex project with information flowing back and forth between groups at several different stages, other workload in each group has to be factored into those milestones. But that's also another reason why timely accomplishment is critical: Delays can affect not only this project, but other assignments in your units as well.

• *Check back frequently.* Planning is great, but it's not enough by itself. As the assignment proceeds, talk to Brian to make sure that his group is getting what they need from yours and to give him feedback about what you're getting from his group. Frequent opportunities to check progress will give you a chance to identify potential problems early and make minor course corrections, to avoid later major ones.

• *Acknowledge contributions.* A significant component of any good relationship is mutual respect. Make sure that Brian knows that you recognize and appreciate the work his group is doing on the project. Identify specific tasks that have been accomplished especially well and let him know that you understand how those contributions add to the success of the project overall. Be sure also to acknowledge his cooperation and willingness to work out issues, without letting them become crises.

• *Look for opportunities to strengthen ties.* Once the assignment is completed, don't go back to your own little cubicle and hide again. Use this assignment as a springboard to a stronger relationship with Brian and his group. Then be alert to opportunities to work together again, either in tandem or in a larger project with several other managers. The stronger and more cohesive your management group becomes, the better you'll be able to withstand threats from outside the organization.

Is doing what you did ever right?

No. A good manager always embraces assignments that will help her build relationships with her peers. It's good for everyone involved.

A tip for mistake-free managing:

One of the reasons you were picked for a managerial position was your ability to work with other people. Many of the same skills that make you effective in dealing with your subordinates will make you successful in building good peer relationships. Your ability to listen empathetically, your cooperation and willingness to participate with others in achieving joint goals, and your skills in leading and eliciting the cooperation of others are all important contributors to the development of good peer relationships, as well as effective relationships with the workers in your unit. Capitalize on the skills you already have to become an even more effective member of the management team.

10-3   The Mistake: Badmouthing your boss, other managers, or the organization

The situation: "I don't know how you can stand working for Mr. Kutya," Rob commented after one of your boss' two hour presentations. "He just seems to go on and on about nothing, but for a very long time. It must be frustrating to have a boss who's so in love with the sound of his own voice."

"You don't know the half of it," you respond. "It's not just that he likes to hear himself talk, but he doesn't want to listen to anybody else. There can't possibly be a good idea in the world unless he thought of it himself. And there's nothing you can possibly say that has any merit. You're right, it is frustrating. But what can I do? The job market out there's not so good these days."

Why was it a mistake?

Your actions are intentional attempts to undermine the authority of your boss. Similarly, badmouthing other managers is a purposeful act. These are clear demonstrations of disloyalty to the organization as a whole. It doesn't matter that the focus of your remarks may be an individual rather than the company. It's your job as a manager to build up the organization—not tear it down.

If your boss hears about your conversation with Rob, he'll probably be very angry, and justifiably so. But even if he doesn't, the attitude of disrespect and disloyalty you've conveyed don't serve the company or you well.

How can you recover from it quickly?

Only by making sure that it's a *single*, isolated incident, never repeated during your tenure with the organization.

How can you consistently do it right from now on?

This one's easy to fix: Just don't engage in this behavior again.

Understand that there's a fine line between being open and honest, even blunt, and being unacceptably disloyal. Many organizations (including the best ones) encourage their employees to look for ways to improve operations and to feel comfortable about pointing out deficiencies and suggesting changes. That's not what's happening in your conversation with Rob. You're not constructively criticizing Mr. Kutya or the organization. You're not suggesting improvements to processes or methods. Your sole purpose in this conversation was to gripe about your boss—not to suggest any improvements.

Even in organizations that encourage open dialogue, the focus of that policy is on allowing *workers* to voice their criticisms and suggestions in public. Managers don't criticize each other or the organization to others. They keep their disagreements "within the family" and present a united front to everyone else, including the rest of the staff.

Although, as a manager, you *can* criticize company operations among the management group, there are two kinds of remarks about your organization or its staff that are likely to get you in trouble (because they'll be perceived as disloyal or, at best, irritating) in *any* setting:

1. *Remarks that are aimless griping.* When you talk about how bad the computer support is (or purchasing, personnel, payroll, or any other support services), when you gripe about the heat, the cold, the lack of ventilation, your office space, the furniture, or the parking problem—these are all problems without a solution.

Every organization gets the same kind of complaints, in mass, all the time, mostly from people at working levels. But, because most of these problems don't have quick solutions or, frequently, don't have solutions at all, most of this complaining is unproductive. So it just wastes time, even among your peers, and keeps you from focusing on the problems for which there are workable solutions.

2. Remarks that are critical of people *rather than of ideas or issues.* It is especially disloyal to the organization to complain about its leaders. There's a big difference, which we've discussed in other chapters, between complaints and criticisms of *people* and complaints and criticisms about ideas, or behaviors, or products, or decisions. While you're free to voice disagreement and constructive criticisms about almost any issue or decision your company's concerned with, criticisms about people is like hitting below the belt

Just as you'd expect to be told about your irritating personal style in private, with no one but you and the person who's trying to help you in the room, that's what other managers and your boss expect from you.

Is doing what you did ever right?

No. Not ever. Public criticisms and complaints by members of the management team are never acceptable.

A tip for mistake-free managing:

Being supportive of your organization and your superiors is not synonymous with being a "Pollyanna," someone who refuses to admit shortcomings or faults in anything at all. It's important that you acknowledge aspects of your company that need improvement—at the same time that you work to make sure those improvements occur. The distinction is often one of focus, between an emphasis on the things that aren't working and an emphasis on the things that are being done to make them better.

Do you harp on the company's poor production figures for the last quarter *or* do you stress the efforts being made by the production divisions to streamline their processes? Do you complain about the lack of heat in the building *or* do you accentuate the positive improvements in office layout that are being made?

There's a middle ground between carping and criticizing on one hand and hiding your head in the sand on the other. That's the ground where you ought to stand.

10-4 The Mistake: Not carrying your share of the load

The situation:	"Aw, I really don't have time to oversee the cleanup of the storage room. That's something we ought to be able to delegate to almost anyone to handle," you urge Eve, your boss.

"That's actually not the case," Eve responds. "Part of the cleanup is knowing what to save and what to pitch. That's not something that can be delegated to just anybody. It requires someone who knows enough about what goes on around here to be able to tell what's important and what isn't. I don't know anybody outside the supervisory ranks who could handle that.

"Of course, you don't need to be right there in the room all the time the cleanup's going on. You could just pop in every couple of hours, sort through stuff."

You acquiesce reluctantly, mostly to get Eve off your back. But by the time cleanup day rolls around, you've wheedled your way out of the job. Claudia, whose group occupies the section adjoining yours, has agreed to oversee the work. Once again, you've managed to duck a tedious chore.

Why was it a mistake?

Why shouldn't you make the most efficient use of your time that you can? Why shouldn't you take advantage of someone else's willingness to handle an unwelcome task? Was that so wrong?

Well, neither the world nor your organization is going to rise or fall by whether you accepted your boss' tasking to oversee the cleanup of a storage room. *But,* you're doing yourself no favors by contributing to the office's perception that you don't carry your fair share. Weaseling your way out of an unpleasant assignment is one of those irritating characteristics that, over time, will win the resentment and disdain of your fellow managers and your boss. That's not a good position to be in.

How can you recover from it quickly?

Before cleanup day arrives, or at the latest, during the cleanup operation, let Claudia know that you're available to help oversee the work after all. Maybe you could plead an unexpected schedule change or a deadline that was met surprisingly early. However you choose to cover for your earlier faux pas, make sure that you pitch in when the time comes and share the load with Claudia and anyone else who's been roped into participating.

Do *not* show up just to kibitz. Your role is that of a willing helper, not an unnecessary commentator or critic. Roll up your sleeves, take off your heels, and start sorting through the mess. Your enthusiastic cooperation, late as it is, is the only way to recover from this mistake.

How can you consistently do it right from now on?

• *Accept tasks from your boss willingly.* Develop a reputation with your boss as someone she can count on to help out when help is needed. Dependability, reliability, and *not* grousing are attributes you value, aren't they? It's no different with your own supervisor.

Every job has its share of "grunt work," work that's repetitious, boring, dirty, or otherwise unpleasant. If your boss knows she can count on you when she needs you, she may even ask less often—just so she won't feel guilty about picking on you repeatedly.

• *Volunteer* occasionally *for an assignment no one else wants.* Don't make a career of being a martyr. ("Poor me" doesn't go very far in winning the admiration of your peers either.) But when you occasionally volunteer for uninteresting or unpleasant assignments, you take the burden off the other managers in your organization. You provide convincing evidence that you're a team player who carries her full load, and you also lead the other managers to follow your example and to volunteer for projects themselves. When everyone handles a few of the unwanted jobs, no one gets stuck with many of them.

• *Acknowledge and support other managers who end up with the unpleasant work.* Let them know that you sincerely appreciate the fact that you're all sharing tasks together. Be careful not to be condescending in your approach, nor to gloat about the fact that you're *not* doing the work. Instead, show your genuine gratitude to your peers who are willing to participate in jobs no one wants.

Is doing what you did ever right?

Getting out of an occasional unpleasant assignment isn't a big deal. The mistake, as we pointed out before, arises when you develop a consistent pattern of behavior that indicates that you're just along for the ride, not a willing participant but a freeloader on the company train.

A tip for mistake-free managing:

How do you react when your workers try to duck unpleasant assignments, feigning overwork or lack of skill or any myriad other lame excuses? Do you accept those rationalizations, or do you set clear expectations and hold your workers to them?

When some people in the organization carry most of the load while others skate free, the same kind of resentment builds that you're trying to avoid among your peers. Eventually, the level of cooperation among your entire staff is affected, teamwork suffers, and it becomes more difficult to get even the critical work accomplished. Even little irritations, like a refusal to clean the storage room, can mushroom into big problems when they remain uncorrected.

10-5   The Mistake: Not looking at problems in depth

The situation:

"Are you sure we need more training?" asks DeAndre. "From what I've seen, people know how to inspect this stuff when it comes in. They just don't take the time to do it."

"No, no," you insist. "I'm sure that if we had a class on inspection techniques we would solve this problem completely."

"I tend to agree with DeAndre on this one," Aimee adds. "It seems to me that the problem is more that we're asking people to do everything at once, and we don't make it clear what we really want. We tell them to inspect everything that comes onto the receiving dock, but we measure their performance just by the number of lines that are processed and stowed. We're sending mixed signals. I think that's the real issue here."

"That may make things worse," you admit. "But it still seems to me that one good training class could take care of this whole thing. We'll try that first, then see where we are." And, with your pronouncement, the discussion ends.

Why was it a mistake?

Clearly, superficial analysis leads to superficial, and ineffective, solutions.

"So what's the harm?" you may ask. "If one solution doesn't work, we can just try another."

Well . . . yes. . . but . . .

Ineffective solutions waste time and money. They *don't* cure the real problem, but they can often lull everyone into believing that they have. And when the problem to be addressed is a critical one, they delay finding the real cause and fixing it.

On a more personal level, you don't want to develop a reputation for superficial analysis. When you consistently shoot from the hip, rather than looking at problems thoughtfully and in some depth, your workers, your peers, and your superiors won't trust your solutions. You lose credibility.

How can you recover from it quickly?

Couple your immediate solution with a more detailed analysis. It may not be necessary to retract your direction to hold the training class. In fact, even if lack of skill isn't the real problem, the class may focus your workers' attention on the importance of exercising the inspection skills they already have.

But, at the same time, ask DeAndre and Aimee to look into the problem more closely: "As I thought about our conversation, I decided that you may be on to something. How would we know whether we have a training problem or a problem with mixed messages on what's important or a lack of incentive to do the inspections? Could you come up with a plan for investigating this?"

DeAndre and Aimee will probably be pleased to have the opportunity to do a little sleuthing, and you're likely to get a much more focused solution to your problem.

How can you consistently do it right from now on?

• *Ask questions—lots of them.* Before you make your decision, gather information from a variety of sources. Ask the people who do the work what they think might be causing the problem. Talk to other managers whose units perform similar functions. Read whatever trade publications or management books and journals you can find that address your problem. If the problem is a major one that has you stumped, consider talking to a consulting firm or to specialists in your industry or at university research organizations for help.

• *Never solve problems in isolation.* Most functions that your group performs are interconnected with other functions—some performed by your group, some performed in other parts of the organization. Recognize that the solution to one problem often affects work performed somewhere else.

Do you know how your functions interface with others? Who uses the material that's being processed through your receiving division? Is performing receipt inspections likely to slow down the movement of material into storage? How will that affect its availability for processing in your production division, or its readiness for shipment to customers? How can you handle those problems?

Even if you can't solve the problems that may be caused further down the line by the changes you're planning to implement, you need to recognize that your actions *do* have repercussions, and make sure that everyone who's likely to be affected knows what you're planning.

• *Explore alternatives.* Model the solution you intend to implement. Ask questions such as: "What if we set aside material that needs to be inspected and have a special team handle that at the end of the day?"

What problems would that solve? What new problems might it cause? How do your staff think that procedure would work?

But don't stop there. Now look at another solution: "What if we set up an 'assembly line' and designate one person inspect an incoming shipment, then someone else process it in, then someone else to route it to preservation and packaging or for direct storage?"

How does that solution compare, positively and negatively, with the first one?

Ask your workers for suggestions, maybe do some structured brainstorming or have a group problem-solving session, and identify several alternatives before you settle on one.

Is doing what you did ever right?

As a matter of fact, sometimes it is. Sometimes it is less important that a manager have the *right* answer than that he have *an* answer. Occasionally, your workers will come to you with a question for which there really isn't a right or wrong answer: "If we have to buy a piece of equipment for a specific project, do you want us to bill it to the customer or to overhead?" "Should we work first on billing problems or on reconciling these accounts?" "Who's going to handle this issue on the Sebring purchase?"

If the answer doesn't matter and your workers are looking only for direction so they can get on with their work, or to ensure that whatever is done is done consistently, in-depth analysis isn't important. Make a decision, so you and your workers can get on with the business.

A tip for mistake-free managing:

Analysis and problem solving are skills, not arts. There are many sources that can teach you basic problem-solving techniques and step-by-step procedures for analyzing issues to reach workable solutions. Training classes, some as short as a day in length, are offered by many training providers. There are also management books that can help you develop analytical skills.

Two skills that are critical for success in management positions (but that sadly, are lacking in many managers) are the ability to analyze and the ability to write. When you've developed both of these skills and demonstrated your abilities to your superiors, you will have made yourself invaluable to the organization.

10-6 The Mistake: Being too narrow in your approach to problems

The situation:

"I hear that your receptionist has started transferring all her calls out to the divisions when she goes on break or leaves for lunch. Why would you have her send all the calls out to us just when our folks are least likely to be there?" Seth complains. "And, from the comments I'm getting, it sounds as if she's not even letting us know when the calls are being transferred. That doesn't sound like good customer service to me."

"Wait a minute, Seth" you reply. "The reception and phone desk is my problem. I don't have to check with you every time I make a change in the way it works. We're not doing anything now that hadn't been agreed to a long time ago. It just wasn't enforced. Instead, the phone just kept ringing off the hook in my section. Now there's at least a chance someone will answer it when Angel is on break."

"I don't disagree that it's your function, and you can run it however you want. But you might want to think about the rest of us and what you're doing to the whole company's image, the next time around."

Why was it a mistake?

Many of the decisions you make affect other parts of the organization besides your own. Similarly, solving a problem you've identified in your own section may require changes in other units as well. In most companies, functions are increasingly interconnected. When you miss those connections, you're probably missing at least half of the real issue.

How can you recover from it quickly?

You can't. But you can learn from the experience so you don't repeat it the next time you need to make a decision.

How can you consistently do it right from now on?

• *Keep the "big picture" in mind whenever you look at problems in your unit.* We've talked before about the importance of understanding your role in the organization as a whole, about keeping abreast of the organization's goals and strategies, about ensuring that the individual actions you take are focused on meeting those goals. Problem solving is a specific application of that advice.

No matter how minor a problem may seem, your solution to it must at least be sensitive to that big picture. And if the issue you're dealing with bears directly on the achievement of a company goal or the attainment of a value that's important to the company, you'll need to be sure that your solution is in complete alignment with what the company is trying to do.

More than anything, this big-picture focus doesn't require that you *do* anything differently. It's simply an awareness of what's important to the company that you need to maintain to be sure your decisions are on the right track.

• *Solicit opinions from other units.* Whenever you're examining a problem that appears to cross functions, be sure to let the other managers know what you're trying to solve and how they're likely to be affected (if at all).

You may want to mention your efforts in staff meeting, or you might want to run any changes in procedure past the other managers before implementing them—either for information or for concurrence. And certainly any time your changes require corresponding changes in process in another unit, you'll need to get agreement in advance.

• *Form an information exchange mechanism with other managers.* This can be in your regular staff meetings, or as a part of the networking you're already doing, or it can be a regular group meeting to discuss those processes you share in common. However you proceed, you need to find regular opportunities to talk to other managers about how to improve operations and resolve mutual problems.

Be ready to trade favors. Perhaps several units can rotate responsibility for staffing the reception desk during lunch and on Angel's breaks. Or perhaps you can agree to cover the reception desk throughout the day in return for help in another area. Keep your eyes open to opportunities to create solutions in which everyone wins.

Is doing what you did ever right?

Many of the problems you address will affect only your unit, and so it's not necessary to look outside the organization when you're solving them. But you need to be aware of the interfaces between your work and that of other groups, so that when larger issues are involved you can address them appropriately.

A tip for mistake-free managing:

How often do you find yourself on the receiving end of the situation we've described here? What happens when the loading dock closes down at lunch time and hangs out a sign, "See reception desk for delivery information" —but no one has let you know that a convoy of delivery trucks is on its way?

When your focus is narrowed on only the work of your own unit, you're as likely to be hurt yourself as to hurt someone else. Looking out for the interests of the organization as a whole is a good defensive measure, not just a "nice" thing to do.

10-7   The Mistake: Ignoring office politics

The situation: "Better watch out for Lucinda, she's making real inroads with the boss," Joel warns. "I've heard that he's thinking about giving her a couple of extra spaces to beef up her staff, mostly because he thinks she's got some uncanny knack for making suggestions that are exactly what he's planning himself. I guess he hasn't figured out yet how transparent he is and that she's just parroting back to him what he's already said before.

"Whatever she does, it sure works. She seems to be getting whatever she wants these days."

"I don't worry about that stuff," you smugly assert. "I do a good job with this unit, and everybody knows it. Competence is the way to get ahead—not a lot of politics and who likes who and who knows who and who's getting ahead of everybody else."

"Well, you may think you're above all that, but sooner or later it's going to catch up with you," Seth cautions. "Politics counts, and not just inside the Washington beltway."

Why was it a mistake?

Seth is right. Politics do count. Office politics is a way of exerting influence. Being good at politics means that you can influence others to do what you want done. Being poor at politics, or ignoring the political overtones altogether, means you'll be much less effective at influencing others.

The longer you're in management, the more obvious it becomes that there's very little that most managers achieve by the exercise of sheer *power*—whether with their own staffs, other managers, or the people above them in the organization. You can hardly ever effectively *order* people to do anything; you can *persuade* them to move mountains. Influence and persuasion are the essence of politics, in the office or anywhere else.

How can you recover from it quickly?

You probably can't. Political skills take time to develop. The next section suggests some ways to do that.

How can you consistently do it right from now on?

There are three essential elements of effective politicking:

• *Exposure.* You can't have the right connections if you don't go where the other people are. This may mean lunching together, going for a drink after work, playing golf on the weekend, whatever. A lot of it can be done during work itself; you can chat with others before meetings or visit them in their offices. Even the conversation you just had in the hall with Seth is a connection you want to foster.

• *Interpersonal skills.* There's a mistaken idea among some managers that just being around "the people who count" is enough. It's not. You need to have the interpersonal skills to carry on an effective conversation. You need to be friendly, relaxed, a good listener, and so on. If you don't think you have these skills, there are good books, videos, and courses on them.

One of the most effective conversational skills you can develop is the ability to get other people to talk about themselves. This is a little more than effective questioning skills, which can begin to seem like a grilling to the person on the receiving end. But good questions are a part of getting people to talk about themselves and the things they're interested in:

> "Looks like the hometown team is a good contender for the pennant this year. Didn't you used to play on the company baseball team?"

> "I saw Chaletta Martin at lunch the other day. She said she's still having headaches over the call center you two set up. That must have been a real challenge."

> Or even the old standby: "How's everything going?" can be a conversational entrée—and you can elaborate on details as you go along.

To be good at politics, you need one other conversational skill: the ability to steer a conversation in a specific direction. When you mingle with other managers, you may not want to talk just about things in general. You may want to make sure, for instance, that Ed Brabender knows that you noticed his report on the new office layout. Or you may want to suggest to Ivy Stangle that she consider one of your employees for the job she's filling, since you're not in a position to offer him a promotion. When you're talking to these managers, you want to be able to guide the conversation smoothly, not just interrupt with it.

You need practice to get good at this, but one technique that's often effective is to move the conversation gradually. Say that you and Ivy are talking about how overloaded you both are with work that you have no staff to handle. You could move the conversation one step to: "I guess you'll get a little relief when you fill that new job in purchasing."

Now, at this point, Ivy may start talking about filling the job, or she might go off in another direction and talk about the glitch in the purchasing subsystem that almost halted her entire operation last week. If she doesn't go with your lead, you can try again: "I've had system problems lately too. Probably couldn't have solved them if it weren't for Scott Munsey. I think he's likely to apply for that position you're filling. You might want to grab onto him if you can. If he doesn't get a promotion fairly soon, I'm afraid we'll lose him, and I have nothing to offer him."

Aside from practice, there are also books and other sources that can help you develop your conversational skills.

• *Reliability.* No matter how much people see you and enjoy talking with you, it won't do you much good unless you are someone they can depend on. This means that

1. they can trust that you know what you're talking about—that you're competent in the areas you discuss.

2. they can trust the truth of what you say.

3. they can trust that you'll do what you say.

These are the elements in the basic prescription for influence. Managers, including your boss, often make decisions on the basis of information from other managers they know and trust. These are the people who have influence. If you want to influence the direction the company takes, and even the direction your own career takes, you need to develop these political skills too.

Is what you did ever right?

This is an area in which there's not really a "right" or "wrong." But there is an "effective" and an "ineffective." If you want to become a more effective manager, you won't ignore the political side of the job.

A tip for mistake-free managing:

If people aren't comfortable around you or don't trust either your competence or reliability, you'll be ineffective at office politics. By constantly exposing yourself to other managers, you'll be reinforcing their low opinion of you. The answer to this is simple: Don't complain about other managers being "too political" or dismiss what goes on in the office as "just politics." Develop the skills in yourself, so you can play on the same field.

10-8   The Mistake: Not understanding and following the organization's culture

The situation: "Today we're going to have a little chat. It's come to my attention that many of you are taking long lunches and breaks, ducking out of work early in the afternoon, letting your kids drop by after school, and generally treating this office as if it were a country club.

"Well, it's not. You may have gotten away with this behavior in the past, but things are different around here now. And here are our new rules . . ."

Why was it a mistake?

If every other manager in your organization allows her employees to do just the things you're complaining about in your workgroup, you're in for a lot of hard feelings and resentment when you try to swim against the tide. Organizations do develop their own culture and climate. It's the product of many personalities and of individual decisions about the image the company wants to project to its customers and to its own staff. These merge over time into a relatively consistent set of norms and expectations.

With each succeeding CEO and senior management staff, the culture might shift a little. But, in organizations where senior staff are handpicked at least in part because they conform to those cultural norms, the organizational climate can remain remarkably stable over even long periods of time.

Your workers come into the company with a certain set of expectations about what it's going to be like to work there, based on their perceptions of the organization's culture. Those perceptions are modified or reinforced, depending on how well their actual experiences match their initial expectations. They shape their behavior to match the culture they experience in the company.

Failing to follow the company's cultural norms is a problem in at least three ways:

1. It ignores the company's "big picture"—its overall goals and strategies. Since an organization's culture is the product of conscious decisions about the company's image and goals, your failure to follow that culture violates those goals. Are you out of sync with the rest of the company in other areas as well?

2. Because workers rely on the norms they've experienced before, your changing the rules midstream means they don't have any sure guide any more. Maybe everyone else in the company can take long lunches and leave early on some days because they're expected to pitch in and work extra hours on other days when workload is especially heavy. If you're so strict about breaks and lunches, does that mean you're not expecting them to work the extra hours either? What is the message you're trying to convey?

3. When you're out of sync with the rest of the company, workers will also tend to compare their situation with other units. If they don't like what you're doing in your unit, they're likely to find a place they like better and leave you. And, if they're in a position in which they can't leave (maybe because there aren't any openings in other units), they'll stick around—but resentful and ready to file grievances and complaints over the slightest deviation from your stated policy. Your unit will take on the aspect of an armed camp.

How can you recover from it quickly?

Find out what practice the rest of the company follows. Ask your boss or another manager: "I just tried to bear down on my group for taking too much time away from work at lunches and breaks. Thought I was going to have a mutiny on my hands. How do you all handle that?"

If you find that the long absences are tolerated as a kind of compensation for the company's expectation that people will be available to work extra on very short notice, you can go back to your unit and explain what you've learned: "I found out that the rest of the company uses longer breaks and lunches to make up for asking people to work extra hours on short notice. That makes sense to me, too, so I'm backing off from what I said before. Let's just not abuse the bargain."

You've made explicit the agreement that your company's management and workers have made (and many workers probably don't know why the practice evolved, they know only that their absences are accepted). You've also helped to set some limits on the practice. Once the trade-off is understood by everyone, each worker can better gauge whether he or she is within norms or is, perhaps unknow-ingly, abusing the practice.

How can you consistently do it right from now on?

• *Become attuned to the organization's culture.* As we said earlier, an orga-nization's culture is shaped largely by conscious decisions about the image the company wants to project to its customers and its own workforce. So it's a part of the organization's overall goals and strategies. You need to become as familiar with the culture of your company as you are with every other aspect of its "big picture." If you're not already, look at the first case in this chapter for suggestions.

• *Ask questions.* Just because you know what the company's practices are doesn't mean you understand *why* things work the way they do. Ask questions—of your boss, other managers, people on your staff who've been around for a while. Questions such as:

> "I've noticed that the professional staff here get all hot and bothered if you expect them to answer a telephone. Why is that?"

> (Maybe because they're not generally expected to answer the phones, but maybe because all their previous managers just got tired of fighting over it.)

> "The second the clock reads 4:30, there's a regular stampede out of my office. When I ask why nobody will stay long enough even to finish the claim they're working on, my folks just say everybody else does the same thing. Is that true?"

> (What "everybody else does" *might* be an excuse, but it might also be a part of the culture.)

> "When I tried to stop these long lunches and breaks, do you know what my folks' argument was? They just said, 'We've always done it this way.' What difference does that make?"

> ("We've always done it this way" *might* be organizational inertia, but it might also be a clue that this is a part of the culture.)

• *Adopt organizational norms and practices.* Once you understand what the cultural norms are and, at least sometimes, why they've developed as they have, incorporate them into your own way of doing business as much as you can. Where they affect the core mission of your unit, adopt them completely. But when a cultural norm is in conflict with your ability to accomplish the basic objectives of your workgroup, it's a slightly different story (although you may still be forced to yield).

• *Negotiate deviations*. Cultural norms are generally established over time to meet a particular set of circumstances in the organization. Whenever you find that a cultural norm doesn't apply to your unit or, especially, interferes with the work of the unit, it should not be treated as sacrosanct. Following the organization's culture does *not* require wholesale acceptance.

It *does*, however, require that you acknowledge your intent to deviate and, wherever possible, negotiate the differences with your unit. You might begin the discussion like this: "I understand that the reason everyone in the company goes along with these long lunches and breaks is that there are so many times when we ask people to work extra hours on short notice. But that doesn't apply to our unit. We hardly ever work extra hours, but we do have to be on duty and productive during all of the normal workday. What can we do that's not too different from the rest of the company, but gets people at their desks most of the day?"

You have good and sufficient reasons for not operating like the rest of the company, but now it's up to your staff to help come up with an alternative that works.

Is doing what you did ever right?

Kind of. There are times when the organization's cultural norms don't apply to the situation you're working in. As in our example, if your unit doesn't work a lot of extra hours on short notice, but performs tasks that require your workers to be productive most of their eight hours, you might have a good case for not following the practice of the rest of the company.

But whenever you deviate from the organization's culture, you at least owe it to your workers to explain what you're doing and why.

A tip for mistake-free managing:

What if the company's culture is one you can't live with? Maybe it drives you crazy to see people lounging on the back dock when you know there are orders just waiting to be filled. Maybe you can't stand "dress-down" days when everyone comes in looking as if they're on the way to the golf course. (Or maybe you can't stand to wear a skirt and heels every day and *want* a dress-down Friday.)

Maybe you're uncomfortable with company practices that seem on the shady side of ethical behavior.

For whatever reason, when your personal style and the organization's culture don't mesh, it's time for a change. And there are only two possible changes. Both are yours, since the chances of your changing the *company* significantly are "slim" and "none."

Either you can decide that you can learn to put up with whatever aspects of the culture you don't like or you can decide it's time to leave. We can't help you make the decision. But we can suggest that, when you go job hunting again, it's as important to check out the culture of the organization you're entering as it is to learn anything else about it.

10-9   The Mistake: Letting the job get to you

The situation:

"I just don't know how much longer I can take this. No one is ever satisfied with anything. Our production figures are stagnant. The boss is on my back to find a solution to this mess with destination inspections. My staff is ready to mutiny because only half of them are allowed to take off Christmas week. I have more deadlines and complaints and whining workers, and griping managers than I can handle.

"I'm not sure why I thought being a manager was going to be so great in the first place. Sometimes I really want to go back to the good old days when all I had to worry about was my own little assignment, and I didn't have the rest of the world breathing down my neck.

"Maybe I'll just hang it up and go someplace else."

Why was it a mistake?

Maybe it's not. But it *is* a mistake to give up too soon. You really did want to become a manager, didn't you? So let's work through this a little more.

Everybody goes through stale periods in whatever they're doing, on the job or off. Marriages go through dull periods, friendships wax and wane, outside interests lose their luster, and jobs get to be too much. Most of the time the dissatisfaction is transient. You just "tough it out" and things get better in time. If you give up too soon, you will have lost a golden opportunity to do something you really like, just because it got a little tough for a while.

How can you recover from it quickly?

You might not be able to. First look at why you're letting things get to you and then follow the advice below for making your life better.

How can you consistently do it right from now on?

• *Figure out what the problem is.* Sometimes the job itself really is the problem. It may have grown to the point where it's overwhelming—either because of the volume of work or because you aren't equipped to deal with the kinds of problems that arise. Or it may be the opposite problem. Maybe the challenge has gone out of the job. You've solved most of the problems there are to solve, at least once. You've seen most of the situations that are likely to come up, at least once. There's nothing left to conquer, and you're bored.

Sometimes the problem isn't the job at all. All kinds of personal events, both positive and negative, can have an effect on the enthusiasm you have for your work. Maybe so much is happening at home that you can't concentrate on work, or maybe the rest of your life is so stagnant that it's affecting your attitude toward the job too.

The first step in curing your dissatisfaction is to identify its cause.

• *Develop coping strategies.* If the problem is that there's too much going on at work or at home, do some soul searching about what really needs to get done and what doesn't. Set aside some time to accomplish one or two nagging chores that are dragging you down. That may mean taking a day off work to finish something at home. Or it may require closing your door and turning off your intercom at work so you can devote uninterrupted time to completing tasks that seem to drag on forever.

If the workload is truly overwhelming, talk to your boss about some relief. Don't whine; just point out what isn't getting done and give her some suggestions for alternative sources of assistance.

What if things are dull and boring? What can you do to liven them up again?

Think about what excited you about the job in the past. The people problems? Trying to do things faster, better, cheaper? Introducing new technology? Taking on assignments that required you to learn new skills?

See how much of those more interesting kinds of work you can introduce into your current job. Many jobs are what we make of them. Managers especially, aside from the occasional crunch, have a lot of freedom to develop their own individual styles. You probably can too.

• *Maintain a healthy distance.* Even a normal workload can become impossible when you begin to take personally every problem and criticism that arises. Remember that no matter how important a job you may hold, it's just a job—not your life.

Here are some indicators that you're not successfully distancing yourself from your job:

1. Do you wake up in the middle of the night because a work problem has suddenly popped into your head?

2. Do you take work home frequently or come into the office on weekends and holidays?

3. Do you carry your briefcase with you nearly wherever you go, even to places not connected with your work?

4. Have you taken fewer than 10 days of vacation time in the past 12 months?

5. Does correcting a worker's performance or behavior make you anxious and nervous?

6. Do you agonize about decisions you've already made?

7. Do you look for acceptance among the people who work for you?

8. Is it important for you to be seen as a "good guy" or "good gal" among your staff?

9. Do you socialize mostly with people you've met through work?

10. Did your reading last weekend consist solely of management and trade journals rather than mystery novels or the sports page?

None of these standing alone indicates a problem. But if several of these describe you, you need to think about whether you're taking the job too seriously. If you are, lighten up a little. Take time just for you—even if it's only an hour or two rather than a day or a week.

Develop some distance between the job and you. When you leave the office each evening, or at least every Friday evening, put your thumb and forefinger to your forehead and rotate them slowly—clockwise. You have just locked the door on your office and your job. Tuck the key to your "work brain" in your pocket and leave it there, all night or all weekend. Trust us, things will still be percolating somewhere back in the dark recesses in your mind. But if they start to push toward your consciousness, slam the door shut and bolt it again. You need the rest.

• *Keep your options open.* What if nothing you do helps? You've rearranged your workload. You've looked for ways to liven up the job. You've managed to distance yourself from the work so that you're not feeling everything that comes up as a personal crisis. But you're still unhappy.

If nothing you do makes it any easier to come to work, then it's time to move on. You may be able to cope with your dissatisfaction for a while, but time will tell. Eventually your dissatisfaction will infect your entire unit. Your performance will suffer and so will the organization's. Your attitude as a manager sets the tone for your whole group, and if you're not happy, chances are they won't be either. So without animosity or hard feelings—and without burning any bridges—it's time to look around for greener pastures.

Is doing what you did ever right?

Of course. Everybody has periods of dissatisfaction and ennui. And everybody's job has periods when it requires attention 24 hours a day, 7 days a week—for a while.

But before you give up and give in, try some of the suggestions we've given you, and soon you should be back in fine fettle again.

A tip for mistake-free managing:

We've talked about how to avoid letting your job get to you, but we haven't addressed the problems that arise when your workers' jobs get to them. Especially if you work in a high-pressure environment (and don't most of us?), your workers are prone to the same feelings of burnout and being overwhelmed as you are. And they need the same opportunities to work through these feelings.

Whenever a worker seems to be "off his stride," let him know that you've noticed the change. Give him a chance to talk about the problem and, if you can, help him identify the cause. Coach him in using some of the coping mechanisms we've discussed. If he can't identify the cause, help him find some professional guidance to assist him in working through the problem. Most of all, give him understanding and some time to work through his own issues.

CHAPTER *11*
MISTAKES IN ESSENTIAL MANAGEMENT SKILLS

11-1   *The Mistake: Not keeping your word*

The situation: One of your workers approaches you: "But you said you'd have the answer for me today on whether I could go to that conference next week. I have to make arrangements for my assignment to be covered, and there's not much time left."

"I know I did, Tom, and I really meant to. But you know how hectic things have been around here lately. I just didn't get to it."

"I've got to be able to let the training director know by tomorrow or I'm going to lose my ticket, and may not be able to get someone to fill in for me on such short notice."

"Ok, I'll let you know tomorrow—I promise."

Why was it a mistake?

It is always and everywhere a mistake to tell someone you will do something and then not do what you said when you said. Do this just a few times and people begin to believe that they cannot count on you. If they cannot count on you, they cannot trust you, and if they cannot trust you they will deal with you as little as possible. This is true for anyone, at any level. It is particularly true for those who work for you.

How can you recover from it quickly?

You find Tom and you say: "Tom, I apologize. I let you down. I'm going to try to get you an answer right now. If I can't, I will get you one as soon as I finish the management meeting tomorrow morning."

Then you do just that. Is it inconvenient to do so? Might you have to work a few minutes extra or take a few minutes from your lunch break? It doesn't matter. Do it.

How can you consistently do it right from now on?

Always keep your commitments. Always *do whatever you say you'll do and do it when you say you'll do it.*

How do you do this. By following these three steps:

• *Step 1:* Think every commitment over carefully before you make it. If you have any doubt that you'll be able to keep it, don't make it. When you make it, make it with the full intention that you will keep it just as you made it. When you say, "I'll do this for you and I'll have it done by next Tuesday," mean it.

• *Step 2:* Keep the commitment and keep it when you said you'd do it.

• *Step 3:* What if something happens that will prevent you from keeping it? Is this something you could reasonably have anticipated at the time you made the commitment? Then why didn't you plan on it and make the commitment accordingly? Is it something you couldn't reasonably anticipate? Then as soon as you know you won't be able to keep the commitment get together with the individual to whom you made it and renegotiate it. Do it as soon as possible; *do not ever wait until the last minute.*

If your commitment was to have a report completed and to another manager on Friday, and something comes up,

> *Say:* "I just found out that I have to do a presentation next Thursday, and it will take me a day to plan for it. I just can't have the report to you by Friday. If I promise you to work on it first thing Monday morning and have it to you no later than Tuesday noon, is that OK?"

> *Don't say:* "Oh, I'm going to have to leave for a presentation I wasn't expecting. I'll get you the report sometime next week. OK?"

If people understand that you normally keep your commitments and renegotiate them as soon as possible when you can't, they will believe they can rely on you and trust you.

What if your boss insists on your making commitments you know you can't fulfill? First, ask why she does this. One possible answer is that you haven't kept commitments to her in the past, so she believes she has to push you to an unrealistic commitment to get something done on time. You can change that only by beginning to demonstrate that your commitments are rock solid, so she will gradually let you set more realistic ones.

There's a particular problem, a psychological one, with commitments to the people who work for you. If you make a commitment to your boss, you have the fact that he's your boss pressuring you even if you don't want to keep the commitment. But if it's someone who works for you, you don't have the same pressure. You'll be all too tempted to tell yourself that it's really OK to let it slide. But it never is, because your workers are dependent on you. If they can't trust you to deliver what you promise, they can't trust you—and everyone is in trouble.

Is doing what you did ever right?

No.

A tip for mistake-free managing:

You can't control many aspects of your work environment. You have company policy, your boss's directions, perhaps a union to deal with. But you can control your commitments; you can make your word your bond. And you can see that every member of your workgroup does the same. Do this, and you will have a solid foundation for everything else.

11-2   The Mistake: Not understanding that workers really are different from one another

The situation:	"Yeah, Terrence, I just can't understand it. I sent all my people to the "empowerment" training; I've discussed with all of them what their authority is and what I expect from them. And now I've got a mess on my hands. Three of my people have really taken to it; I don't ever have to worry about them. Two others like the autonomy all right, but they keep going off on tangents and I have to corral them and bring them back. Six or seven of them are showing maybe a bit more initiative, but they're mainly just keeping on as they've always done. And poor Bruce; he's in my office asking for help at least twice as much as he used to. I just don't know what's happening!"

Why was it a mistake?

For too many organizational programs, management texts, consultants, and management training courses act as though one approach will work with all workers (and their managers). It won't—as the manager in the example above found out.

In fact, people aren't alike, and since workers are people, workers aren't alike. Some want autonomy; others want to be told what to do. Some like to take chances; others avoid risks as completely as they can. Some want a pleasant workplace more than anything else; others want to get ahead as quickly as possible. Some judge every job by the its pay level; others are far more interested in whether the job is interesting. And on and on and on.

One of the first tasks of any manager is to get to know his or her workers as individuals and understand how they're different from one another. Not doing so is a fundamental mistake.

How can you recover from it quickly?

You can't. Understanding your workers and how they differ from one another takes time and effort. However, you can get started quickly.

How can you consistently do it right from now on?

Let's look at how a manager who understood the differences among her workers might deal with the problem of different reactions to increased worker autonomy:

> "Cherise, you're taking to this like a duck to the water. Please make sure you're coordinating with everyone you need to; otherwise, just let me know if you run into a problem I can help you with."

> "Joel, I really appreciate the incentive you're showing these days, but you seem to be going in a different direction from the rest of us. I know you want to be independent, but I can't let you unless you're willing to work with the rest of the group. You need to meet with Billy Joe and Juanita and make sure that the three of you are coordinating your efforts. If the three of you can work it out, I won't have to keep bugging you."

> "Hank, you're doing an OK job, just as you always have. But you were telling me you want one of the senior positions in the branch, and I can promise you that just performing 'OK' won't get you there. Would you like to talk a bit about how you might improve so that you're competitive?"

"Bruce, I think you're not very comfortable in the workgroup these days. It looks to me as if you don't really like making decisions on your own, and if this is true, we may need to talk about your transferring to some other unit."

The manager knew her people well enough to approach each one in terms of what he or she values: independence, promotion, safe performance, whatever. Here are a few suggestions on how you can do this successfully:

• *Learn to recognize and appreciate the differences.* It's important to recognize similarities among workers, and it's important not to exaggerate the differences among them. But it's at least as important to recognize and understand the differences. If Hank's major concern is getting promoted, it's probably a waste of time to make his work space more pleasant. Then take another step: Appreciate the differences. Don't complain because Bruce doesn't take the initiative the way Cherise does. But do understand how he's different and look for the positive possibilities in the difference.

• *Use the differences positively.* This is the goal an effective manager works toward: How to use his or her workers so that their strengths are maximized and their weaknesses compensated for? Cherise can probably do any job more quickly than Bruce, but Bruce can do a routine task that would bore her, leaving her time free for more demanding work. To the best of your ability and theirs, you divide up assignments so that the requirements of the job match not only the abilities but the interests of the workers.

• *Allow people room to grow.* Noticing differences can lead to stereotyping. It's all too easy to pigeonhole each of your workers and keep them on the same duties and tasks. Guard against this. People really do change and grow. Who knows—Bruce may actually walk in one day and ask you to give him a small project to do completely on his own. And Hank may turn down a promotion because the work he's doing in your group is more interesting.

It's good to let people grow; it's even better to encourage them to do so. Most people don't make giant changes in what they want from a job. But they do change. When the change is in a direction you want, help make it easy. Perhaps Joel is beginning to work more enthusiastically with others. Great. Make sure he knows you've noticed this and want to see him continue. The more each member of your workgroup grows, the greater the contribution he or she can make to the overall effort.

Is doing what you did ever right?

Only if your group must follow very rigid work rules.

A tip for mistake-free managing:

Most organizations understand that people are different, but they also understand that in certain ways they must be treated alike. The rules for proper behavior, for instance, can't be modified to fit each individual's preferences. Nor can a manager expect high performance from one worker while letting another get by with marginal work.

One of the most difficult jobs of management is balancing the need to treat people uniformly with the fact that they are genuinely different and need to be treated differently. Sadly, there's no easy answer. However, it will help you if you keep these two questions in mind when asked to make an exception for someone:

1. Would I be willing to make this exception for everyone?

2. If not, can I clearly explain the circumstances under which I will and will not make the exception?

This won't completely solve the problem—by a long shot—but it will get you going in the right direction.

11-3   The Mistake: Concentrating on mistakes, not learning

The situation:	"Emma, I really thought you knew better than to commit the unit to a deadline without checking with me."
	"I thought that we needed to be responsive to our customers, and I didn't see any reason why we couldn't. .. ."
	"I don't really care what you thought here. You know that I don't want any commitments made unless I've personally approved making them. Do you understand?"

Why was it a mistake?

What did Emma learn from this encounter? To check with you first, yes. She also learned not to try to think for herself. She *didn't* learn why it was important to check with you and why her action might have caused problems for the work-group. And you didn't learn what her reasoning was when she agreed to the dead-line. In short, nobody learned anything much, and Emma mostly learned the wrong things.

How can you recover from it quickly?

Make sure you've gotten over any anger at the incident, then call Emma in. (Even better, go to her work site if you can get some privacy there.) This is how the conversation might go.

> *Manager:* "Emma, I was hard on you a few minutes ago, and I don't think I needed to be. You're a good worker. I should've asked you why you thought it was a good idea to make the commitment to the deadline. I'd like to know."

> *Emma:* "Yeah, I didn't like that at all. I know your policy, and I follow it almost every time. Remember, though, when Mr. Limon said in the depart-ment meeting last week that getting the Exacta audit done was the most impor-tant thing on the department's plate? Well, I knew that nothing was going to happen until we got our summary to Ms. Givens' unit, and I didn't see why we couldn't get it done easily by when they wanted it."

> *Manager:* "That's good thinking, and you had the right goals. But let me tell you where the problem is. We got hit by a new requirement just yesterday that I haven't had a chance to discuss with the group yet. We can make your deadline, and we will honor your commitment. But it's going to take some shuffling around. If I'd known what Tom Limon wanted, he and I could have worked it out so we wouldn't have been quite so disrupted. See why it mat-ters, as good as your intentions were, that you check with me first . . ."

How can you consistently do it right from now on?

Some workers simply don't pay attention to direction and policy; they pre-fer to do things their own way. You do have to get strict with them at times, or even help them transfer to a job where they can have more independence. Most work-ers, like most managers, aren't this way. They want to follow policy and direc-tions, but they also want some room to exercise their own judgment.

How do you ensure that they do what you need done without simply becom-ing "yes-people?" The conversation above is a good example of how you might go about it. These are the steps:

• *Step 1:* Make sure the individual knows that he or she has made a mistake. *Don't* tell yourself that it was just this once and that it won't ever happen again. The quicker you deal with the situation, the easier it will be to resolve. The manager in the example did this; the problem is that he or she stopped there, without going on to the next two steps.

• *Step 2:* Find out why the worker made the mistake. The individual's reasoning may have been good (Emma's was) but incomplete. The individual may have seen an aspect to the situation you'd overlooked. He or she may have reacted impulsively, without thinking it through. Or there may have been any of a hundred other reasons.

• *Step 3:* Now that you know why the individual did what was done, you can relate your policy not only to the situation but to the individual's approach to it. You can point out to Emma that her reasoning was good but that she didn't have enough information. If the worker noticed an aspect of the situation that you overlooked, you can thank him or her for noticing it and then see what needs to be done. If the worker ignored the policy and reacted impulsively, you may have a more serious problem, but now you know what it is and you can start dealing with it.

In short, if you follow these three steps both you and the worker will learn, and each of you will be able to perform more effectively next time. The worker, because he or she understands your policy better. You, because you understand the worker's attitude and approach more completely.

Is doing what you did ever right?

Almost never. Occasionally, you may get a worker who ignores your best attempts to help him learn. Reasoning, encouragement, counseling—none of them seem to work. As a last resort, confronting him sharply, and perhaps angrily, when he ignores direction or policy may get his attention. He may or may not improve, but perhaps he will begin to pay attention. If not, you've probably done everything you can to salvage him.

Remember, though—this is a last resort. It's never where you begin.

A tip for mistake-free managing:

Some workers want to come to work as late as possible, put forth as little effort as possible, and get out of there—particularly if the pay is low and the work is boring. They don't understand what the world of work is all about. Do your best to enforce the rules with them and try to get at least the minimum performance you need.

Happily, they're in the minority. Most workers genuinely want to do a good job—one they can feel proud of. In return, they want to be treated with respect and allowed to use initiative. If they're treated in the same way as the kind of worker described in the last paragraph, though, they quickly become that kind of worker. In other words, you can help them develop their commitment to do a good job, or you can squash it.

That doesn't seem to be a hard choice, does it? When you treat workers with respect, expect them to want to do right, and help everyone learn as quickly and effectively as possible you're halfway home already.

11-4   The Mistake: Judging workers, not their behavior

The situation: "Lee, don't you care even a little bit about doing a good job?"

"Yeah, I do my job."

"You do a halfway job. You just don't care. I don't know if it's a 'Generation X' kind of thing or you simply don't like to work. But you're surely not the kind of worker we need around here. Either you change big time or you're going to be working for someone else."

Why was it a mistake?

You know, I know, everyone knows that it's tremendously difficult if not impossible to change the way we are. At least it is if you put the problem that way. When the manager attributes Lee's performance to the way he is, he or she sets both of them up to fail. Lee will probably fail because he doesn't want to change who he is and doesn't know how to do it anyway. He will also probably fail because the manager doesn't expect him to change who he is either.

If the manager focused on Lee's behavior instead of his character, at least a little space for change would get created. We are all capable of changing a wide range of our behaviors, as long as we know what the behavior is that we need to change and have a reason for changing it. If Lee and his manager focus on specific behaviors, then Lee knows just what he has to do and can make a decision whether to do it or not.

How can you recover from it quickly?

In this case, the manager almost certainly cannot recover quickly. Lee brought a set of problem behaviors with him to the workplace, and the manager has been busily reinforcing the idea that the behaviors are a direct result of Lee's character. Perhaps the behaviors can be changed, but it will take time to change them.

How can you consistently do it right from now on?

Look what the manager said about Lee as a person. "You *don't care* even a little bit about doing a good job. You're a *'Generation Xer'* or you simply *don't like to work.* You're not *the kind of worker* we need around here. Either you *change big time* or you're going to be working for someone else." Translation: "The problem with you is the person you are." Ow!

Instead of focusing on the kind of person Lee is, follow these steps and concentrate on what he's doing (or not doing):

• *Step 1:* Identify the specific job behavior that needs to change. In Lee's case, this was the misroutings and the backlog.

• *Step 2:* Use supporting data. Your opinion ("I don't think you're doing a very good job") is far less effective than data that demonstrates the performance deficiency ("I see you've been late with your morning report three times this week"). The manager had a report that showed where Lee's problems were.

• *Step 3:* Stick to the problem. Stay with the deficient performance, and insist that the worker do the same. He or she won't want to and will quite possibly distract you to other issues ("You're picking on me," or "You just don't like me.") You may want to explore these issues, but *after* you've dealt with the performance issue. In the brief example above, Lee didn't get around to raising a distraction, but he might have in the next sentence.

Step 4: Make sure that the worker leaves the room with the responsibility for the improvement. Our example ends with the manager making the first step in this direction. The manager should have gone on to get a specific commitment from Lee of what he was going to do and when he was doing to have it done. Not what he was doing to *try* to do, but what he was actually going to do. "I'll cut the mis-routings in half by the end of the month." You may also have to make some commitments; in Lee's case, for instance, some of the routing data may have been incomplete or misleading. But the worker has the responsibility for improving.

Is doing what you did ever right?

No—not even with good workers. A "good" worker is good because he or she performs well. Focus on the performance. Don't say "You're a great worker." Say instead, "I really appreciate the way you always meet your deadlines." Your comment not only focuses on performance but gives the worker some concrete information on the behavior you value.

A tip for mistake-free managing:

Performance has four elements: the performer's intent; the performer's visible behavior; the organization's support for the behavior, and the result. You need to make clear to workers what you intend them to accomplish. You need to support the result you want (in Lee's case, you need to make sure he has the information he needs to correctly route the items). You need to know what the actual outcome was. Then, when you've done all three of these and you're not getting the result you want, you and the worker need to identify where his or her behaviors are deficient and what needs to be done to correct the deficiency. Then it becomes the worker's responsibility to change the behaviors.

None of this has anything to do with the worker's character or inner nature. That's the worker's business. You and the worker concentrate on his or her performance and how to improve it.

11-5   The Mistake: Not getting the facts first

The situation: "Carlos, you sent copies of our presentation to headquarters when I told you specifically not to!"

"Not really. Joe Tombeau called and asked me if I'd. . . ."

"I don't give a hoot who called you. You know that I said not to do it!"

"I know, but Joe called and said that he really need-ed . . ."

"I told you I don't care who called. You knew you weren't supposed to do it, and you did it anyway. I don't know what I'm going to do about this. Get out of here and let me think."

"But . . ."

"We're done. Leave—before I get really angry!"

Why was it a mistake?

Did Carlos disobey his boss? You don't know—and neither does his boss. And because he didn't first get the facts, his boss may have chewed out a good employee without any real reason. This kind of behavior by a manager is down-right poisonous to his or her workgroup.

How can you recover from it quickly?

That depends. Are you good at apologies? If so, call Carlos back in (or find him at his work site), apologize for acting before you knew the facts, and ask him to tell you his side of the story. The next section will provide you some useful sug-gestions on how to handle the conversation.

How can you consistently do it right from now on?

This is an example of how the discussion with Carlos should have gone:

"Carlos, I heard that you sent a copy of our drawings to Headquarters. Did you?

"No, at least not the way you mean it. Joe Tombeau called and asked for them. He said his boss was getting nervous, and he wanted to give him a quick briefing. I told him I'd call him back and went looking for you. But I couldn't find you. From what Joe said, things sounded serious, so I asked Marie if she could get the summary slide done quickly—you know, the one that lays out the benefits. She did, so I sent it to Joe and asked him to use it just with his boss. Honest, I didn't mean to do anything wrong—I just figured we needed to do something, and this was all I could think of."

Now Carlos' boss has at least the core facts. Do you think he would react as he did above and chew Carlos out? Of course he wouldn't. Even if Carlos made a poor decision—and it's not at all clear that he did—he made it for all the right reasons. At this point in the discussion, it's pretty clear what Carlos's boss should say:

> "I'm not sure yet whether that was the best thing; we need to talk about it a little. But I really appreciate your trying to handle what sounds like a sticky situation. Thank you."

> *Then* they can discuss whether Carlos made the right response.

When you hear that someone has apparently made a serious mistake or let you down or violated policy or direction, your natural response may be to assume the person did what you heard and act immediately. Unless you really enjoy apologizing to people or like workers who want as little to do with you as possible, this is the worst possible reaction.

So what do you do? You follow these steps:

• *Step 1:* You recognize that you have a limited account of what happened—and that's not enough to make a decision on.

• *Step 2:* You get the emotion out of your system. Take a walk, finish a report, close your office door and yell at the world. Do whatever you have to do, but calm down before you try to handle anything.

• *Step 3:* Unless you have a specific reason to believe otherwise, mentally give the worker the benefit of the doubt. Doing so will lay the groundwork for getting the facts, and it will probably help you calm down much sooner.

• *Step 4*: Meet with the worker, tell him what you heard, and then let the individual present his side of the story. Listen carefully and actively and ask questions. Walk a line between rolling over and simply accepting what he says—his account may be very biased—and making him feel that he's getting the third degree. Take whatever time it requires to understand how he sees the situation.

• *Step 5:* If you need to, get more facts. Now you're ready to deal with the situation.

Is doing what you did ever right?

Put yourself in Carlos' shoes. Your boss accuses you of something and then doesn't give you a chance to give your side of the story. How would you feel? Would you want to take any initiative the next time? Would you want to keep working for this person?

In other words, acting in a situation like this without getting the facts first is always wrong.

A tip for mistake-free managing:

Please take this seriously: Some of the most critical mistakes managers make occur because they acted before they got all the relevant facts. Yes, when you confront a worker he may lie to you. Yes, a worker may rush around trying to cover up what happened before you can catch up with her to talk with her. But for every time something like this happens—at least in a reasonably well-run organization—there will be a dozen or a hundred times when the information you begin with will lack crucial facts. And if you act on this incomplete information, you will take the wrong action.

This doesn't mean you can't be tough with your workers. It doesn't mean that you fall into "paralysis by analysis" and keep collecting facts long after you have what you need. It simply means that you want to make intelligent decisions—and you get the facts you need to do so.

11-6 The Mistake: Trying to manage by criticism and fear

The situation: "Benita, did you really think I'd accept this lousy report?"

"I didn't think . . ."

"That's exactly the point—you didn't think! You just stuffed the data into the report without any real plan. I can't make any sense of it."

"Perhaps if you'd let me show you how it's organized . . ."

"If you have to show me, it's not organized well enough. Do you want to keep your job here?"

"Why . . . yes . . . of course."

"Then you'd better shape up. Now go back and do this right and have it back to me by tomorrow—or else."

Why was it a mistake?

Two reasons. First, when workers are consistently criticized and threatened, they respond by looking for safer and safer ways to perform. Benita may have had a creative idea or two in the report; you can bet that she won't have them in the revision. Nor is she apt to take much initiative in the future. She'll do her best to find out exactly what you're expecting and then she'll give you that—no more, no less.

Second, when workers get only criticism they get little information on how they can perform more effectively. Look at the example. Does Benita know what her boss means when she says that the report isn't organized well enough? No. Does Benita know how to change it so it's more what her boss is expecting? No. She knows she has to do something different, but she hasn't gotten the slightest clue what this is—except that the report needs to be "better organized."

Does this mean that a manager has to spell out in detail for every worker what she wants? At first, yes. If Benita hasn't done this kind of report before, or hasn't done it for this customer, she may need some very specific guidance. Then, as she gets more familiar with the report, she should need less and less. If she doesn't? That's another question. It has nothing to do with overall management style.

How can you recover from it quickly?

Whether you can recover completely is doubtful, but you can help the situation immediately. Either call Benita back in or go to her work area (if she has some privacy). You might want to apologize for being so curt with her; that's your choice. Then the discussion should go something like this:

> *Manager:* Benita, I couldn't see how you'd organized the report, but I believe you said that you had and you could show it to me. Would you please do that for me now?

> *Benita* explains the way she's organized the report.

> *Manager:* OK, you did it by topic area. I guess you've done it that way for a lot of the analytic reports you've done." (Benita nods.) "I can't fault you for that, but Headquarters doesn't want the reports they get done that way. They want a good Executive Summary, followed by . . ."

Now the manager has recognized what Benita has done and begun giving her specific guidance on how the report should be organized.

How can you consistently do it right from now on?

Managers often believe that the best way to get good performance is to be very critical of everything their workgroup does. This doesn't work, because it substitutes criticism for three other vitally important aspects of a manager's job:

1. *Setting standards.* You don't get good work by criticizing it into what workers have already done. You get good work by having clear standards, ensuring that workers know these standards, and then evaluating their work products with them against the standards.

2. *Providing feedback.* Feedback isn't something you give a worker once or twice a year at appraisal time. Feedback is the information you give a worker constantly on his or her performance, in time for the individual to improve that performance. And criticism isn't feedback. Good feedback is objective, based on standards that both the manager and the worker know.

3. *Recognizing performance.* If you say nothing to workers, they will assume that what they're producing satisfactory work. Standards and feedback help this situation, but they're not enough. If a job is satisfactory, tell the worker it's satisfactory and thank him or her for it. If it's above satisfactory, make sure the worker knows that, too. You also recognize less-than-satisfactory performance and deal with it. But if you have an at least average workgroup, you should be praising workers on the average at least four times for every time you criticize them. At least.

Now, how do you use this information? You follow these guidelines:

1. You base your management style not on criticism and fear but on encouragement and support. You cannot drive people to do their best, but you can successfully encourage them to do it. In the example at the start of this case, the manager should have found at least two or three aspects of Benita's report to praise. Don't be phony, praising mediocre or slipshod work. And don't make it general: "I really like the way you work" doesn't provide much guidance on what you really like.

2. You set the highest standards the situation will permit. Ideally, you would have a standard for each type of report. If not, you should at least have general standards such as "All reports will be written in ordinary English and will avoid bureaucratese." Standards often work best if they're developed with your workers. Whether they're jointly developed or not, your workers should be familiar with them.

3. You work out ways for workers to get direct feedback on what they do. If your organization produces a great number of reports, you may want to establish the practice that everyone has at least one other worker review each report he or she does. You should also create the kind of team atmosphere in which Benita would feel free to go to another worker and ask if a report to Headquarters was

different from the kind she was used to. If you have to provide some of the feed-back—for instance, if you gave Benita some special conditions and wanted to ensure that she met them—learn to give it objectively, without criticizing.

Is doing what you did ever right?

Not often enough to even think about.

A tip for mistake-free managing:

You will get the most from your workgroup and from individual workers in it, if you see your basic job as supporting them so that can be successful. They produce the work of the unit, not you, so do everything you can to insist that they do it well and then enable them to do it well. This isn't always sweetness and light, though. At some times and with some workers, you do need to make it crystal clear that performance isn't up to snuff.

Perhaps the best way to approach this is to think of yourself as a coach. Great coaches aren't unemotional or wimpy. But they dedicate themselves to drawing forth great performance from the individuals and teams they coach. They understand clearly that their success depends on the team's performance. So does yours.

11-7   The Mistake: Being defensive to criticism

The situation:

"Boss, I don't really mean to be critical," Robert began hesitantly, "but the information you provided me for the Knudsen project wasn't enough. I had to spend one whole morning asking around to get enough information to start working the project."

"Now, look—I don't need the likes of you telling me how I should run this organization. I've been in this job for five years, and I know what people need. If you'd just listened and done exactly what I told you, you'd be fine."

"That's what I've been tying to say—what you told me by itself was misleading. It just wasn't enough to . . ."

"That's enough from you! I gave you what I had and what you needed. I don't need you second-guessing me. Now don't come griping at me again."

Why was it a mistake?

Did the manager really give Robert enough information? Neither of them will ever know. Robert had a work concern. The manager took it as a personal attack and responded accordingly. And that basically cut off the flow of information between them. It also alienated the worker, which isn't trivial.

How can you recover from it quickly?

This is another case where you can salvage at least part of the situation. Wait until you get over your defensiveness and anger (defensiveness is a form of anger). Then meet with Robert. Apologize or make excuses or do whatever seems right to start the conversation. Then ask him about the information he needed and why the information you gave him wasn't enough. If it wasn't enough, and especially if it was misleading, thank him for bringing it to your attention. Ask him to bring the next situation like that to your attention quickly and promise you won't react defensively again.

How can you consistently do it right from now on?

Defensiveness is a common disease of organizations—and it is a disease. When managers and workers are consistently defensive, the quality and amount of information and new ideas drops off dramatically. As a result, no one can do a really effective job.

What causes you and others to be defensive? It happens when someone criticizes you and you feel attacked. What makes you feel attacked? More than anything else, it's insecurity—the feeling that if you admit a mistake you will suffer for it. When an organization or manager rules by fear (as in the case just before this one), it creates this kind of anxiety. So does an organization that holds very high standards but doesn't provide enough time, support, or training so that workers—or managers—can meet them.

How can you overcome defensiveness in yourself and in your workers? First, you need to understand that for the time being you are going to react emotionally. Just because you make up your mind to change, this change won't happen overnight. You'll have to catch yourself again. If you can do it, we recommend strongly that you admit the emotion, get it out of the way, and go on from there.

If you did this, the encounter in the example in this case might have gone this way:

> "Boss, I don't really mean to be critical," Robert began hesitantly, "but the information you provided me for the Knudsen project wasn't really enough. I had to spend one whole morning asking around to get enough information to start working the project."

> "Now, look. [Pause.] Give me just a minute, Robert. I'm trying to learn not to overreact when one of you all bring up something like this with me. [Pause.] OK—I'm ready to listen to you now. You said I didn't give you enough information about the Knudsen project? Tell me some more about that."

> "Well, you told me it was important, but you didn't tell me *how* important it is. I waited until this morning to call to set up the meeting and ran into a buzz saw. They were expecting me to drop everything and fly up there today."

> "Wow—you're right, I didn't make that clear to you. And, frankly, they didn't make it clear to me. I sure am glad you called this morning and didn't put it off any further. Now tell me some of the rest of it. . ."

Note that information is flowing between the two of them. They're both learning better how they need to deal with each other, and how to handle truly hot projects.

But suppose Robert really was just trying to pass the buck. Suppose at one point he had said: "Well, when you said it was important I just didn't understand it was *that* important."

He may be acting defensively himself and trying to make excuses for his performance. You don't accept that from him any more than you expect him to accept it from you. What do you do? This might be your response to his comment: "Oops, Robert—I thought we all understood that when a project is important it means we call the customer as soon as possible to get the details."

These examples may help you deal with specific situations, but you need to practice not being defensive all the time. If you want your workers to stop being defensive, the best way to achieve that goal is never to be defensive with them. And with most bosses, never being defensive is the best strategy. Just keep telling yourself that you can never get too much information, and being defensive will always keep you from getting information. Don't be a stop sign. Be a sponge.

Is doing what you did ever right?

No. Even if your worker is trying to shift the blame for his poor performance onto you, your defensiveness won't help.

A tip for mistake-free managing:

Managers and workers don't just decide to be defensive, any more than they simply decide to stop being defensive. Defensiveness is a protective reaction, one designed to protect the individual from an attack.

This chapter briefly mentioned some of the reasons why individuals get defensive. You want too do what you can to keep that defense reaction from kicking in. You want to demonstrate open, receptive behavior that makes it easy for workers to speak their mind to you. (Remember, no matter how open you are you don't have to agree with them.) You want to make it easy for them to bring problems to you immediately, not after they've festered and gotten far worse. And the more open you are, the more open most of your workers will be with you. (One or two may not; you handle them as individual performance problems.) And if you've never experienced it before, we promise you you'll be amazed at the difference it makes in both the work atmosphere and in performance.

11-8   The Mistake: Not building a trusting atmosphere

The situation:	"OK, Regina where's the prototype you were supposed to have for me today?"
	"I never said I'd have it for you. I said I'd *try*. And I did try. But it's going to take us at least another day and maybe two to get it finished."
	"Oh, no it won't. You wanted a couple of extra days, but I told you clearly I wanted it today."
	"And I told you just as clearly that we couldn't make it by today. There were just too many people to clear it with."
	"I don't want excuses—I want results!"

"And I don't want to be set up for failure. You're not blaming this one on me!"

Why was it a mistake?

If you look at the discussion, you see that it's shot through and through with distrust. The manager doesn't trust Regina to perform effectively, and Regina doesn't trust him. If this is a typical conversation, the entire workgroup is shot through with distrust. This guarantees that work will not be done efficiently and probably not effectively because everyone is too busy making sure he or she can't be accused of anything. As you know if you've worked in a distrustful organization, you can't constantly play CYA (Cover Your Anatomy) and still produce much that you're proud of.

How can you recover from it quickly?

You almost certainly can't. If you have led your workgroup into this kind of pervasive distrust, there's no way you're going to correct it overnight. One of the serious problems is that anything you say or do to try to establish trust will be distrusted by the workgroup.

How can you consistently do it right from now on?

We can put this another way: How can you build and maintain trust in a distrustful atmosphere? And particularly when you may have created the distrustful environment in the first place? Here are some practices to follow:

• *Begin to take workers at their word.* The dialogue at the start of this case end made it clear that the manager didn't do this. What might he have done when he originally negotiated the deadline?

"Regina are you *sure* you can't have that prototype by Tuesday?"

"I'll try but I'm almost certain we can't get it done by then. If nothing else, half the world has to coordinate on what we're doing, and you know how long that takes!"

"OK, I'll take your word for that. When can you have it done? And remember how important it is to the division."

"I know. I'll try to have it to you on Wednesday morning, and I absolutely promise that we'll have it done by noon Wednesday."

"I'll be expecting it then."

Notice that the manager tested to make certain that Regina didn't feel she couldn't commit to the earlier date. Then he insisted on an absolute commitment to the date she picked. That's normally a reasonable solution.

• *Start managing by encouragement, not criticism and fear.* In a distrustful environment, everyone distrusts everyone else. No one wants to be blamed for anything, so workers hide everything they can from you until the last moment. How do you stop this? Shift from blaming individuals to encouraging them.

• *Listen.* Listen to workers when they try to explain why they made mistakes, missed deadlines, or otherwise let you down. Listen to them when they think you've let them down. Listen to them when they suggest changes, or believe you're not being fair, or . . . You don't ever have to agree; listening doesn't require that commitment. But you do have to hear. And you do have to communicate that you heard. Then take the action that seems best—and workers will usually accept it, because they know you listened to them.

• *Be open with your workers.* Will a project be inspected particularly carefully? Be sure they know this and be sure they know how to perform the project successfully. Is the workgroup going to be stuck with extra work? Let them know, sympathize with them, then challenge them to find ways to do both the old and new work effectively (and listen carefully to their suggestions). Create a situation in which they know that you will share what you know with them so that they can come to you as their best source of information. Don't be defensive. And, for heaven's sake, don't ever lie to them because one lie can destroy the trust that it's taken years to build.

You may want to look at the cases before this one in this chapter. Many of them illustrate management behaviors that create and maintain distrust and provide detailed suggestions on how to change them.

Is doing what you did ever right?

Creating trust is one of the most basic responsibilities of a manager. It's as critical to a workgroup's effective performance as gasoline is for a car's performance. If you don't create it, or if you allow it to disintegrate, you've failed at a basic responsibility.

No, it's never right.

A tip for mistake-free managing:

Any worker who has performed in both a high-trust and a low-trust environment can tell you, at length, the difference trust makes. A trusting workplace makes every contact easier, less stressful, and more productive. It makes real cooperation possible. It helps people grow. It cuts out the need for the destructive game playing you so often find. It helps everyone be responsible at the same time that it makes it possible for them to depend on others. It makes the workplace a far more pleasant and satisfying place to work. And it makes it possible for every member of the workgroup, yourself included, to perform at the highest level possible.

Need we say anything else?

11-9   The Mistake: Not making the workgroup mission clear

The situation: "But I thought our job was to load and check all of the new software for the department," Lionel said, a slightly puzzled look on his face, "and then help them when they have problems with it."

"Load and check it, yes. But after we finish that they're on their own until the time comes to load a new version or reload what they have when they get in a new machine."

"You mean we're supposed to transfer the software to their new machines? I don't think anyone has ever called me to do that, and I can't remember ever doing it." Lionel was looking completely puzzled now.

"Yeah. We do the transferring so that we can get all the files carried over without losing any of them. If we don't do it for them, the users are apt to lose or corrupt key files."

"I know—I spend a lot of time working with them after they've done the transferring, trying to get the system working right again. What you're telling me I should be doing and what I've been doing don't seem to resemble each other too much!"

Why was it a mistake?

This one shouldn't take a lot of explaining. If the mission isn't clear, your workers aren't going to be doing what you expect, which means that they're not going to be concentrating on what you think is important.

It can also cause problems such as your boss calling you in and asking: "Why have I gotten three calls this week from organizations that need help moving files? Don't your people know how to do their jobs?"

Finally, unless you keep the mission clear you can absolutely count on your workers starting to do something different. If the mission is repetitive but workers can do something else that's more interesting at least some of them will. If the mission doesn't include a particular service but customers keep asking for it at least some of them will start providing it. Because each worker is an individual, before long everyone is performing a slightly different set of tasks. Not only are they not doing the mission you thought they were, they're not even doing the same mission.

How can you recover from it quickly?

Fortunately, you can get started on fixing this problem right away. There are other ways to begin, but we suggest this one:

Call a group meeting. Make its purpose clear, so no one gets overly anxious.

Ask all workgroup members to write down what they believe are the most important tasks they perform. Give them plenty of time and make it clear that you're looking for information, not for someone to blame for something.

Write their answers on a white board or on flip charts. Be prepared to be surprised and expect that they will also.

Now, from all the answers, you can identify those that are really part of the mission. Then you and everyone else can agree that this is where the unit should be spending its time. (What if you genuinely need to be doing some of the non-mission tasks? See the next section.)

How can you consistently do it right from now on?

First, expect that you need to hold meetings like the one above frequently. How often is "frequently"? That depends. Maybe it's monthly, especially if you're in a dynamic and changing atmosphere. Maybe it's quarterly, if the organization is very stable. Annually, only if the organization is truly stagnant. You may also find that you need to hold unscheduled meetings (like the one above), especially if there've been a rapid series of changes in the organization.

Second, don't expect that the mission is going to stay constant. One of the basic purposes of the meetings is to find out how things are changing "out there." When you find that the work has changed, take time to explore the changes.

Third, you can see how important it is to keep your boss up to date on any changes in your workgroup's mission. It's important that you and your workgroup have met, so that you have detailed information from them *and* you understand the situation the way they do. It's just as important that you think carefully about what you've learned so that you can make good recommendations to your boss.

Is doing what you did ever right?

It's one thing for your workgroup to depart from its mission if it believes it must do so to meet rapidly changing conditions. It's another for this to happen without your keeping up with it. If you don't keep up, that's always a mistake. If you stay on top of events and let the mission evolve for a while, though, that may be an effective way to handle the situation. Just ensure that what's actually being done isn't too far different from what your boss and the rest of the organization expect.

A tip for mistake-free managing:

A clear, worthwhile mission is the heart of workgroup performance. A traditional workgroup needs it; a team can't function effectively without it. If you want worker commitment to the mission, it must be clear to them. And when you and the units you work closely with understand your missions clearly, it makes working together that much easier.

Note that we say a mission needs to be clear and *worthwhile*. If what workers are supposed to do is clear but they don't see much use in doing it—well, don't expect much commitment from them. Keeping the mission clear is a necessary start. Then you need to see that each worker understands why the mission is important and deserves his or her best efforts. And if you can't communicate that clearly with them, perhaps you need to explore just how necessary the mission is and, if necessary and possible, do something to change it.

11-10 The Mistake: Not training and developing workers

The situation:	*Monday:*	"Cheryl, I appreciate that Pauline Ashton has promised you that if you transfer to her group she'll send you to three major training courses this year, but is that really enough of a reason to leave us?"
	Wednesday:	"If that's the way it is, Velda, go ahead and call Mr. Newley and tell him we just can't get him that report by the end of the week. Be sure he understands that we want to do it, but Boris is the only one who knows how to build that kind of spreadsheet and he's off 'til next week."
	Friday:	"Kit, I'm afraid we're going to have to cancel the word processor training you were scheduled for next Tuesday and Wednesday—we're just too shorthanded for me to let you go."

Why was it a mistake?

We've compressed three events a bit more than they might actually happen, but the consequences of not developing workers are clear:

1. The workgroup has lost a worker because she couldn't get training in new skills. (Because of this, she may have been getting really bored with her job.)

2. The workgroup couldn't produce a report quickly enough for a customer because only one person knew how to handle that kind of spreadsheet. (Mr. Newley may or may not have accepted this as a valid reason for not getting the report.)

3. A worker couldn't get training she needed because the workgroup was too busy. (This was both cause and effect. The workgroup was too busy because it was undertrained. Then, since the manager couldn't spare another worker go to training, he perpetuated the situation.)

In short, not developing your workers catches you in a vicious cycle.

How can you recover from it quickly?

You can't do much for Mr. Newley. You can attempt to bargain with Cheryl and make her at least as good an offer as Ms. Ashton has. (There's a double problem here. First, it's never good practice to get into a situation where you have to bargain to keep a worker. Second, Cheryl will quite possibly not believe the training will ever happen.) And you can change your mind quickly and see that Kit gets her training. (Of course, with the bind created by lack of training, you may genuinely be unable to spare her for the training.)

How can you consistently do it right from now on?

Simple: See that your workers get the training they need to do their current jobs and the development they need to prepare them for more demanding work and better jobs.

How do you do this, particularly if your workgroup is already stretched thin because it lacks training? Here are some suggestions:

• *Make training and developing workers a high priority.* You know that you will do whatever is a high priority for you. Sometimes training and development slips through the cracks, though, because it isn't pressing enough. It seems that it can always be put off, while today's work absolutely has to be done today.

Only you can change this situation. You *plan* on a certain number of hours of training for your workgroup. How many hours? How badly do individual workers need training? You can answer that in part from the next paragraph. But plan training and development—don't try to allow for it at the last moment. If necessary, negotiate the amount of training with your boss; you want her support if someone complains he can't get what he wants because one of your workers is off on training.

• *Help workers prepare individual development plans.* Many organizations have elaborate individual development plan programs. Perhaps you've worked for one of them. You don't need anything that bureaucratic (though a well-run organizational program can be immensely helpful to you). Call your workers together and ask them to participate in the process both to identify training they need to do their current jobs and for development opportunities they want so they can advance in their careers.

Then meet with each worker. Discuss with the individual the training he or she needs as well as the development that would be useful. The two of you may not agree. That's OK. You need to spend some time understanding *why* you disagree—to help you each get a better picture of the situation. Then list the training and development, list milestones for it as best you can, and each of you keep a copy.

• *See that workers use the training they receive as quickly as possible.* It seldom helps to send someone to training that the individual won't use for weeks or months. (Think of your own experience. What happened when you went to an exciting course, but then had no chance to apply what you learned?) As much as possible, schedule courses so that the person can start applying at least part—and preferably all—of what he or she has learned immediately. That's the most effective single step you can take to ensure successful training.

• *Do as much cross-training as possible.* The workgroup couldn't do the spreadsheet for Mr. Newley because Boris was off, and he was the only one who knew how to build that kind of spreadsheet. If you ensure that you cross-train everyone possible, that won't happen as much in the future.

Here you can count on significant worker motivation. Most workers are anxious to learn other jobs, particularly if it makes their work more interesting and might help them prepare for a promotion.

In one organization we know, the manager made an agreement with all of her workers that if they finished their week's work by noon on Friday they could spend Friday afternoon cross-training on higher-paying jobs. Not only did everyone finish by noon Friday, but absenteeism and quits in the unit were dramatically lower than in comparable groups.

Is doing what you did ever right?

In the short run, you may sometimes have to forgo training to get the work out. In the long run, it never works. So don't do it.

A tip for mistake-free managing:

Training is not the answer to all of your problems. Training by itself is almost never the complete answer. (Training, for instance, won't motivate workers or provide them with good job standards.) But almost every problem requires training before it can be completely solved.

Development is even easier to put off than training, because workers don't need to use the skills they learn to do their current job. Its long-run impact, though, is often greater. Particularly in our rapidly changing world, developing workers to prepare them for new and more challenging duties is a survival necessity.

It doesn't hurt to get known as a manager who trains and develops so well that his or her best people keep getting offered promotions. You may have a problem holding on to your top-flight performers, but you'll be extremely competitive in hiring their replacements. People will want to come to work for you.

11-11 The Mistake: Not helping new workers develop self-management skills

The situation:

"The young people I hire in here these days just aren't dependable. Are you having that same problem, Gerrie?"

Gerrie, another manager at your level, nods her head vigorously. "I have to look over their shoulders constantly. You can't believe how often I give one of them a project and then come back the next day to find out they haven't even gotten started."

"What are we going to do about this? At best, I think I get something like 80 percent of the work out of them I got out of my group eight or ten years ago."

"I wish I knew. I threaten them, but it doesn't help. And as soon as I find one that's reasonably productive, he leaves for another job."

Why was it a mistake?

The two managers in the example don't understand what their problem is. They may have workers who lack motivation and a work ethic. The workers may not be as well trained as they would hope. But none of these are the basic problem. The workers they're getting lack self-management skills. They don't know how to organize their time or their work. And if no one teaches them self-management skills, very little else will help.

How can you recover from it quickly?

There isn't any way.

How can you consistently do it right from now on?

• *Expect that workers will learn to manage themselves and make the expectation clear to them.* You might want to have a talk with each new worker that goes something like this:

> "I expect everyone here to manage themselves. What does that mean? I expect you to be able to plan your day and follow through on your plan. When I give you an assignment, I expect you to do it or be able to ask me or another worker the right questions to find out how to do it. I expect that you will do your job without my always looking over your shoulder, which is what I expect you want, too.
>
> "We find that many of the people who come to work for us here haven't had a lot of experience at managing themselves, so we'll do everything necessary to make up for this. We'll send you to training, then help you use the training back here on the job. If you put some time and effort into it, you'll pick it up quickly and fit right in. And remember, the better you get at it, the more independence you'll have and the more fun your job will be."

• *See that every new worker gets training in self-management.* This training is becoming more and more widely available, though it may not be called "self-management" training. Look for training that will teach workers how to organize themselves and their day, how to make realistic plans and follow them, how to set goals and motivate themselves to achieve them.

A quick note. If you currently have a number of workers who lack self-management skills, you might want to send them to the training as a group. They can help one another apply the skills and support one another when the going gets rough (as it occasionally will). You might even want to find another manager or two with workers who need the training and have the course brought in.

However you do it, start now to see that it's done.

• *Give assignments that require the worker to use the self-management skills immediately.* Students quickly forget even the best training unless they can apply it quickly. Plan the training so that they'll use it when they return to the workplace. You might have an assignment ready for each person when he or she returns—one in which it's clear how the individual can apply what's been learned. For instance, you might ask that he or she develop a plan for a project and discuss it with you. If you have other workers who are skilled at self-management, they might help you—see the last item in this section.

Just see that your workers use what they learn and keep using it.

• *Notice and recognize every improvement in self-management, no matter how small.* Nothing is more important than this. Don't wait for individuals to become fully self-managing before recognizing their effort. Has someone who couldn't identify where to start a project before learned how to sketch out a beginning series of steps? Notice it and recognize the individual for having accomplished it.

Then recognize each step further on. As individuals become more and more proficient at self-management, you'll need to give them less and less recognition—but ensure that they continue to use the skills and recognize when they're using them successfully. You also want to remind individuals every so often, at whatever stage of progress, how far they have come from where they began.

• *As more and more workers become proficient at managing themselves, have them help train new workers.* Here you begin to get a double payoff. Not only do individuals become proficient at managing themselves, but they can help you train others to be self-managing. They'll probably enjoy this. Just as important, they'll understand how to approach workers without self-management skills since they were once there themselves.

Is doing what you did ever right?

Not unless you enjoy micromanaging, high turnover, and constant frustration.

A tip for mistake-free management:

Studies have shown that many individuals entering the workforce these days don't want to be supervised, yet they often lack the self-management skills required to perform without supervision. At the same time, many organizations are structuring themselves to require more autonomy from workers at all levels. This creates a real bind, especially for first- and second-level managers.

What do you do about it? First, apply the suggestions in this case. Actively help your workers learn to manage themselves.

As you do this, though, keep two points in the forefront of your mind. First, the reason many individuals don't manage themselves is that they don't know how. Lack of self-management is first a *competence* problem. When individuals lack competence, it does no good to yell at them or get frustrated when they don't display self-management skills.

The second point is this: They have had no reason to be self-managing. No one expected it of them, so they didn't need to learn how to do it. In short, the fact that workers don't manage themselves is also a *motivation* problem.

If you want workers to learn to be self-managing, you must help them develop the competence at the same time that you give them an incentive. Neither will work by itself.

11-12 The Mistake: Not networking with other managers

The situation:

"We missed you at the department managers' shindig yesterday."

You turn around to see Eileen Watkins, a supervisor from the Finance Branch. "Yeah, I really wanted to be there, but I had to get some paperwork done. You know there's no end to it."

"Not in our branch, anyway. But we still missed you. Billie Marks had an advance copy of the new policy on employee removal and we spent a lot of time going over that. She and I and Sam Epps are going to ask the department chief to let us make a presentation on it—it just makes it too hard to get rid of someone who's causing a problem."

"Well, I sure wish you luck. If I can do anything to help, just let me know." You wave goodbye to Eileen and turn into your office.

Why was it a mistake?

For three reasons:

1. Many of the best-known changes in organizations for the last decade— TQM, self-managing teams, downsizing—have resulted in reducing the number of first- and

second-level managers sharply. This happened because top management didn't see that it was getting real value from these levels of management. When first- and second-level managers know each other well and work together well they not only do their jobs better but are in a position to point out this value to higher management.

2. Managers at these levels share many of the same problems. It's much easier when you can call another manager and find out how he or she handled the problem than to have work out the answer for yourself.

3. When you know other managers at your level, work with them, and help them with their problems, you build strong relationships. As some of these managers get promoted, their good opinion of you may result in better assignments and even a promotion yourself. And if you're the one who gets promoted, you know which other managers you can rely on.

How can you recover from it quickly?

If you've neglected networking, there's no quick solution to the problem. Strong relationships don't blossom overnight. But start immediately to begin building relationships with other managers.

How can you consistently do it right from now on?

Networking means building connections. To build those connections with other managers you need to (1) spend time with them and (2) be genuinely helpful to them. How do you accomplish this?

- *Spending time with other managers*:
1. Attend any and all management meetings that are open to you. Even if the topic is deadly dull, other managers will see you there. You may particularly like one or two other managers and be tempted to sit with them most of the time. Don't! This will give you a clique, which other managers will resent and which will limit you.

2. Learn how to work a room. Find someone who's really skilled at schmoozing and watch her. If the individual's really good, she'll engage in a brief but meaningful interchange with all or most of the people in the room, in a way that acknowledges them, not her. When you work a room you don't tell everyone about your latest accomplishment or brag about your kids. You focus on the people there. They're much happier talking about them-

selves than in talking about you—and you'll learn a great deal more than if you did most of the talking. The same rule goes for all conversations: Learn to listen well.

3. Schedule lunches with other managers. You can do it on a "catch as catch can" basis and hope to run into someone in the cafeteria or wherever. But it works much better to set up a calling list and call one or two managers a week to suggest lunch.

- *Being genuinely helpful to other managers:*

1. Through meeting with other managers and getting to know them, get to know their important problems and concerns. Willie may be having trouble with a hot love affair in the office that's turning frigid. Delrina may be deciding whether to give one of her workers another chance or simply let him go. And Tomas may be in trouble with his manager because his workgroup is getting further and further behind. If you're going to be helpful, you need to know where your help might be used.

2. When you see a situation in which you might help, volunteer—but do it in a way that leaves the other manager free to refuse. "Willie, I had almost the same thing happen a year ago. Would it help if I told you how I handled it?" Don't press, but if you can be helpful, follow through.

3. Always begin by being helpful to other managers, but then don't be afraid to ask them for help when it's reasonable. Strong relationships involve give and take on both sides; start by giving, but move toward a balanced relationship.

Is doing what you did ever right?

There's no question of right and wrong here. Failing to network isn't wrong, it's non-productive. Like it or not, we base most of our important decisions on who we know and what we know about them. (If you really want the straight skinny on something, do you go to the organization's Corporate Communications Office or a manager you know and trust?) Networking helps you be more effective and builds a reservoir of talent you can call on. Not networking loses you both of these.

A tip for mistake-free managing:

Even though organizational manuals and a great deal of management training overlook them, relationships are the way work gets done. Strong relationships depend on individuals who know one another well, are willing to help one another, and can depend on one another.

Keep one point in mind, though: The closer the relationship, the better the individuals understand one another. If you enter these relationships solely for what they will get you, that will begin to show. If you're an egotist who keeps bringing the subject back to himself or herself, that will begin to show. And if you're a shallow, conventional thinker who never really comes to grips with the hard issues—well, that will begin to show as well.

The moral? The more open and honest you are as an individual, the more powerful your network will be.

INDEX